superconnected

THE INTERNET, DIGITAL MEDIA, AND TECHNO-SOCIAL LIFE

Second Edition

SAGE was founded in 1965 by Sara Miller McCune to support the dissemination of usable knowledge by publishing innovative and high-quality research and teaching content. Today, we publish over 900 journals, including those of more than 400 learned societies, more than 800 new books per year, and a growing range of library products including archives, data, case studies, reports, and video. SAGE remains majority-owned by our founder, and after Sara's lifetime will become owned by a charitable trust that secures our continued independence.

Los Angeles | London | New Delhi | Singapore | Washington DC | Melbourne

superconnected

THE INTERNET, DIGITAL MEDIA, AND TECHNO-SOCIAL LIFE

Second Edition

Mary Chayko
Rutgers University

Los Angeles | London | New Delhi
Singapore | Washington DC | Melbourne

FOR INFORMATION:

SAGE Publications, Inc.
2455 Teller Road
Thousand Oaks, California 91320
E-mail: order@sagepub.com

SAGE Publications Ltd.
1 Oliver's Yard
55 City Road
London, EC1Y 1SP
United Kingdom

SAGE Publications India Pvt. Ltd.
B 1/I 1 Mohan Cooperative Industrial Area
Mathura Road, New Delhi 110 044
India

SAGE Publications Asia-Pacific Pte. Ltd.
3 Church Street
#10-04 Samsung Hub
Singapore 049483

Acquisitions Editor: Jeff Lasser
Editorial Assistant: Adeline Wilson
Production Editor: Laureen Gleason
Copy Editor: Amy Hanquist Harris
Typesetter: Hurix Digital
Proofreader: Victoria Reed-Castro
Indexer: May Hasso
Cover Designer: Gail Buschman
Marketing Manager: Kara Kindstrom

Printed in the United States of America

Library of Congress Cataloging-in-Publication Data

Names: Chayko, Mary, 1960–, author.

Title: Superconnected : the internet, digital media, and techno-social life / Mary Chayko, Rutgers University.

Description: Second Edition. | Thousand Oaks : SAGE Publications [2017] | Revised edition of the author's Superconnected [2017] | Includes bibliographical references and index.

Identifiers: LCCN 2017033031 | ISBN 9781506394855 (pbk. : alk. paper)

Subjects: LCSH: Information technology—Social aspects. | Internet—Social aspects. | Digital media. | Information society.

Classification: LCC HM851.C4335 2017b | DDC 302.23/1—dc23 LC record available at https://lccn.loc.gov/2017033031

This book is printed on acid-free paper.

SFI label applies to text stock

17 18 19 20 21 10 9 8 7 6 5 4 3 2 1

CONTENTS

ABOUT THE AUTHOR

Dr. Mary Chayko is a sociologist, Teaching Professor of Communication and Information, and Director of Undergraduate Interdisciplinary Studies at the School of Communication and Information (SC&I) at Rutgers University. She is also an affiliate member of the graduate faculty of the Department of Sociology, an affiliate member of the faculty of the Department of Women's and Gender Studies, and a Faculty Fellow in Residence at the Honors College, all at Rutgers University. Dr. Chayko has been honored as a Rutgers University Faculty of Arts and Sciences Distinguished Contributor to Undergraduate Education.

Dr. Chayko received a BA in Communication and Psychology from Seton Hall University. She also earned an EdM in Counseling Psychology and an MA and PhD in Sociology from Rutgers University.

For over 25 years, Dr. Chayko has been researching the impact of the internet and digital technology on community, society, and self. She is the author of *Portable Communities: The Social Dynamics of Online and Mobile Connectedness* and *Connecting: How We Form Social Bonds and Communities in the Internet Age*, both with SUNY Press, as well as many published articles. With Corey Dolgon, she coedited the anthology *Pioneers in Public Sociology: Thirty Years of Humanity and Society* for Sloan Publishing. She speaks widely on techno-social life, and in 2017 keynoted the multidisciplinary international conference "Re-Thinking Community" in Dresden, Germany.

This book features a companion blog: http://superconnectedblog.com. The blog features short podcasts written and recorded by Dr. Chayko to supplement each chapter of the book, providing an additional point of access to the material (as supplementary "listening"). It also includes lecture slides and questions for discussion to accompany each chapter, created specifically for the book's second edition. Additional updates and items of interest are also found on the blog.

Please feel free to use the hashtag #superconnected to discuss the book and interact with Dr. Chayko on Twitter!

Dr. Chayko can be reached at mary.chayko@rutgers.edu, on Twitter @MaryChayko, and via the book blog http://superconnectedblog.com and her website http://marychayko.com. The website contains excerpts from her published works, media appearances, photos, and even some of her music. In her spare time, she is a singer and flutist in a folkie, social justice–oriented band with fellow sociologists Jim Pennell and Corey Dolgon. Selections from the group's CD *Songs of Peace and Justice* can be heard on the website.

For Marco
because he's family

1 SUPERCONNECTEDNESS

superconnected

The first thing you should know about this book is that the title is partly a misnomer. Yes, our societies are *superconnected*, and so are we—never in human history have so many been connected to so many others, in so many ways, with such wide-ranging social implications. But sometimes it is assumed that the whole world is wired, living in a state of electronic connectivity, and that's just not the case. There are places in the world, such as much of southern Asia and sub-Saharan Africa, in which internet access, computers, and even electricity are seriously scarce. About 15% of the world's population does not have regular access to electricity, and although cell phones have penetrated the developing world to a much greater extent than computers have, they are used in much more limited ways than they are in more technologically developed areas, mainly because owners are often hindered by inconsistent internet access, unreliable service, and the inability to regularly charge their phones (Gronewold, 2009; International Telecommunication Union, 2014; McKinsey & Company, 2014; Pew Research Center's Global Attitudes Project, 2012; World Energy Outlook, 2016).

So when we talk about technological connectedness via the internet, digital and social media, and mobile phone use, as we will throughout this book, we must keep in mind that these things are not equally available to or experienced by everyone. More than half the world—3.9 billion people, or 52% of the world's population—does not have internet access. And social divisions and differences influence whether and how people go online and make connections, even in highly developed countries such as the United States and Canada. Most people who do not have regular internet access live in rural areas where poor infrastructure, health care, education, and employment opportunities impede internet adoption and use. They are disproportionately low income, elderly, illiterate, and female. About one fourth of the offline population is illiterate. Others are offline by choice (Dutta, Geiger, & Lanvin, 2015; Ferdman, 2014;

International Telecommunication Union, 2016; Luders & Bae Brandtzaeg, 2017; McKinsey & Company, 2014).

Internet and technological connectedness reflect the ways in which social factors like socioeconomic status, educational background, race, ethnicity, gender, age, sexual orientation, and so on play out in the physical world. This is because the *online*, digital world is not a separate entity from the *offline*, physical world. It is part of it. Online activity can make more visible and amplify concerns, problems, and divisions that are part of social life in physical space, and it can raise concern about new issues, too. But the digital world is in every way real and is deeply integrated with everyday lived experiences and with the future of our societies—and ourselves—which makes it critically important to examine and understand.

Though obstacles remain to worldwide digital access and to the full realization of the potential of these technologies for all, the internet and digital technology still afford tremendous opportunities for social connectedness and social change. They have become embedded in nearly every facet of modern life, including cities, cars, home appliances, lighting and heating products, and health and lifestyle monitoring. In all kinds of spaces, from the global to the local and everything in between, individuals and their communities and societies have become interconnected, their lives dramatically affected, their environments increasingly saturated with technology. So in the end, the title of this book still seems appropriate . . . because to an extent previously unimagined, and with the almost unlimited potential for more, the world has indeed become technologically and socially *superconnected.*

the internet . . .

The internet is a global network of circuits, tubes, and packets of data that connect countless billions of computerized devices and, thus, the people that use these devices (Blum, 2013). In doing so, it provides a gigantic, complex, always growing and spreading infrastructure for the sharing of information. I will not be capitalizing "the Internet" in this book, preferring to use the lowercase *i*, due to my determination that the internet has become such an integral part of so many lives that it seems no longer necessary to consider it A Special Thing That Deserves Capitalization (in conjunction with the Associated Press stylebook [Associated Press, 2016], and following similar arguments made by Steve Jones [in Schwartz, 2002]; Markham & Baym, 2009; and others).

Many services are carried along this global network, including email, social media, and the World Wide Web. The *web* is not the same thing as the *internet*, though the terms are often used interchangeably. The web is a system of hyperlinked pages and documents that exists *on* the internet. Put another way, the internet is a huge network consisting of many, many smaller networks and operations, including the web. Using internet services, people find one another, learn about one another, exchange information and social support, work, play, and become connected, so copiously and completely, that we can say they have become *superconnected*.

Computerization is required for these operations to work and for smaller networks to detect one another and become interlinked. There are many types and sizes of computers that work through many types of devices. Some computers are so tiny that they can be carried in our hands. Cell phones and smartphones are really best thought of as tiny computers that enable digitized, portable communication.

Some communications that are exchanged on computerized and mobile devices, such as texting, gaming, and instant messaging via SMS (short messaging service), are facilitated by cellular and satellite networks rather than the actual internet—that is, these networks may not technically be part of the internet. But they are digitized and serve to connect people; they contribute to the techno-social life that this book examines. An exploration of internet use is therefore very much a study of all kinds of communication practices mediated by computerization (called *computer-mediated communication*, or *CMC*), so this book will encompass all these ways that people can become electronically, digitally connected.

... digital media ...

Media are the means by which pieces of data, which aggregate as information, are stored and then communicated to others. Media are considered to be digital when data are communicated via computerized networks in bursts of invisible energy (bits) as opposed to being communicated face-to-face without computerized mediation (in what might be described as an *analog* fashion). As information is digitized, countless bits of data are represented and stored by computers as digits—zeroes (representing *off*) and ones (representing *on*).

There are limits to this; not everything can be digitized. When an experience is considered to be analog, the senses—taste, smell, and touch—can be more fully engaged. Subtle interpersonal nuances that could not be coded and transmitted numerically, both tangible and intangible, can be detected. Still, tremendous amounts of information can be digitally stored and transmitted by computers, making digital communication a generally efficient, cost-effective means to transmit information and communicate. The word *digital*, then, and the corresponding modern condition of *digitality*, have come to refer to computerized phenomena, media, and environments and have even been applied to circumstances and life itself in the age of computing.

As technology advances to create more and more ways for people to become connected and to impact the world around them, a full complement of technologically enabled activities has transformed everyday life. Even people who do not personally go online much (or ever) or who do not use social media have had their lives changed dramatically by the global internet, digital media, and mobile media revolution. This book looks at a wide array of these changes and impacts, focusing on the experience of living in a digitized, superconnected society.

As we explore the internet and digital and mobile media, distinctions among them and among various ways of accessing them online will not necessarily be drawn unless they are relevant to the topic at hand. The terms *online* and *digital*, for example, will refer broadly to connectedness via computerized technologies and do not imply exactly how a user accessed the connection. When the mobile, portable nature of this activity is most relevant, we'll tag the activity as *mobile* or *portable*, but we will not refer to every act accessed on a mobile device that way, for while digital communication often occurs via portable mobile devices, being "on the go" may not always be the most salient aspect of the act. When people have an experience in physical space, it will be said to take place *offline*, and when an interaction takes place in physical space, it will be called *face-to-face*. Digital devices can, of course, bring people's faces into one another's sight lines, but *face-to-face* has become shorthand for the analog experience of physical togetherness.

These terms are quite imperfect, for all these kinds of activities "melt" into one another and are thus not discrete. For example, we can be face-to-face and online with someone at the same time, texting him or her from across the room. We can feel that a person is more fully and vibrantly present in an online, digital interaction than in a hurried or nondescript offline, face-to-face one. At this writing, though, these are the terms most often used and understood to convey these complicated realities. More precise terms will eventually evolve, so we must remain flexible in our nomenclature and open to always learning more about this rapidly changing field.

We must also remain mentally flexible as we attempt to understand the concepts that underlie the terminology. Individuals often have experiences that are not neatly categorized as digital *or* face-to-face, as online *or* offline. They may use digital technology in combination with more traditional means of interaction in forming and maintaining relationships. Binary categories have serious limitations as we attempt to understand modes of interaction that overlap and intersect one another. As we explore more fully in Chapter 3, the online and offline are generally experienced in combination with one another. They are enmeshed. People are often so deeply, so comprehensively affected by the infusion of technology into their everyday lives that a highly useful way to think about these lives—these spaces and experiences and relationships and communities and societies—is that they are *techno-social* (see Brown, 2006; Chayko, 2014; Ito & Okabe, 2005; Willson, 2010; and Zeynep Tufekci's blog, technosociology.org).

... and techno-social life

Those who live in environments saturated with technology can find that nearly every aspect of life is affected: They can travel great distances with relative ease; horrific diseases that might once have claimed their lives can be survived; and they can fairly effortlessly learn about, communicate with, and get to know people who might have otherwise remained forever strangers. Faraway friends, relatives, and acquaintances can relatively easily become part of one's everyday life. Even those whose experiences with technology are more rudimentary are still profoundly affected in the global digital society.

A *technology* is the process or technique of making something that allows human beings to share their knowledge, perform a task, or fulfill a function (see Jary & Jary, 1991). It can also be thought of as a tool or invention that, once created and used, is intended to solve a problem or improve on past understandings of how to do something. It differs from *science* in that science is primarily directed toward the discovery of knowledge for its own sake, while technology represents a deployment of knowledge to get something done (Volti, 2014, p. 64). Whether in transportation, construction, the arts, or—our primary interest here—communication, technologies help to spread ideas, advance knowledge, and make new modes of production and products possible. These technologies lead, ideally, to progressively more effective and useful inventions that enhance the ways that people live, and they lead, inevitably, to progressively more complex societies.

A technology can be as basic yet critical to communication as the process of writing or drawing, or it can be something more tangible and more mechanically intricate, such as a computer, camera, or software. Even a pen or pencil is a technology. We usually think of something as *high-tech* when some kind of machine or modernized industry is involved and consider it to be *low-tech* in less mechanized conditions.

Information and communication technologies (ICTs) have become embedded in the way people live, the way they think, the way they associate with others. Nearly half of the world's population uses the internet, while 65% of the world's population uses mobile phones, with penetration in developing areas growing at twice the rate as in more developed areas. High-speed, always-on *mobile broadband* technology is used in about one third of mobile subscriptions. Increasingly, the internet and mobile phones are used to establish *social networks*—pathways between people that can be used to obtain and share resources, opportunities, and information (*social capital*) and to form connections and communities (boyd & Ellison, 2007; Castells, 2011; ITU, 2014, 2016; Pew Research Center's Global Attitudes Project, 2012; Rainie & Wellman, 2012; Statista, 2017a; Zichuhr & Smith, 2013).

Furthermore, approximately 2.5 billion people—about one third of the world's population—use social media (Statista, 2017b). When individuals gain internet access, social networking is generally one of the first online activities they undertake, and social media platforms have become indispensable for social networking. Technology is used for social purposes constantly, and for many, indispensably, as has been the case for eons, given that media has long had a social component (McKinsey & Company, 2014).

Social life—living in tandem with others, in relationships, in families, in communities—is one of the aspects of people's lives most profoundly changed when information and communication technology enters the equation. The internet and digital media connect people together in ways both mundane and significant. They help bring people into one another's awareness and allow them to discover commonalities and contact one another.

The technologies that contribute so much to the shape and texture of our lives were designed and invented and built by people and are continually shaped by people as well—by the collective actions of all those who create and use technologies. It is not useful or accurate to think of technology as an entity doing something *to* people and then to blame the technology when things go wrong or get complicated. This is called *technological determinism*, and as a way of understanding technology and its effects, it has many limitations.

When technological determinism is employed, *agency*—the ability to act and make choices—is assigned to the technology itself. Technological determinism doesn't adequately capture the human element: the personal choices, the actions taken, the gratifications that are met, the humanity that is at the root of all tech creation and use. Human agency, of course, is often limited by the structures that influence or constrain one's ability to freely act (such as one's position within an organization or the larger culture). While structure can constrain agency, it is through the actions cumulatively taken and the decisions cumulatively made by people in a culture that structures are built in the first place and then change over time.

A technology does not have the property of human agency. It cannot think and act on its own accord, independent of human and social forces. To assume that it does and to therefore blame or credit a technology for consequences that emerge in connection with its use is a less-than-helpful way of understanding how technology intersects with our social worlds. Still, technological determinism is invoked fairly frequently as an explanation for a social condition. We explore many issues in this book—such as online harassment, online surveillance, and compulsive internet use—in which technological determinism has been proposed by some as an explanation of the problem. In each of these situations, we will consider the range of possible factors that can contribute to the condition, and I ask you *not* to leap to the conclusion that technology in and of itself is the cause of the problem.

Societies face serious social problems—crime, violence, poverty, war, environmental destruction, all kinds of inequalities. Since rapid technological change has *accompanied* these problems, it can sometimes seem to have *caused* them. But to understand and work toward solutions for social problems is a complex endeavor for which simple causal frameworks are rarely sufficient. Furthermore, when two things are associated or related or correlated in some way, it does not necessarily follow that one has caused the other. Technology and society (and *society* should always be thought of as a collection of actual, acting, decision-making people who share space or goals or a common fate) are in constant interplay. People develop and use technology today in ways that affect how technology will be developed and used tomorrow and in the days, years, and decades to come.

It is also helpful to be aware that technology reflects and often advances the interests of those who create it and fund it. It is not neutral—it is not *just* a thing or a tool—but something that can disproportionally benefit those who make it, profit from it, or control its use. Exploring how the invention and use of technology is related to forces like political power, social class differences, and organizational dynamics is called the *social constructivist* approach to the study of technology. This approach can explain much about the ways that technology comes to develop and flow (or not) throughout a society and how it can impact individuals, relationships, communities, organizations, industries, and whole societies (see Volti, 2014).

When technology is seen as a combination of devices, skills, and these larger social structures, such as organizations, businesses, or governments, it is considered a *system.* In technological systems, these elements are interconnected and result in particular patterns and impacts of use. The development of these various elements is generally an uneven process, for when one part of the system changes, it can generate tensions in other parts of the system that must be resolved (Volti, 2014). For example, as tools to create and publish photos, stories, music, and videos have become available to individuals, and as people's skills using these tools have developed, the industries that seek to control how these technologies are used and monetized have felt great tension and have looked to regulate the technologies more strictly, which can create tensions for individual users in return. Human social systems are dynamic and often unstable, so such tensions are prevalent in modern technological communities and societies.

Human experience is at the same time technologically infused and highly social. Life is *techno-social* in the fullest sense of the word. I hyphenate this word to call equal attention to both the technological and the social and their equivalent importance in the examination and understanding of modern life (see Chayko, 2014). The technological and the social are in such intimate interaction, constantly influencing one another, that we really must consider their impact on one another in depth. So let's take a closer look at both the "techno" and the "social" aspects of techno-social life. First, the techno.

technology, mediation, and the diffusion of innovation

Information and communication technologies (ICTs) carry ideas and information from one person to another. When this process occurs, it is called *mediation* or *technological mediation,* and the technology itself can be considered a *mediator.* For centuries, people have used technological mediation to help them shape their thoughts into the stories that they tell others, whether via mass, large-scale mediation (TV, movies, newspapers, books); medium-scale, or meso-scale, mediation (using social media or blogs to reach dozens or a few hundred people, perhaps); or small-group, small-scale mediation (emailing or texting between two people or among small groups, telephoning or video chatting, or the more personalized use of blogs or social media). People can learn about those who lived in the past from all kinds of media, such as books, encyclopedias, photos, letters, and historical movies. People who live miles apart can come to know a great deal about one another. In all these ways, technology allows people to share the products of their minds with one another and, in the process, links people together across space and time (see Chayko, 2002).

Information and technology spread throughout societies through a process called the *diffusion of innovation* (see Rogers, 1962/2010). Whenever a new idea, technique, or technology—an *innovation*—is initiated by a creator or *innovator*, it begins to make its way (or not) through social networks. One possible outcome, if it spreads widely and successfully, is that a new way for people to become connected may develop. If very successfully diffused, as with the internet and digital media, new *norms* (expected behaviors), new *values* (beliefs), and a new kind of culture can develop.

Change agents—people or organizations that initially take interest in an innovation and influence others to do the same—may decide to adopt the technological innovation, use it, and tell others about it. A relatively small percentage of these *early adopters* tend to embrace innovations quickly and easily and enjoy being on the cutting edge of the culture. They were the first to buy and use personal computers or cell phones, for example. These are the people that are first in line to try the newest products and to learn the lingo that surrounds them. They start and set trends.

As others in the society are exposed to and react to the innovation, they too make decisions about whether or not to adopt it. The *early majority* tends to adopt the innovation once they see it being used and decide that it has some value, while the more conservative and practical *late majority* waits until it has been in wide circulation and seems to be becoming an essential part of daily life. Collectively representing about two thirds of the population, these individuals and groupings adopt new technologies at a pace they feel comfortable with. Collectively, they determine its popular success.

A small percentage of the population, generally estimated at about 16%, lags quite a bit behind the others. Some may never adopt the innovation at all. Rather unflatteringly called the *laggards*, these are the people who resist the adoption of an innovation as long as they can. They may feel comfortable with the status quo and see no reason to make a change, they may not be able to afford the invention, or they may not care about the usefulness of the invention, unable to imagine how it could benefit them. Even in North America, there are still some people who do not use computers or the internet (Rainie & Wellman, 2012, pp. 46–47).

When an innovation successfully takes hold, it spreads beyond the early adopters and can be said to be diffused throughout the society. It can be said to be well diffused when enough people—called a *critical mass*—make it part of their lives. In time, social norms, such as how people work, play, and conduct their everyday lives, may change. Eventually, the process can become self-sustaining, and the new idea or technology can be said to have taken root in the culture (Rogers, 1962/2010).

As a technology begins to spread, its impact can be felt more and more widely. It can inspire related or competing innovations, and the original technology itself can undergo adaptation. Problems may be identified and overcome (or not), and changes to design or use can be proposed and implemented. These adaptations can be at least as consequential as the breakthrough innovation, but they often represent small, steady, *incremental* advances, as opposed to large, *disruptive* changes that alter with startling impact whatever came before. In all kinds of industries, it is steady, modest improvements to existing technologies that most often result in large cumulative gains (Volti, 2014, p. 43).

This process does not necessarily advance because a new device or process is determined to be superior to another or is more exciting or fun to use. Certain groups can strongly influence the selection process, deciding, for example, that a technology meets their needs or deserves their funding. Policies and laws can be passed that favor one technology or process over another. People can use purchasing or political power to make their preferences known. This is why it is so useful to think of technologies as parts of social systems consisting of a number of disparate and diverse agents (sometimes called *actors* in this kind of formulation) and elements.

It is also instructive to consider how power flows through these social systems and the social networks that circumscribe them. In social networks, sets of individuals are linked in some meaningful way by physical or digital pathways along which social support, resources, and even relationships themselves (all of which can collectively be viewed as *social capital*) can flow and be exchanged. When digital, ICTs allow information and messages to be sent along these pathways. Interpersonal power and influence flow through networks as well.

When you share a photo of yourself on Facebook or some other social media platform, for example, you are sending a message that communicates something about you. With Facebook (via a computer or mobile phone) acting as technological mediator, that message is transmitted to others. But think about what actually occurs within that simple act—and consider the power of Facebook as you share that photo. Do all of your friends have an opportunity to view it? What about the non-Facebook population or those who rarely check it? What about those friends of yours that Facebook has decided (via a formula called an algorithm) will not see your news feed? Are your friends equally empowered to know and receive what you are sending? What if some individuals who do see your photo comment on it in a way that you had never intended (perhaps making fun of something you found serious or pointing out the flaws in a picture you thought flattering, for example). Have they grabbed some power—perhaps the power to change the meaning of the message? What if others tag or repost the picture or share it with someone you never thought would see it? What if the photo then receives another whole bunch of comments from people you don't know? What if some of these comments cause you distress? What if Facebook or an outside organization repurposes your photo as an endorsement of a product that you may or may not be comfortable being associated with? There are any number of ways that we relinquish power over our ideas and images when we share them via internet and digital media networks.

In this book, we consider who has the power to determine how digitized messages will be shaped and sent, in what contexts, and with what effects. "Every technology is both a burden and a blessing," said communication theorist Neil Postman (1993, p. 5), who then went on to remind us that these blessings and burdens are not distributed equally. There are winners, Postman says, and losers, as technologies are invented, adopted, and used. It is not always clear who will win and who will lose, and, for that matter, it is not always clear exactly *what* will be won and lost. Postman suggests that we ask ourselves, "To whom will the technology give greater power and freedom? . . . Whose power and freedom will be reduced by it?" (1993, p. 11). For all the rhetoric regarding the benefits of technological innovation that has arisen since the word *innovation* began to be widely used in the 1940s and the process has been focused upon, social inequalities are still pronounced (Vinsel, 2014), and solutions to the problems that can result are elusive.

Technological innovations can have an influence far beyond what their creators, early adopters, or anyone else could have imagined. Once a technology is created and unleashed on the world, anything can happen, and these changes are to a great extent unpredictable. It is impossible to know exactly how technology will be rolled out, received, and used and what it will mean for a community or society as a whole. In other words, because human beings are deeply embedded in technological systems, they, and their social lives, can be affected by internet and digital media use in any number of unforeseen ways. This is why this book examines the "social" part of techno-social life right alongside, and in direct connection to, the "techno."

sociality, or being social

Human beings are inherently social—that is, we gravitate toward one another to fulfill many of our needs, including safety, shelter, sustenance, companionship, and love. Left to our own devices, cut off from one another, we would be underdeveloped intellectually and emotionally. We would be much more vulnerable to danger. The world is better faced in the company of others.

People's tendency to form connections and bonds with one another, and to live life in concert with others, is called *sociality*, and a great deal of this can be accomplished via digital technology. To form social ties and bonds, people must coordinate their actions, and even their thoughts and emotions, with others. To do this, they must locate and get to know one another and determine the extent to which interpersonal similarities, commonalities, and synergies exist. And it is not necessary to be physically face-to-face with another person for all of this to occur.

As technology mediates between and among people, it facilitates the flow of information from person to person and from network to network. This allows people to discover the kinds of commonalities that can inspire social connectedness. Contrary to what some assume, the use of internet, digital, and mobile technologies does *not* tend to deter face-to-face interaction. Rather, it *prompts* face-to-face interaction, making it more likely to occur (Chayko, 2014). This is a consistent finding, backed up by study after study, that seems counterintuitive to some, but it is a key fact in the study of techno-social life (see Boase, Horrigan, Wellman, & Rainie, 2006; Chayko, 2014; Wang & Wellman, 2010; Zhao, 2006).

By enabling more and more people to form and maintain social connections, and even to make dates to get together physically, the use of digital technology has had an overall positive impact on sociality (Chayko, 2008, 2014; Tufekci, 2012). Some people get to know others *better* when their contact with them is primarily digital as opposed to face-to-face. Distance can enhance closeness. Mobile media use allows contact and connectedness to occur nearly any time, in any place; people can be available to one another much of the time and engage in frequent interactions that make the relationship hardier and more likely to be continued face-to-face.

Moreover, those who use the internet and digital media most often are those who stay in closest contact with their friends face-to-face. They use the technology to check in on friends and family members and post updates so all can remain "in the know." They use the tech to arrange get-togethers. They are more likely to have close relationships and confidants and to form local, neighborhood relationships than non-internet users, too. As we discuss in greater depth in Chapter 7, internet and digital media use make it much easier to make and maintain social contacts and relationships, both online and offline.

While the internet and digital media—and mobile and social media, in particular—enhance users' abilities to remain connected to one another, some people have an aversion to or difficulty in making connections via digital means (Tufekci, 2010). Technologies cannot be expected to have a uniform effect on all who use them. Still, most internet and digital media users—especially those who frequent social network sites—are open to experiencing sociability, conviviality, and even deep, meaningful connectedness when they go online. Many receive or exchange substantial amounts of social support, help, and resources (Ellison,

Steinfield, & Lampe, 2007, 2011; McCosker & Darcy, 2013; Sproull, Conley, & Moon, 2005). At the same time, risks and dangers exist online, as they do in every interpersonal setting. These are also explored in this book.

Given the human desire and need for togetherness and the ability of technology to serve as an interpersonal mediator, it makes sense that people would turn to technology to bring them together so they can experience sociality even (or especially) when they are separated by space and time. Doing so has become a routine use of the internet and digital media and explains much about the tremendous expansion and popularity of these technologies. Accordingly, individuals in technology-rich communities and societies tend to live *techno-social lives.*

this book

Technological superconnectedness and the role of the internet and digital, social, and mobile media in people's lives is a fascinating topic that has interested thinkers from many walks of life. Scholars in a number of academic disciplines—from sociology, communication, and psychology to media studies, information science, computer science, philosophy, the humanities, and many more—conduct research and/or develop theories that can help all of us understand it better. Nonscholars and writers interested in the topic, including technology experts, inventors, and critics, also have much to say that is thought-provoking and important. Ideally, as you read this book and absorb its ideas, you will have a lot to say about techno-social life as well.

In writing this book, I examined a wide array of this research, writing, conversation, and debate, bringing together and synthesizing ideas, understandings, and findings from many relevant fields. While much of this literature reflects research and theory on technology-rich, information-intensive North American societies that can be applied to tech-rich information societies globally, I sought and included, and the book will speak to, many studies of lower-tech societies across the globe as well. The result is an overview of techno-social life that draws on a wide variety of perspectives and findings, focusing on communities and societies that are characterized by a steady flow of communication technology and information, while contrasting this with lower-tech life.

I also drew upon my own research, which spans over 25 years; some of this research is highlighted in published articles and talks, and some can be found in my books *Portable Communities: The Social Dynamics of Online and Mobile Connectedness* and *Connecting: How We Form Social Bonds and Connections in the Internet Age* (2008 and 2002, respectively, both with SUNY Press). This research was qualitative in nature, comprising over 200 extended, open-ended, multi-phase face-to-face and electronic (email) interviews I conducted for a range of projects that contributed to the aforementioned books. Portions of these interviews are shared here to illustrate relevant points, including additional material to enhance *Superconnected*'s second edition. These excerpts appear primarily in chapters that focus on themes with which my prior research has been most concerned: the social dynamics and implications of the online experience (Chapters 3 and 9) and the nature of the identities, connections, and communities formed in internet and digital media use (Chapters 6 and 7—see Chayko, 2002, 2008, for delineation of these projects and their associated methodologies and findings).

This book invites you to consider many dimensions of techno-social life and superconnectedness and to think about (and discuss and write about) how *you* and those you care about have been affected because the study of social life and society is most engaging when it is personalized, seen through the lens of *your own* life. Anyway, society *is* you, it's not some abstract mass or huge, faceless throng—it's a living, breathing, learning, interconnected bunch of people, like you and your friends, like me and mine, like all who share a common space or identity or purpose. Society is *all* of us, going about our daily lives, trying to understand what's happening and how the world works. So society is always alive and in motion, and the study of it is always personal.

We'll begin with a short history of how internet and mobile technology developed, became so deeply embedded in so many people's lives, and helped create the modern information age (Chapter 2). We'll then travel through the techno-social environment and the rich complexity of the online experience (Chapter 3). We'll examine online information sharing and surveillance (Chapter 4), global impacts and inequalities (Chapter 5), and the influence of the internet and digital media on socialization, growing up, and the always-developing self (Chapter 6). We'll learn more about friending, dating, and relating online (Chapter 7); the techno-social institutions of family, health care, religion, work and commerce, education and libraries, politics and governing, and the media (Chapter 8); and some of the benefits and hazards of 24/7 superconnectedness not covered in other chapters (Chapter 9). Finally, we'll look at the future (or, more accurately, the *possible* future) of techno-social life (Chapter 10).

So let's get started by stepping back in time a little bit. We'll find out how the internet, mobile technology, and digital and social media were conceived and invented and how they, and related services and apps, have become so central to so many lives. You'll notice society beginning to change in ways that continue today, becoming *your* world and your life—your superconnected techno-social life.

2 CREATING THE INTERNET AGE

a (very) short history of information and communication technology

Communication is much more than an act of technological mediation, or even a process of writing or talking. Communication is prehistoric, preliterate, preverbal, and even nonverbal—think of how much is communicated by body language. Prior to the invention of words and writing, people sent messages to one another using gestures, grunts, cries, and crude symbols such as cave paintings, stone carvings, and smoke signals. Then, as now, these messages were probably imperfectly received and interpreted, but they speak to the timeless human desire to communicate with one another, to be seen and known and understood.

In prehistoric times, before records of these processes could be kept, communication consisted primarily of gestures, grunts, and body language. Slowly, communication became verbal and more complex; grunts became words and words became spoken languages. Formal languages began to coalesce and spread, probably between 150,000 and 350,000 years ago, though it could have been even earlier—it is extremely difficult to pinpoint with accuracy things that happened before written records were kept (Perreault & Mathew, 2012). Famed communication theorist Marshall McLuhan has compared language to transportation technology, invoking French philosopher Henri Bergson in writing that "language does for intelligence what the wheel does for the feet and the body." Language enables the intellect to "move from thing to thing," McLuhan said, and allows people's thoughts and ideas to be transmitted and to be more easily shared (McLuhan, 1964, p. 83; see Chayko, 2002).

When languages began to take root, people could share information with one another more widely but also more concretely. At first, they'd share easily memorized facts, such as lists of kings or names of clans, that they thought important to pass along to future generations. When they did so, those facts could become fixed in people's minds and in the collective memory of the group. It would then become more important for future group members to know such facts—and knowing them would become part of their role and identity as group members. Sharing information in this way became part of how people related to one another and helped connect them to one another.

Somewhere around 5,000 to 8,000 years ago, in Mesopotamia, China, or Egypt, formal systems of writing began to appear, originally to simply keep count of things and record business transactions. Technology external to the body, such as bones and shells dipped in plant juice or animal blood, recorded information on available surfaces (Gabrial, 2008). Phonetic elements and alphabets emerged as well. This allowed people to communicate with even greater specificity and breadth. People were freed from having to retain everything they knew in their minds; now that they were able to write much of it down and pass it along, messages could be more complex, more abstract, and could have greater longevity. People who lived at different points in time could learn in greater detail about those who had come before them. It became possible to form detailed, complex social connections that would span time and space (see Chayko, 2008, pp. 10–13).

Words and symbols were etched into stone and clay and then later printed on parchment, cloth, and paper with styluses and ink. These early forms of media (software, really!) allowed data and messages to be stored and communicated to others. Hand-printed and copied scrolls, books, pamphlets, and newspapers—the first mass media, intended to reach larger audiences—followed. These documents were painstakingly prepared and copied by hand until the invention of movable type, in which molds of original pages were cast in a material such as clay, wood, or, most durably, metal, allowing them to be printed and reprinted.

In or around 1450, Johannes Gutenberg introduced a mechanical movable type machine called a printing press and ushered in the era of mass production and communication. Books, including the Bible, could now be mass-produced—indeed, they could become bestsellers. The technology quickly caught on; within 50 years, tens of millions of copies of books had been printed. Pamphlets, newspapers, and magazines soon became set in movable type as well. The mass-media era was now swiftly underway, ushering in a time of rapid social change, as political movements (like the American Revolution), social movements (civil, labor, and women's rights), and the beginnings of public education all gathered large-scale strength with the ability to widely disseminate ideas and information. Since this time, ICTs have helped bring about social changes small and large and have, in fact, become indispensable to such causes, as we discuss further in Chapter 5.

In the early 1800s, technologies that allowed the harnessing of electric power, such as electromagnetism and batteries, became sufficiently advanced that practical applications of electricity followed. These applications included many that facilitated the sending of messages electronically, such as the phonograph (which was originally acoustic), Morse code, telegraph, telephone, and the mass media of film and radio. Messages could now move much more quickly from one place to another, and people could begin to discern the meanings and motivations of those who sent them. The 1900s brought improvements on the prior century's innovations, plus television, videophones (oddly, a very early invention that never really caught on until the era of the webcam), computers, and giant brick-sized, early-model cellular phones (which did not have computerized capability beyond telephony and are discussed later in this chapter, along with mobility in digital communication). Interestingly, as new technologies are invented, they do not necessarily supplant those that came before but are often used in combination with them, sometimes inspiring changes in how the existing technologies operate or are used (see Dunbar-Hester, 2014; Jenkins, 2006; Volti, 2014).

By the 1900s, data could be stored and shared so widely, in so many ways, that the word *media* had many meanings. It could be defined by the type of platform used to deliver it (broadcast, print, digital, mobile, social/interactive, multimedia), its content (news media, advertising media), or its recency (traditional media, new media). To speak of *the media* is generally to reference the totality of all these types of media. And one of the newest and most important forms of the media that could reach many people nearly instantly—the internet—was on the horizon.

a (not quite as) short history of computing and the internet

The forerunners of modern computers actually date back thousands of years, when people began to develop nonmechanized (and later mechanized) means to count and calculate sums, document and catalog information, and automate critical functions. More modern systems to organize and classify great amounts of information owe much to Melvil Dewey's Dewey Decimal System, a classification system developed in 1876 to organize books and other library resources, and Paul Octet and Henri LaFontaine's Universal Decimal System of 1895, which attempted to collect, organize, and share "the world's information" in a comprehensive international document center. Octet also envisioned systems in which books could be read with the use of screens and a keyboard, and numerous individuals could view an event remotely, à la videoconferencing (Google Arts and Culture, 2013).

The first known use of the word *computer* actually referred to an individual who, in the early 1600s, was considered extremely adept at arithmetic and talented at computing. Such a person would be called a "computer" for short. Now, of course, when we think of computers, we think of machines that are programmable, perform complicated tasks, use digital encoding, and can be linked to other computers so that information can be transferred from one to the other.

Computers became more modern and began to fit this vision throughout the mid-to-late 1800s and into the early 1900s. Notable advances were made by Charles Babbage, who in 1837 designed the first programmable mechanical computer; Ada Lovelace, considered to be the first computer programmer (1840s); Herman Hollerith, who in the 1880s invented the keypunch machine that launched information processing; and Alan Turing, who in 1936 designed the first electronic digital computer.

Many consider the modern age of computing to have begun in the 1930s and 1940s. Engineer and mathematician Vannevar Bush began thinking about how machines could automate human thinking, and, in 1931, he built a huge, almost room-sized machine called a differential analyzer that could analyze differential equations. In 1945, a landmark article titled "As We May Think" that he wrote and published in the *Atlantic Monthly* magazine described how a machine called a memex might extend human memory by making links between documents (presaging computerized hyperlinking), allowing a person to build "a trail of many items," occasionally inserting "a comment of his own, either linking it into the main trail or joining it by a side trail to a particular item" (Bush, 1945). Bush's work was constrained by the level of technology of the time, and he died before the web and hyperlinking were invented, but his ideas directly inspired those who actually built the internet and the web.

In the 1950s, a number of computer scientists, psychologists, physicists, and other scholars began to imagine and develop interactive computers of the type that the internet would use. Some, led by computer scientist John McCarthy, concentrated on the development of *artificial intelligence*, or computing systems able to perform tasks that would otherwise require human intelligence, such as visual perception, speech recognition, and decision-making. McCarthy and his colleagues conducted research into *artificial intelligence* that led to the development of computers that could best human beings in games like checkers and chess and solve problems of logic. The U.S. Department of Defense funded much of this research, clearly committing to the importance of "smart machines." In 1954, American inventor George Devol laid the foundation for the field of robotics with the first digitally operated and programmed robot, named Unimate, which worked on a New Jersey assembly line. An extension of artificial intelligence, *robots*, guided by computer programs, would take on rote tasks that could be automated, but they would also, as we shall see, take on more complex tasks over time and become more lifelike.

At the same time, other researchers, such as psychologist J. C. R. Licklider, realized a particular need for the development of computers that could perform the more mundane steps of multistep tasks. He envisioned a human–computer partnership, or symbiosis, that would feature a "very close coupling between the human and the electronic members of the partnership" (Licklider, 1960, p. 4). Licklider described all kinds of possible uses for computerization, including digital libraries, e-commerce, and online banking, and he also envisioned a point-and-click system for using the computer.

Licklider's fellow pioneers in interactive computing began to develop the technologies needed for networked computing to become reality. Doug Englebart, who was strongly influenced by Vannevar Bush, set forth a vision for a human intellect augmented by computers and then created a research lab at which the technology for hyperlinking and the computer mouse was developed. A method by which blocks of data could be transmitted, called packet switching, was developed, independently, by Paul Baran in the United States and Donald Davies in the United Kingdom. Computer hardware, software, and the programming codes that would instruct computers what to do became increasingly more sophisticated. Protocols for connecting computers together, network standards, and assigned domains began to spring up. Conditions were ripe for an internet to be born.

What we now think of as the internet actually began as an initiative of a Department of Defense agency responsible for the development of technology for military use. It is called the Defense Advanced Research Project Agency, or DARPA. A computer research team at DARPA, including Licklider, Baran, Leonard Kleinrock, and project manager Larry Roberts, all of the Massachusetts Institute of Technology (MIT), began to invent and test various models. Similar research was also underway at RAND, the global nonprofit research and development organization that conducts military and weapons research, and at the United Kingdom's National Physical Laboratory (NPL), where Donald Davies worked. In 1965, working with Thomas Merrill, Roberts connected a computer in Massachusetts to a computer in California with a low-speed, dial-up telephone line, creating the first wide-area (though tiny by today's standards) computer network. Roberts called this idea of networked computers the ARPANET (Leiner et al., 2009).

Several academic institutions soon became keenly interested in this project. ARPANET computer sites were set up at University of California, Los Angeles; University of California, Santa Barbara; the University of Utah; and the Stanford Research Institute. Paul Baran argued strenuously and ultimately successfully that the internet's nodes, or annex points, should not feed directly to a single centralized source, but be distributed so that the whole network would not collapse if one portion of it were to fail and so that it could not be taken out all at once in an enemy attack. Coordinated activity among these sites—mostly the sharing of resources and performance of mathematical functions—began in 1969, and in 1970, additional computers were added to the network. The system was successfully introduced to the public and demonstrated by Robert Kahn at the International Computer Communication Conference in 1972.

ARPANET evolved into what we know as the internet, as research continued not only into the means of connecting and networking dispersed computers but into the possible uses of such a network. Interested researchers, business professionals, and government and military users began using these computers to share information with one another. An initiative called BITNET attempted to link all academic mainframe computers. Domain names were requested of Elizabeth "Jake" Feinler at Stanford Research Center's National Information Center (NIC), and massive paper directories of the ARPANET and documents that detailed how the system worked were published. "The NIC was like the pre-historic Google," Feinler now says. "People came to us for everything" (Metz, 2012).

Once the ARPANET was up and running, applications could be developed, and almost immediately, a platform people could use to interact was developed. In 1972, Ray Tomlinson, a defense department engineer, sent the first email message (he has since forgotten its contents, he says!) and made the highly influential decision that the @ symbol would be used as the electronic locater symbol. Larry Roberts wrote an email utility program, and almost immediately, people began creating mailing lists, allowing groups of people with similar interests, such as science fiction devotees or wine tasters, to share information and engage in discussions. "We could see instantly that email was a *social medium*, in addition to simply being an interoffice memo system," recalls Vinton Cerf (as cited in Standage, 2013, p. 219, emphasis added). The simple but powerful ability to exchange messages electronically quickly became one of the most popular uses of the internet, eventually becoming an everyday activity for billions of people (see Rainie & Wellman, 2012).

In 1974, the term *internet* (short for *internetwork*) was first mentioned in a document on transmission protocols by Vinton Cerf, Yogen Dalal, and Carl

Sunshine (1974). Before long, it would become obvious that one of the internet's most enticing uses would be neither military nor academic, nor even particularly industrial, but *social.* Experimentation into other kinds of applications, such as gaming, file sharing, and voice communication, began. Some early group messaging and bulletin board systems existed (see social networking and social media, discussed later), but relatively few people thought to or were able to use them. Computers themselves were not common, and neither were the slow, sometimes expensive dial-up connections that were required to connect them to other computers and networks of computers. Few had the specialized knowledge needed to operate them, for graphical, "windows-like" modes of network navigation (like point-and-click interfaces) had not yet been invented.

Still, small local computer networks (LANs) sprang up, and throughout the 1970s, larger ones appeared. Some researchers, business professionals, and members of government and military organizations began using these computers and the young internet to share information with one another. At the same time, computers were coming down in size and in price. The invention of the microprocessor—a small chip that contained most of a computer's circuitry—allowed computers first to fit on the top of a desk, and then, years later, in one's hand.

In 1973, IBM and Hewlett-Packard introduced the first of these desk-sized programmable computers. These were mostly used for scientific and research purposes. Other early personal computers were introduced by Xerox, Commodore, Radio Shack, and, perhaps most famously, by Steve Jobs and Steve Wozniak, who created the first Apple computers in 1976 in Jobs's family garage. During this time, Microsoft founders Paul Allen and Bill Gates began to develop an operating system to allow computers to interpret and execute their coded instructions. By the late 1970s, early adopters were purchasing personal computers, and these computers were becoming successfully marketed, although their uses were still quite limited.

In the late 1970s, a packet switching system called X.25 began to spread internationally, and a worldwide network infrastructure was spawned that reached from the United States and Europe to Canada, Hong Kong, and Australia. By 1982, protocols by which data could be transmitted and received (called TCP, transmission control protocol, and IP, internet protocol) were standardized. Computer scientist Radia Perlman introduced advancements that permitted data to be moved and managed more easily and networks to scale and self-organize. The resultant worldwide network of interconnected networks became widely referred to as "the Internet" (always with a capital *I* back then; it was also sometimes called the information superhighway). In 1985,

The National Science Foundation Network funded five large, interconnected supercomputing centers that would become connected to regional networks and to colleges and universities, along with the equipment and circuits needed to facilitate connection to this network. This sprawling network (or network of networks), called NSFNET, became considered the "backbone" of the modern internet (Cyber Telecom, 2014).

Though the internet as we know it today was taking definite shape, still only about 10% of Americans in 1983 owned personal computers, and only about 10% of those people—approximately 1.4% of the U.S. population—were using the internet to send and receive messages (Rainie & Wellman, 2012, p. 60). The applications and uses of computers were still not apparent, and their operation was slow and cumbersome. There was also a big structural obstacle: The National Science Foundation's acceptable use policy forbade *any* personal or commercial use of the NSFNET "backbone" network (although smaller connecting networks could formulate their own policies). The larger network, the internet itself, was supposed to support research, education, and nonprofit firms only. But before long, this policy was challenged. The internet would not be contained.

In 1990, one of the regional networks connected to the internet, a Michigan network called MERIT, proposed to the National Science Foundation that the commercial potential of the internet be explored. A for-profit corporation was permitted to develop and own computers and transmission lines and to solicit customers. Though this development was not without controversy (indeed, congressional hearings regarding the appropriate future of the internet were held), commercial internet service providers were eventually allowed to become part of the quickly expanding network, whose infrastructure and services were now being frequently updated. Communications-based corporations such as Sprint, AT&T, IBM, and MCI helped fund and establish the needed technology to expand and privatize the internet. CompuServe (1979), Prodigy (1984), and America Online (AOL; 1985) began offering service packages and the means for people to "get onto" the internet, and Microsoft began developing and providing browsers and servers in addition to its operating system. In 1995, the National Science Foundation ended its sponsorship of the project, and the internet could be considered privatized (Harris & Gerich, 1996).

Although private companies began to become involved as vendors or service providers, there was no central or global agency controlling the internet—not the Department of Defense, not a research think tank, not a university. Crucial to the successful development and identity of the internet was its open and distributed architecture. Openness, of course, has its benefits and its drawbacks.

Malicious programs written and programmed to disrupt the operation of computers and networks, called *computer viruses*, began to be written and deployed. Malicious code called *malware* could spread rapidly from computer to computer, erasing hard drives, stealing data, or monopolizing the screen with a graphic that would not go away. Junk email, or *spam*, that could potentially damage a computer could be sent simultaneously to countless accounts (Naughton, 2012). In time, malware- and spam-blocking services and filters became sophisticated enough to derail a good portion of these problems, but, as we shall see in Chapter 4, hacking and computer crimes now proliferate.

Still, the openness of the internet, considered critical to its functioning and social applications and central to its very identity, was preserved through each iteration and innovation that allowed it to expand. Each link in the network could stand on its own; the larger network did not rely on any one portion for it to work. When a "web" of services and applications began to diffuse across the still relatively young internet, its impact was immediate and profound.[1]

the web is born

As recently as 1990, the internet was still a relatively small-scale phenomenon. There were probably fewer than 5 million internet users worldwide. "Only people with specialized knowledge could find what later came to be called 'web sites,'" Rainie and Wellman have pointed out, "and only real specialists could build them" (2012, p. 61). Though the internet was technically open for business, it was difficult to navigate and work within, and so its *affordances*—its possible opportunities, effects, and benefits—were still largely unknown. The internet was still strange, incomprehensible territory.

All this changed with the development of the World Wide Web (WWW) during the 1989 to 1991 time frame. The WWW was the brainchild of Tim Berners-Lee, a British engineer who worked for the European Organization for Nuclear Research (called CERN) and who had begun developing what he called the "WorldWideWeb"—originally all one word. It was, and still is, a collection of documents that are linked together through a system called *hypertext*, which had been invented without a context for widespread usage by American engineer Doug Engelbart and his team at the Augmented Research Center back in the 1960s. Hypertext contains *hyperlinks* that allow the user to click easily and nonlinearly from one bit of data to another and has become a central feature of internet use. By ensuring that documents could be embedded with hypertext links that would take users anywhere on the web, Berners-Lee saw to it that one portion or branch of the web would not be able to dominate or overtake the entire system. Documents could be linked and interlinked in a sprawling, weblike structure, hence the name—which soon became abbreviated to "the web."

Just as important as Berners-Lee's technical and intellectual contributions to the web and the internet was his determination (and that of CERN) that the web be decentralized and available for free for anyone to use. In 1993, CERN made web technology available to the world at no cost to any particular organization—a key moment in internet history that meant that unfettered access to it would be the web's most striking and enticing feature. Aided by the internet's open architecture, this would herald the web's worldwide (though not universal) spread and influence. The Telecommunications Act of 1996 called for all U.S. classrooms, libraries, and hospitals to become connected to the internet. Thanks to the invention of email and data transfer technologies (including files, chats, phone calls, and streaming video), the web became a place where people began to congregate, to reach out to one another, to be social, and, eventually, to build networks and share media.

Technologies that supported the widespread development of the web were rather quickly invented and enjoyed rapid adoption and diffusion among computer users. Mosaic, a web browser that was graphical and easy to use, supplanted the clumsier text-based browser Gopher in 1993 and was soon followed by the even-easier-to-use graphical Netscape Navigator. Now, people could travel or "surf" the web without possessing specialized knowledge and skill. Web pages became visually interesting entities—simpler versions of what they are today, but much more colorful and refined than the earliest versions. The Digital Millennium Copyright Act (or DMCA) of 1998 governed the use of copyrighted content in the United States, shielding websites from liability for users' possible copyright infringement (though contested content had to, and must still be, taken down temporarily). Web directories, such as Yahoo, began to catalog things on the web. Early versions of web-based commerce and banking were offered.

Search engines, which provided a means for people to find what they were looking for on the web, soon followed, but they were not immediately seen as critical tools. The internet was envisioned as "an infrastructure of connection, not of sorting or of organization," Christian Sandvig has noted. "To the typical Internet user of that era, computers did not usually sort content in any way that was meaningful. They did not sort (recommend) music or movies, email was not automatically highlighted as 'important' or 'spam,' and search engines were not particularly useful" (2015). In fact, the success of AltaVista, the first important search engine, launched in 1994 following earlier engines WebCrawler and Lycos, was not foreseen. The prevailing belief was that it was not possible or necessary to efficiently sort and catalog the web (Sandvig, 2015).

Google, developed by Stanford PhD students Larry Page and Sergey Brin in the mid-1990s, became available to the public in late 1997 and took web searching to the next level. Rather than ranking search results by the appearance of the desired search term, Google determined a website's relevance by the number of pages that linked to it (the PageRank system). In 2001, Google revolutionized the process of web searching again by developing complex, rule-based formulas, or *algorithms*, that sorted and organized information even more efficiently. Over time, these algorithms became progressively more sophisticated, allowing searches to become personalized in order to supply you—the searcher—with links that would be of greatest interest to you (and learning quite a bit about you in the process—we explore the implications of this in Chapter 4).

These innovations paved the way for the development of increasingly interactive software, media platforms, and specialized programs called applications, or *apps*. People with special interests from a wide range of backgrounds began to create the intricate and sophisticated web pages, sites, and blogs that now populate so much of the web. The imagination of many was caught with this stream of innovation, and ways to create content and associated technologies became more apparent, available, achievable, and inexpensive. The shaping of the internet by people without technical expertise was underway.

However, the internet was still not, and *is* still not, universally accessible. The technology that would facilitate internet connectivity began to penetrate Europe in the mid-1980s (due to the efforts of Daniel Karrenberg, among others), Asia in the late 1980s (the pivotal work of Kilnam Chan), and Africa in the 1990s (a joint effort of many, including Tarek Kamel in Egypt, Mike Lawrie in South Africa, Shem Ochuodho in Kenya, and Charles Musisi in eastern Africa). Still, as noted in Chapter 1, only about half of the world's population uses the internet today, and there is much to be done to bring, especially, sub-Saharan Africa and the poorest areas of Asia and Latin America online. In many areas of the globe, the electronic (and physical) infrastructure is still underdeveloped or too expensive for all but the richest citizens to access. Furthermore, authoritarian or totalitarian regimes may censor or filter the internet, denying people the ability to freely access and disseminate information. Mobile phone communication, however, is spreading more quickly and widely, even in developing areas of the world, providing many individuals with internet access they would otherwise not be able to obtain (we discuss global impacts and inequalities, and the implications of these inequalities, in Chapter 5).[2]

a deep, "dark" web is also born

Almost as soon as the ARPANET was assembled, small, isolated networks that were not cataloged and could not be detected on the network by usual means began to appear. Sometimes called the "darknets," these secretive sites increased in number throughout the 1980s and did so exponentially when the internet as we know it today began to take shape. Requiring special encryption, illegal activity often occurred on these sites, such as file-sharing of copyrighted materials, illegal gambling, and the exchange and use of illegal pornography, including child pornography. As such websites would not appear on search engines, someone who wanted to visit one would need to know the URL and type it in manually, which seemed to offer some level of identity protection and anonymity.

The early 2000s saw the release of Freenet, software that facilitated passage to untraceable websites and areas of the internet, and HavenCo, a means for hosting restricted data. In 2005, the U.S. Naval Academy released Tor, a software that concealed, and could spoof, the location and IP address of users. While intended to protect the identities of American dissidents in repressive countries like China, Tor also served to provide cover to those who wanted to visit "dark" and often illegal sites on the internet without being detected or identified. With the wider use of Tor, software piracy exploded. In 2005, up to half a million movies were illegally streamed each day, and illegal copying and use of such software as Microsoft's Office was rampant. It was estimated that companies lost over $34 billion in 2005 due to activities in what was by then being referred to as the *dark web* (McCormick, 2013).

Since this time, the dark web has only expanded. In 2009, *Bitcoin*, an untraceable digital currency, was developed and introduced, and it would become the most widely acceptable currency of its kind, well suited to participation in illegal activities and growing illegal businesses (among other, more acceptable uses). Marketplaces for the buying and selling of illegal drugs and weapons were set up and began to do brisk business. Data hacking could more easily serve destructive purposes, as hacked data could be dumped into sites on the dark web and then be used to harm or blackmail. In the Ashley Madison data hack of 2015, for example, individuals who joined and used the site to conduct extramarital affairs found their data hacked and moved to the dark web, where a payment of $2,500 in Bitcoin was required to prevent their infidelities from becoming public. Criminal hacking and cybercrime began to proliferate (see Chapter 5), testing the resources and tech skills of law enforcement at local and national levels.

The dark web is also used for a variety of political and terroristic purposes. Those in totalitarian regimes may use encryption and uncataloged sites to organize revolts and communicate with the outside world—behaviors that become all the more urgent when regimes forbid their citizens use of the internet. Citizens of all countries may use these sites to hold conversations and organize movements that they wish to keep secret from those in power. And there has been a precipitous rise in recent years in the use of the dark net by extremist and terrorist groups to recruit members and organize and carry out their destructive acts.

The dark web is a subset of the *deep web*, which has become the term used for all websites and activities that are not ordinarily accessible to internet users. This includes databases, registration-required pages and sites (including those used for online banking), and those that are behind paywalls. There are many such sites and pages, and their number grows exponentially each year. Most are not harmful but are simply not available without special registration—that is, they exist "deep" in the web. Also, versions of websites and pages that are not ready to go "live," or that were once live but have since been deleted, can still exist, be archived, and potentially retrieved as part of the deep web (Egan, 2017; McCormick, 2013). This is what is meant when we are told that "nothing ever truly disappears on the internet."

wireless and mobile communication

One of the biggest advancements in information and communication technology, and in digital technology in particular, has been the development of the ability for people to communicate wirelessly. By making the mediated world and all that it offers portable—accessible nearly anywhere and at any time—wireless and mobile technologies have become an essential component of life in modern societies and in many ways characterize these societies. Though we think of mobile (or cell, and now smart) phones as the first and most important of these technologies, they were preceded by many innovations that allowed individuals to move farther and farther away from one another in physical space and to still establish and maintain social connections "on the go." These innovations include roads, railroads, cars, planes, stone tablets, pen and ink, books and newspapers, transistor radios, and handheld cameras, all of which help make portable communication possible. The continuous invention of ever-smaller, ever-more-portable devices with which we can communicate reflects the desire of many modern individuals to access information and enjoy social connectedness while on the move.

Wireless communication dates back to the late 1800s, when electromagnetic waves, which make wireless connecting possible, were discovered. Radio waves were used for electronic transmissions via two-way radios, such as citizen band (CB) radios, and for the sending of telegrams. Later came radio and TV shows and global positioning systems (GPS), used to determine location in cars, boats, and aircraft. As of the mid-20th century, cellular, satellite, and other wireless networks became the foundation for modern mobile telephones, computer connectivity, Wi-Fi, and wireless broadband internet.

Mobile phone technology first appeared in the form of car phones, which made their debut appearance in 1946. They were enormous and expensive and, of course, limited by the technology of the time. Though they were mobile, they couldn't use the cellular and transistor technology that had yet to be invented and perfected, so calls were more like CB-radio transmissions in which one person had to wait for the other to finish talking before continuing the conversation. Others could easily listen in. The earliest phones were the size of a suitcase, and "the only call one could make would be to the service station, as the power required to make a call actually killed the car battery" (Dead Media Archive, 2011).

Motorola led the development of the modern mobile cell phone that was not anchored to a car. Engineer Martin Cooper made the first mobile phone call in 1973 in New York City. The phone weighed almost two and a half pounds, and its battery lifetime was only 20 minutes, but that wasn't too much of a problem, Cooper has been quoted as saying, "because you couldn't hold up the phone that long" (John Dixon Technology, 2012b).

It took until the 1990s for enough radio frequencies to be assigned that mobile phones could become a viable mass technology and even longer for the size and price of phones to come down so that they could enjoy wide acceptance. Not until the 2000s did phones become truly "smart"—able to serve as mini–entertainment and information centers, with text messaging and web browsing as standard features. Four "generations" of mobile phone technology (called 1G, 2G, 3G, and 4G—introduced approximately 10 years apart) have been designated to mark differences in the capabilities of these phones. Improvements have included the ability to transfer calls from one cell site to the next as the user travels between sites during a conversation (in the first generation, 1G, introduced in 1981) and the replacement of this kind of circuit switching by the internet's packet-switching technology, which enabled a higher density of streaming audio, video, and phone calls (4G, in 2012).

But enabling phone conversations is no longer the primary purpose of a smartphone. In the late 2000s, cell phones and smartphones began to feature full keyboards rather than just embedding letters within number keypads, and wireless data price plans began to come down in price, both of which enabled text messaging to become a mainstream activity. *Texting* was, and is, a relatively simple, convenient, and unobtrusive way to communicate. It can be done silently in the midst of any number of activities and environments, often without others aware that it is happening. Texting is such a convenient and efficient way to communicate that it allows, for many, near-constant interpersonal connectedness (a state that we examine further in Chapter 9).

The proportion of the American population that texts has risen dramatically in recent years, while using cell phones for voice conversations has decreased just as dramatically. From 2006 to 2011, the percentage of the adult American population that texted nearly doubled, rising from 31% to 59%, and this number continues to increase (Rainie & Wellman, 2012). More than 75% of American teenagers text, with older teens sending an average of over 100 texts a day (Lenhart, 2012). As modern smartphones are really minicomputers that include cameras, word-processing capabilities, internet access, and numerous apps, one wonders whether mobile "phones" may eventually be called something else.

Mobile phones have now diffused across the globe, reaching even into traditionally poor, rural, or low-population areas that might not otherwise be able to use the technology, although in such areas people are much more likely to use a rudimentary phone that may not be able to access the internet, and it is not uncommon for several people to share a phone (for more on global digital communication, see Chapter 5). Many mobile web users rarely or never use a desktop, laptop, or tablet to access the web. Advancements in mobile tech and the technology of *virtual reality* or *augmented reality*—immersive nonphysical environments that simulate the physical and often require special headgear or other external technology—have also brought about a huge increase in online games and gaming, many of which are enjoyed on mobile devices (John Dixon Technology, 2012a).

early online networking

A bunch of individuals (or groups or organizations) can be said to be *networked* when they are connected or tied together such that they have some relationship to and influence over one another. To consider entities networked is to be able to trace and chart the many ways, some subtle and some even invisible, that this occurs.

Online social networking is often described as one of the most recent applications of the internet and the web, but it actually predates both. The first computerized interpersonal social networks arrived in the mid-1970s. They had great historical significance in terms of facilitating the exchange of messages among physically separated people, and there was an incredible sense of excitement that accompanied their use in those early years. The feeling of being part of a grand social experiment—a pioneer on a brand new frontier—was frequently invoked among those developing this new kind of social interaction in those not-so-distant times. They seemed to sense, correctly, that they were at the vanguard of a revolutionary form of sociality.

Many consider Murray Turoff to be the "father" of social, interactive computing. In his work in the early 1970s, first for the government and then as a professor at New Jersey Institute of Technology, he designed several initiatives that allowed dispersed individuals to share information via computer. Perhaps the most well known of these (developed with Starr Roxanne Hiltz, also a professor at NJIT and Turoff's spouse) was a teleconferencing system called the Electronic Information Exchange System (EIES), which included very early versions of online educational courses. Interestingly, it also encouraged face-to-face meetings among its users. Many who designed the online networks that followed EIES have mentioned how influential this early online initiative was in their conception of what it might mean to be digitally connected and networked.

One way that people could be networked online was via a system whereby someone would electronically post a message and someone else could respond. At first, this exchange had to be asynchronous—in fact, in these early days, it could take days or even weeks for a response to appear! Some very early 1970s experiments that allowed the exchange of messages included Community Memory, which used hardwired terminals in various neighborhoods near Berkeley, California, to allow people to submit and respond to questions; PLATO, developed at the University of Illinois, which allowed people to share "notes" (at first education-oriented), play games, chat, network, and eventually spread these messages around the world; and the computerized bulletin board system (CBBS), which originated in 1978 in Chicago, Illinois, and was intended from the start to be accessible to the larger public through dial-up access. Thereafter, post-and-response setups were often called bulletin board systems, or BBSs, and, eventually, simply message or discussion boards or forums.

Online gaming was born and gained steady popularity in the 1970s as well. Some games were adventure based and encouraged their players to create what have been called virtual "worlds" together. These games were and are called MUDs (multiuser domains), MOOs (multiuser object-oriented domains), or MPORGS (multiplayer online role-playing games). In them, large numbers of users cocreate meaningful domains or environments in which they interact, play games, and form relationships, including romantic and cybersexual relationships. Players depend on one another to create and inhabit the game space or "world."

Prior to the development of graphical interfaces, these worlds were text based only and did not feature images or avatars. Still, they gave the player the sense that he or she was in a multidimensional environment. The sprawling, cocreated environment provided a "place" for people to not only play the game but to get to know one another as well, which was (and is) a critical aspect of the gaming experience. Rudimentary graphics and a host of interactive games (such as Dungeons and Dragons in 1974) and "worlds" (such as The Sims, a "life experience" video game in 2000) followed. Participants felt truly immersed in social interactivity and sometimes in virtual reality experiences that felt—and, indeed, were—very real.

Very early entrants into the world of social networking were usually "techies"—people with above-average interest in computing or gaming (or they wouldn't have had knowledge of and access to the still-rare computerized technology in the first place). They needed patience to deal with extremely slow data transfers and waiting time for responses and were both curious and interested in connecting in this brand new way. These persistent early adopters and users gave this new experience, this new techno-social activity, a chance to take off and grow.

In 1980, a somewhat different way for people to share and discuss articles and posts was invented by Tom Truscott and Jim Ellis at Duke University. Called Usenet, it was originally intended only for the use of those at Duke and at the University of North Carolina. It used the ARPANET rather than the internet. Usenet had no single central authority or server. It was, instead, a sprawling, decentralized way for groups of people interested in different topics to find one another in text-based, categorized newsgroups; to post and retrieve articles and messages; and to discuss these communications in a free and uncensored way (as it had no central authority that could censor it, though newsgroups were moderated). It spread fairly widely fairly quickly. Unfortunately, due to its open and uncensored nature, an unfettered spread of pirated and illegal material and pornography throughout the system eventually threatened its position as the premier online social network. That, plus competition from the discussion groups and forums beginning to proliferate on the internet, many of which were characterized by graphical interfaces that were easier to use, spelled the downfall of Usenet. Usenet eventually moved to the internet and become so decentralized that it couldn't be simply shut down all at once. In fact, it still exists, though it cannot claim any kind of dominance as a social network. A whisper of its former self, as of 2010, Usenet was no longer even operational at Duke University.

In 1984, physician Larry Brilliant convinced Stewart Brand, publisher of the liberal magazine *Whole Earth Review*, to join forces to create a unique online social network that would be part community and part business. Brilliant's idea was simple (and brilliant?): "Take a group of interesting people, give them the means to stay in continuous communication with one another, stand back, and see what happens" (Hafner, 2004). This experiment would pay off big; appropriately named the WELL (Whole Earth 'Lectronic Link), it resulted in a quirky, unique social network characterized by intense exchanges among members, many of whom shared their lives with one another in great depth and provided all kinds of support to one another, including, at times, the sending of money and the initiation of face-to-face meetings. The WELL would influence nearly every form of social networking that followed, including an early online community for college students called Tripod (established in 1992) and GeoCities (1994), a site which allowed users to create websites modeled after urban areas.

Throughout the 1980s and 1990s, the WELL grew in size and scope, and the spirit of the WELL—the idea that the internet could be highly social—began to permeate the common consciousness. In 1994 and 1995, the *wiki*—a web application in which groups of people could collaboratively build and edit documents and sites online, even in real time if they liked—was invented. AOL's Instant Messenger (AIM; founded in 1997), which allowed participants to chat with one another in real time, was becoming extremely popular. Blackboard (also founded in 1997), an educational course management system, provided a structured means for teaching and learning to occur online. And blogging had begun to make the web a kind of personal, albeit public, space for expression.

The very first blog, though it was not yet so named, is generally credited to Swarthmore student Justin Hall, who began posting online about his life in 1994 at links.net (which, as of this writing, is still in active operation; see Hall, 2014, and Silleson, 2014). Such sites, soon to be called weblogs (for they "logged the web"), and later known as just blogs, consisted of collections of links, diary-like musings and confessionals, information dissemination, or some combination of these. Beginning in 1999, the platform Blogger provided individuals with a simple way to create and share blogs, thus helping to popularize the practice. As the internet was still not widely understood, many wondered why anyone would choose to share private thoughts and feelings online. Indeed, in 2002 blogger Heather Armstrong was fired for complaining online about her job as a web designer and graphic artist, an early example of the potential pernicious consequences of online sharing. Still, within a few years of the birth of Blogger and other blogging and journaling sites like Xanga and LiveJournal, blogging had become widely accepted, and by 2006, more than 40 million blogs had been published on the internet (Standage, 2013, p. 228).

The birth of Wikipedia came in 2001, and wikis and collaborative practices, such as video, audio, and text conferencing, continued growing. Wikipedia is an extensive expression of the gathering of large amounts of information in an easy-to-access place. It is similar to an encyclopedia (from which its name is partly derived), but it is continually updated by the over 20 million users (or "editors") who contribute to it (most of whom are males with tech skills; see Hargittai & Shaw, 2015). It began as a supplement to and later replacement for the more professionally edited online encyclopedia Nupedia. Wikipedia is also notable for using *open-source* software, which means that its content is freely distributable and reproducible. Such a system can compromise reliability and safety for openness, but those who oversee Wikipedia attempt to minimize inaccuracies, providing oversight of entries and requesting additional information when needed, and the accuracy of entries ideally improves over time. It is not a foolproof system, nor is it a gold-standard tool for research, but when used with a critical eye, it can be an excellent starting point for the exploration of a topic. It also, at this writing, has no corporate biases, as it does not accept advertising and claims that it never will.

These early networking systems were significant not only because the technology that would connect people online was proving to work but, very importantly, because of the strong and *real* sense of community that was invariably the by-product whenever they were established. Those who communicated via these online networks very often came to feel bonded—like members of a community or club in which they were genuinely, often deeply, engaged. It was, for sure, a new way to initiate sociality. Early pioneers on what John Perry Barlow called the "electronic frontier" were showing everyone else that time spent online could come to have a social, communal quality that was real and meaningful (Goldsmith & Wu, 2006, p. 17). Soon, this quality would practically be synonymous with the internet.[3]

full-featured social network sites (SNSs) and social media

In the very late 1990s and around the turn of the 21st century, a number of sites sprang up that were sufficiently different from earlier experiments that they began to be known by the specialized name *social network sites* (SNSs; boyd & Ellison, 2007). These sites were different from those that preceded them in that their users could easily see and articulate lists and profiles of "friends" and "followers." These friends and followers were typically people that they already knew, or knew of, personally. Members on SNSs also had the capability to create profile pages, substantially personalizing their use of the site. Compared to sites that had existed in the past, they were generally easier to use and became more and more user-friendly over time.

These sites also differed from those that came before in their scale. They could serve the one-to-one or one-to-many functions of communication equally smoothly, giving them both a personal and a "mass-media" feel and function. Material on these sites could generally be easily shared and reposted, and information and profiles could be accessed by search engines. SNSs are sometimes called new media, but their social functions are so profound and prominent that the moniker that has really stuck is *social media*, especially for those platforms with obvious media-sharing capability.

The first site generally considered to provide all these functions, and therefore to be the first full-featured SNS, may have been 1997's Six Degrees. Though AIM featured buddy lists, members of Classmates.com could affiliate with their high schools or colleges and search for people to connect to, and though some early dating and community sites allowed the creation and posting of profiles, Six Degrees was the first to combine all these features. It was also, perhaps, a bit too "ahead of its time" (boyd & Ellison, 2007). While it attracted millions of users, they were so widely geographically dispersed that good-sized networks of people who knew one another face-to-face failed to form. One of the first truisms of online social networking began to become apparent: People mostly use online social networks to maintain and enhance connections with people they also know face-to-face.

The next widely used SNSs were organized around journaling (LiveJournal), community interests (AsianAvenue, BlackPlanet), business (Ryze), and virtual worlds (Cyworld). In 2002, Friendster was launched; this SNS had the explicit goal of helping friends of friends (and friends of friends of friends, and so on) come into contact and possibly meet. Friendster's rapid growth created problems both technically and culturally as the company struggled with how to keep up with facilitating the functions users seemed to most want, and users became disenchanted. Interestingly, just as Friendster's popularity was fading in the United States, it took off in the Philippines, Singapore, Malaysia, and Indonesia. Its success, for a time, helped convince many groups to launch their own SNSs, and from about 2003 or so, there was an explosion of such sites (notably LinkedIn, Tribe.net, and MyChurch).

Social network sites were also becoming organized around the sharing of media. Before long, media-sharing sites such as Flickr (photo sharing) and YouTube (video sharing) added social-networking features to their sites and became full-fledged SNSs and true social media sites. Today, social media and social networking are in many ways synonymous since most SNSs allow (indeed encourage) both media sharing and networking and users often perform these activities together. MySpace, which launched in 2003 as a full-service SNS, was particularly welcoming to music and bands. People began connecting with others based on their musical preferences and all kinds of other shared interests. The most popular SNS of its time, MySpace grew in size as its members (increasingly teenagers) encouraged their friends to join. In time, it was sold to a corporation and was implicated in several underage sex crimes and scandals; it subsequently lost much of its status as a top SNS.

The decline of MySpace coincided with the rise of Facebook (initially, "thefacebook"), which would eventually become the world's largest and most influential SNS. Established in 2004 as a Harvard-only site by Mark Zuckerberg, assisted by other Harvard students, it spread to other colleges and high schools in 2005 and to professionals and then the wider world beginning in 2006. As of this writing, it is by far the most populated and well-known SNS, with about 2 billion users and over three-quarters of a billion daily users (Sedghi, 2014). Some, however, feel that its growth has come at the expense of the intimacy and "coolness" that characterized the early Facebook.

Decisions by Facebook to commercialize the site with advertising, embed its "like" buttons throughout the internet, and allow numerous applications to become activated and used in conjunction with the site in what has been called "frictionless sharing" have been criticized as eroding intimacy, community, and even democracy at the expense of monetization. In the 2016 U.S. presidential election, demonstrably false "news" articles, ads, and fake accounts that looked like they were associated with real people but were really robotic ("bot") accounts, likely Russian, were developed to deliberately spread misinformation that may have impacted Facebook users' opinions and actions with regard to the election. Many people now rely on social media, and Facebook in particular, to provide them with information regarding current events and the news (for more on "fake news" and current journalistic trends, see Chapter 4). In a September 2017 Facebook post, Mark Zuckerberg issued an apology, apparently for not being more vigilant regarding these issues, writing, "For the ways my work was used to divide people rather than bring us together, I ask forgiveness, and I will work to do better" (Oreskovic, 2017). In October 2017, Facebook turned over more than 3,000 Russia-linked ads, most with divisive messages, that had appeared on its platform during the campaign. The controversy highlighted the role and responsibility of social media platforms for the content posted on them—a controversy that will surely be playing out in the months and years to come, and may result in the increased regulation of social media companies.

Facebook also develops and uses algorithms that help determine much about who its users are and how to best reach them and encourage them to become more deeply engaged in the site. Then it begins to make money from (*monetize*) their participation—usually through the gathering and selling of their data (see Chapter 4 for more on data mining). Other social networking sites, such as Twitter and Pinterest, do the same. An SNS can also make money through selling advertising or stock in its company.

Facebook has proven that social networking can be very big business. Social media and networking sites and blogging sites are now plentiful. Some, such as Twitter, Instagram, and Foursquare, and blogging sites like WordPress, Blogger, and Tumblr, have become popular and influential, with users numbering in the millions. Social media specialists, designers, writers, and managers have joined computer scientists, information technology professionals, and other tech careerists in becoming a large and rapidly growing sector of the modern workforce. It should be noted, though, that much web content is contributed and shared free of charge on many sites and blogs, complicating the situation for those who wish to be paid for such work. More and more people are finding jobs in these "knowledge industries" (Machlup, 1962), in which not goods, or even services related to goods, but the production and exchange of ideas—in fields like education, science, and the mass media—predominate.[4]

the triple revolution of the 2000s

The ever-increasing prominence of the internet, mobile communication, and social media networking has catalyzed nothing less than a revolution in social connectedness that has come about largely since 2000. Social network researchers Lee Rainie and Barry Wellman call the confluence of these three advancements the *triple revolution* (2012). Societies at all levels of technological sophistication have been affected.

Prior to this century, it was relatively rare to access the internet with broadband service or wireless technology. Mobile connectivity and social media were in their infancy. Now, nearly half of the world's households are connected to the internet, and mobile phones, often kept by users' sides or even attached to their bodies allow their users to access information and entertainment at the touch of a button and to make social connections via text messaging, phone calls, and on social network sites (Katz, 2003; Katz & Sugiyama, 2006). Nearly seven in 10 Americans use social media sites such as Facebook, Instagram, Twitter, Pinterest, and LinkedIn, skewing toward individuals who are college educated and have higher incomes (Pew Research Center, 2017; Pew Research Center's Global Attitudes Project, 2012). When people obtain internet access, social networking is one of the first activities they tend to engage in. This is true even in less developed areas of the world.

Starting in the 1990s, all kinds of specialty services and sites began to jockey for a place on the internet. Online radio stations (beginning in 1994) and retailers such as Amazon (1994) and eBay (1995) found audiences alongside online gaming, hobbyist sites, and pornography. Sports, news, entertainment, and celebrity gossip sites proliferated. In 1999, Shawn Fanning launched a peer-to-peer file-sharing program called Napster that ushered in a new era in music sharing, distribution, and production. Though it would be shut down two years later due to legal issues surrounding copyright and ownership of the music, it introduced a culture of music dissemination via the internet and digital media that iTunes (2001), YouTube (2005), and streaming services like Netflix and Hulu (both 2007) exploited with great success (see Chapter 4 for more on Napster, the making and sharing of media, and the dynamics of this participatory culture).

As the web began to experience massive growth in the mid-1990s, investments in broadband capacity began to increase so that there was enough *bandwidth*, or information capacity, to meet the demand. At the same time, large internet service providers and companies like Microsoft, Google, and Amazon required vast computing power, servers, and online storage. The result was *cloud computing*, one of the most significant computing developments of the 2000s. Cloud computing is "a model for delivering on-demand, self-service computing resources with ubiquitous network access and location-independent resource pooling" (in Naughton, 2012, p. 149). That is, all this digital activity and storage occur in a nonphysical space that exists independent of any hardware and can be accessed from any computerized device. However, serious vulnerabilities exist when data are digitized and remotely pooled.

Information of all kinds began to be generated and spread in abundance. Increasingly collected in large databases, the management and analysis of these big datasets—popularly called *big data*—became ever-more critical, especially as knowledge began to accumulate exponentially (Gleick, 2011; Schilling, 2013). As information had become a "primary good" in tech-intensive societies, members began to feel called upon to produce and act on information nearly constantly (Dyson, Gilder, Keyworth, & Toffler, 1994). Skills in accessing, critiquing, and authenticating information became critical. As a result, such societies are sometimes referred to as *information*, *knowledge*, *information-network*, or *network* societies.

The triple revolution is indeed a global revolution. While the benefits of digital technology still disproportionately benefit those who are more powerful, and many are still denied full access, the technology can provide a mechanism, a pathway, for networks to develop and resources to flow to the less powerful. For example, initiatives to bring computers, internet connectivity, and digital literacy to underserved areas have in many cases aided economic conditions and empowered local communities and groups (Alkalimat & Williams, 2001; Hampton, 2010; Haythornthwaite & Hagar, 2005; Haythornthwaite & Kendall, 2010; Mesch & Talmud, 2010; Newman, Biedrzycki, & Baum, 2012; Schuler, 1996; Schuler & Day, 2004).[5]

This overview of the history of communication technology and media has focused on what is really a small slice of human history—the actions and attitudes that have propelled the creation of technology-rich, computer-saturated societies. We should keep in mind as we reflect on the history of information and communication technology that technology is shaped as much by those who adopt and use it as by its official inventors. Many technologies end up being used in very different fashions than their creators imagined. Perhaps one of the most notable examples of this is the printing press, intended by Gutenberg as a means to mass produce the Bible. Gutenberg was a staunch Catholic and would surely be astonished, and probably appalled, by some of the decidedly nonbiblical content that his technology now helps to produce and popularize. Alexander Graham Bell's telephone invention was intended by him to be a kind of hearing aid, and instead, it has been used for people to communicate across distances and is now at the center of a mobile communication revolution. It is the people in a society—you and me, along with the more socially and technologically powerful, of course—who determine the paths that these technologies will take and the type of societies they will help to create.

Technology brings a critical set of realities to our everyday lives. Think of the ways your life would be different—at the individual, small-group, organizational, and societal levels—if computerization was not impacting it. Your relationships, your online and offline environments, and the experiences you have in them would be different in countless ways. Even *you* would be different. In the next chapter, we take a close look at how techno-social environments are inhabited—how tech-influenced spaces are constructed and experienced. As always, you are asked to personalize what you learn, to apply it to your own life, and to seek to better understand the lives of those who may live in different circumstances but likely have similar needs: to survive and find meaning in our complex, rapidly changing world.

notes

1. For a more detailed history of computing, the internet, and the web, see Computer Hope (2014), Cyber Telecom (2014), Griffin (2000), Leiner et al. (2009), Hafner (1998), Internet Society (2017), Naughton (2012), Rainie and Wellman (2012), Standage (2013), and Stewart (2014), all of which contributed to the foregoing.
2. See note 1.
3. For a more detailed history of early social networking sites and full-featured SNSs and social media, see boyd and Ellison (2007), Computer Hope (2014), Curtis (2011), Cyber Telecom (2014), Hafner (1998, 2004), Naughton (2012), Ofcom (2008), Rainie and Wellman (2012), Standage (2013), and Stewart (2014), all of which contributed to the foregoing.
4. See note 3.
5. Portions excerpted from Chayko (2014).

3 INHABITING A DIGITAL ENVIRONMENT

sociomental spaces, cultures, and societies

Human beings have always used media and technologies—whether they be cameras, print and electronic media, or computers and mobile devices—to build the environments in which they live and form their relationships. When these environments are digitized, they are always potentially portable. And since they can be accessed by mobile phones and other forms of portable technology (tablets, laptops, wireless devices, even wristwatches, glasses, and implantable computer chips), they can be constructed and carried along wherever an individual goes. Portability is one of the most salient features of a digital environment.

These spaces, and the activities, bonds, and connections formed within them, can also be described as *sociomental* because the connectedness is interpersonal (the *social* part) and relies on cognitive rather than physical activity for its creation and maintenance (the *mental* part). Even people in the closest of face-to-face relationships are sometimes physically separated, so all social connectedness has a strongly sociomental component. But social spaces in which numerous interactions and relationships are developed via a variety of cognitive acts are predominantly sociomental in nature (see Chayko 2002, 2008).

One of the very first sociologists, Emile Durkheim (who helped establish the field of sociology), claimed that a society not only transcends the individual; it also transcends the physical. That is, societies are, at their essence, large, collective, nonphysical entities. Durkheim (1893/1964) taught that a society is a "conscience collective"—a collective, shared *consciousness* (mind, or awareness) and, at the same time, a collective, shared *conscience* (morality, or tool for determining right and wrong). Note the subtle but important difference between *consciousness* and *conscience*; in Durkheim's native French, the word *conscience* translates as both "mind" and "morality." This is important because it means that one of the all-time premier theorists of what a society is—someone who has influenced the thinking of millions and who was a primary force in the development of sociology as an academic discipline—has theorized a society as being both mental *and* moral at its essence. For Durkheim, a society encompasses both of these nonphysical states simultaneously and indissolvably and thus (though he did not use the exact word) would be considered a sociomental entity.

A society is made up of the thoughts, ideas, information, norms, values, beliefs, and morals of all of its members. It is a veritable "soup" of mental ingredients, plus the material products created by its members, such as art, books, buildings, and clothing. Collectively, we call these mental and material products the *culture* of a society. People's lives shape, and are shaped by, these products in a process so penetrating and constant that those groups of people who share cultural products are often themselves called a culture. And yet a society, and a culture, is even more than all of this. Something special, almost indefinable, happens when human beings get together. A group "effervesces" and produces an energy, a force, a "vibe" all its own. It is not only mental and moral; it is alive with energy and emotion (Durkheim, 1912/1965).

Though the internet was centuries away from invention when Durkheim was alive, his insights set the stage for the sociomental nature of digital groupings to be better understood and for digital groupings to be considered real, legitimate social units. Other sociological theorists, including Georg Simmel (1908/1950), George Herbert Mead (1934/2009), and Charles Horton Cooley (1922/1964), wrote extensively about the strength, consequences, and reality of *social, mental* groupings. Such groupings, they claim, are the bedrock of society, literally life-affirming and life-saving. People are far worse off (even more prone to suicide, Durkheim famously evinced [1897/1966]) when they are not firmly integrated within social groups and societies that have strong, cohesive *norms* (expected behaviors) and *values* (beliefs).

All social connections and groupings, including those that originate face-to-face, exist in their most complete form in the minds of their members. Social groups are almost always either too large or too widely dispersed, or their participants too busy, for members to get together face-to-face more than occasionally (if indeed then). Just because a social bond or grouping can be described as face-to-face does not mean that the people involved in it spend massive amounts of time physically together. In fact, in a fast-paced, mobile society it may be the case that people do not gather together very often at all. But that does not mean that they cease to be connected when they are not gathered. Groups persist even in the dearth or absence of physicality and even as members come and go (see Anderson, 1983; Cooley, 1922/1964; and Simmel, 1898, on the persistence of social groups).

Digital spaces—social media sites, websites, chat areas, discussion boards, online games, workspaces, classes, conferences, and hangouts, even the spaces in which we share email and text messages—are sometimes called *virtual*. Digital work teams and organizations, in particular, are commonly described as virtual in nature. The use of the term *virtual* is misleading, though, for it implies that something is almost, but not quite, real. And where digital spaces are concerned, that is simply not the case. As sociologist W. I. Thomas has classically stated (in what has come to be called the Thomas Theorum), if people "define situations as real, they are real in their consequences" (Thomas & Thomas, 1928). Digital experiences and the spaces in which they take place are quite real and have real, definite consequences. For this reason, many consider descriptors such as *sociomental*, *networked*, and/or *digital* preferable to *virtual* in describing these spaces and societies (see Chayko, 2008; Dyson et al., 1994).

why not cyberspace?

You may have also heard digital space referred to as *cyberspace*. Activities associated with such spaces have also received the *cyber* prefix—for example, cybercrime, cyberpunk, cyberbullying, and cybersex. But many scholars are moving away from calling digital spaces *cyber*, and the story of why this is happening is rather interesting because it is the inventor of the word *cyberspace*, science fiction writer William Gibson, who now warns against its misinterpretation and misuse.

Remember, it was not very long ago that the online experience was brand new and highly unusual. In the 1980s and 1990s, people struggled to define and describe what was then a brand-new experience. The most powerful description—the one that stuck—came from Gibson, who, in his 1984 novel *Neuromancer*, stated that when people use computers a "consensual hallucination" could emerge. This collaborative kind of hallucination would exist, he said, in a "notional space" that seemed to be located behind and beyond the computer screen. Gibson called this environment *cyberspace* (1984, p. 69), borrowing the prefix *cyber* from *cybernetics*, which is the study of how various kinds of systems and networks function. *Cyber* has since come to suggest something computerized or modern, of the computer era.

In the early years of trying to understand and predict the impacts of computer use, it was important to have collectively understood concepts with which to describe it. It still is. But the conception of cyberspace as a "consensual hallucination" has become increasingly problematic over time because the experiences and consequences of computer use are now widely understood to be completely real. Computerization is many things, but it is rarely hallucinatory.

Let's follow Gibson's thought process in some depth as he discusses where the term *cyberspace* came from and then consider the possibilities and limitations of the term. Gibson has said of writing *Neuromancer* that

> I was painfully aware that I lacked an arena for my science fiction. . . . I needed something to replace outer space and the spaceship. I was walking around Vancouver, aware of that need, and I remember walking past a video arcade, which was a new sort of business at that time, and seeing kids playing those old-fashioned console-style plywood video games. The games had a very primitive graphic representation of space and perspective. Some of them didn't even have perspective but were yearning toward perspective and dimensionality. Even in this very primitive form, the kids who were playing them were so physically involved, it seemed to me that what they wanted was to be inside the games, within the notional space of the machine. The real world had disappeared for them—it had completely lost its importance. They were in that notional space, and the machine in front of them was the brave new world.
>
> The only computers I'd ever seen in those days were things the size of the side of a barn. And then one day, I walked by a bus stop and there was an Apple poster. The poster was a photograph of a businessman's jacketed, neatly cuffed arm holding a life-size representation of a real-life computer that was not much bigger than a laptop is today. Everyone is going to have one of these, I thought, and everyone is going to want to live inside them. And somehow I knew that the notional space behind all of the computer screens would be one single universe. . . .
>
> But what was more important at that point in terms of my practical needs was to name it something cool, because it was never going to work unless it had a really good name. So the first thing I did was sit down with a yellow pad and a Sharpie and start scribbling—infospace, data space.

> I think I got cyberspace on the third try. (as quoted in Newitz, 2011)

Computerization, of course, has since migrated from huge plywood video games and barn-sized consoles to interfaces that are smaller and more portable. But William Gibson's view of cyberspace as the universe "behind all the computer screens" was, and still is, critical to helping us envision, understand, and define the environment and the experience of becoming involved in computer use.

As Gibson himself has stated more recently, though, this universe has changed from this original notion, and dramatically so. "Cyberspace, not so long ago, was a specific elsewhere, one we visited periodically, peering into it from the familiar physical world," he wrote. "Now cyberspace has everted. Turned itself inside out. Colonized the physical" (Gibson, 2010). In other words, Gibson notes, the space behind the screens has become enlarged and intersects with—even encompassing at times—the physical. Incidentally, Gibson believes that Google is the primary "architect" of this new universe (Newitz, 2011).

But a more damning critique of *cyber*, and therefore of *cyberspace* as a construct, is found within Gibson's own description of cyberspace in the first paragraph of the previous extract, in which he shares his sense that "the real world had disappeared" for the children playing computerized video games. This was an early view of and a widespread worry about computer-mediated communication (CMC) and internet use. Mass media and computer use were often seen as generating pseudo, imaginary, or parasocial (one-sided) connections rather than genuine, potentially reciprocal ones (see Beniger, 1987; Caughey, 1984; Giles, 2002; Horton & Wohl, 1956). As clear evidence of the authenticity of these connections and the reality of techno-social life began to mount up, though, it became apparent that cyberspace was anything but a hallucination, consensual or otherwise. It was real—and very, very real in its consequences (see Thomas & Thomas, 1928).

As researchers learn more and more about how real and consequential digital environments are, and how authentically they are experienced, the term *cyberspace* is becoming less and less precise a descriptor. Along with other *cyber*-prefixed words, it has become subject to misinterpretation. Phenomena described as cyber can too easily be seen as less than real, their qualities and consequences seeming to derive more from their connection to computerization than from the behavior itself. For example, cyberbullying can seem to be harmful *because of* the technology by which the behavior takes place rather than due to the harassing behavior itself, which would be harmful delivered in any form. Cyber infidelity can seem to be caused by one's habit of spending time on the computer rather than by the decision to betray a partner during that time, which many would find hurtful in any context. The *cyber* prefix implies that the technology in and of itself is what matters most about a tech-related phenomenon and causes its outcome rather than the person using the technology, which, as we have seen, is called technological determinism. Bullying, harassment, cruelty, and betrayal are harmful and troubling in any context—digital or face-to-face—and are the handiwork of humans, not machines.

At this writing, the term *cyberspace* seems to be fading from use (Rennie, 2012), but technological determinism is still very much present. Examining the range of ways in which people use and are impacted by digital technologies is a more fruitful course of action than blaming the technology. The adoption and use of terminology that encourages such examination would be widely beneficial. In digital contexts, as in all contexts, words matter.

online communities, networks, and networking

Much research has been devoted to the study of how communities and networks operate in these digital, sociomental spaces. Community, perhaps the most sociological of all concepts (Wolfe, 1989, p. 60), is also one of the slipperiest. It can describe a group of people who live within a specific geographical area, and at the same time, it can refer to the intangible, often highly emotional sense of belonging to such a group (see Bell & Newby, 1974; Chayko, 2002, 2008, 2014; Fernback, 2007; Gottschalk, 1975; Hewitt, 1989; Hillery, 1968; Hunter, 1974; Parks, 2011; and Scherer, 1972, for discussions of this distinction). It can also be appropriated by organizations hoping to reap the benefit of the term's warm connotations for commercial and marketing purposes (Baym, 2010, p. 74; Preece & Maloney-Krichmar, 2003).

But a community is far more than warm connotations. Both good and bad things happen in communities, and these things—and these spaces—are not always warm and fuzzy. To become and feel part of a unit larger than oneself, whether that unit has spontaneously arisen or been deliberately constructed, has a wide range of consequences for individuals. Being a part of groups and communities that we can turn to in good times and bad helps people live a balanced, healthy life, even as it provides that life with infinite complications.

Communities are constituted of, and provide for their members, regular, patterned, personalized social interactions. In them, people develop a shared identity, culture, purpose, and fate, as well as feelings of togetherness and belonging. All of this is critical to helping individuals find meaning in life and form interpersonal attachments. These qualities have been considered by sociologists to be key components of community since the earliest days of the discipline. And the internet and digital media readily inspire and facilitate the creation and establishment of communities (see Cooley, 1922/1964; Durkheim, 1893/1964; Simmel, 1908/1950; and, more recently, Amit, 2002; Anderson, 1983; Baym, 2010; Bell & Newby, 1974; Bellah, Madsen, Swidler, Sullivan, & Tipton, 1985; Bourdieu, 1985; Chayko, 2002, 2008, 2014; Erikson, 1966; Fischer, 1982; Hampton & Wellman, 2003; Hillery, 1968; Jones, 1995; Kanter, 1972; Mazlish, 1989; Parks, 2011; Shibutani, 1955).

Online communities are "social aggregations that emerge from the Net . . . to form webs of personal relationships" (Rheingold, 1993, p. 5). They can exist wholly online or can have a face-to-face component. When asked to describe the social groupings they form or encounter online, people often invoke the word *community*, as did the overwhelming majority of those whom I interviewed in my *Portable Communities* research exploring the social dynamics of online and mobile connectedness (2008). They repeatedly referred to the online groups to which they belonged as communities, even though I did not use the word in my initial interview questions to them. Furthermore, these groupings were invariably described as close and meaningful (Chayko, 2002, 2008; see also Baym, 1995, 2000, 2010, pp. 64–75; boyd, 2006, 2007; Cavanagh, 2009; Cerulo, Ruane, & Chayko, 1992; Chmiel et al., 2011; Haythornthwaite & Kendall, 2010; Kendall, 2002; Licklider & Taylor, 1968; Parks, 2011; Poor, 2013; Rotman & Preece, 2010).

In my research, I question people about spending time in online spaces and the experience of being part of online groups. Although they mentioned facing various difficulties, including quite serious problems like harassment and stalking (which we'll discuss in more depth in Chapter 7), they reported many more feelings of closeness, supportiveness, and community. Over and over, they gave me responses such as these:

> I feel I am part of a tight-knit community that cares about one another.
>
> My group is an extremely tightly bonded community that simply cannot be found in normal daily life.
>
> There is a feeling of camaraderie and belonging, a real sense of being able to help so many more people than ever possible before the advent of the internet.
>
> It is relieving to have this place to vent and be able to get feedback and sympathy. (Chayko, 2008, pp. 7, 54)

It should be noted that not all individuals form these kinds of online connections and communities with ease. Some people seem to be more likely than others "to accept online friendship formation as possible, or even desirable," sociologist Zeynep Tukekci suggests in her study of friendship on social network sites (2010, p. 176; see also Tufekci, 2008). She calls those who form online connections less easily and less often the cyber*asocial* and notes that for such individuals, "face-to-face interaction has inimitable features that simply cannot be replicated or replaced by any other form of communication" (2010, p. 176). This does not mean that the cyberasocial necessarily refuse to use all digital technologies—they may be more comfortable using technology in some circumstances, such as to coordinate plans, more than others, such as to hang out online or to broaden their social networks (Tufekci & Brashears, 2014). It should not be assumed, then, that everyone uses digital tools and participates in digital contexts similarly, with the same aims.

Online groupings are so often considered to be genuine communities by those who create them in part because ICTs (information and communication technologies) are pervasive, reaching into every corner of our lives, giving those who use them a very strong "sense of place" (Hampton, 2016; Meyrowitz, 1985; see also Polson, 2013). Storytelling via oral and written communication is known for its *transportedness* (Biocca & Levy, 1995; Gerrig, 1993; Kim & Biocca, 1997; Lombard & Ditton, 1997; Radway, 1984). In providing persistent, pervasive forums for the telling and retelling of stories, social media specializes (as do the mass media of television, radio, books, etc.) in mentally transporting people who share similar ideas and interests to similarly envisioned environments.

Stories shared via technological mediation tend to be envisioned as occurring in a specific place where members "gather" (Kim & Biocca, 1997; Lombard & Ditton, 1997; Morley & Robins, 1995; Schwartz, 1981). As my interview respondents put it,

> The most important function of this forum is it is a *place* where rock fans can *gather* to celebrate the band they love and talk about everything music! It is a place where we can all express our passion for our favorite band. This is where I speak to friends I have not seen in a while, where we keep each other posted on what's going on in our lives, or just talk nonsense; *it's our little gathering place*. (Chayko, 2008, p. 24)

The place-based metaphor gives members a common image they can use to make their digitally mediated experience more collective, more visible, even more tangible (Hampton, 2007; Lambert, 2013; Parks, 2011).

Online groupings, then, are readily referred to and experienced as communities in which people gather and form social bonds. And "communities are clearly social networks," sociologists Barry Wellman and Keith Hampton contend (1999, p. 648). A social network is essentially a set of pathways along which social support, resources, and social connections are exchanged and develop. We can almost see these kinds of social capital "flow" from person to person as we identify these pathways and the social ties that emerge, and study the structures, cultures, and communities that are created (Yuan, 2013; see also Adams & Allan, 1998; Amit, 2002; Cavanagh, 2009; Lee & Lee, 2010).

The study of social networks harkens back at least as far as the teachings of Georg Simmel (1908/1950), who at the turn of the 20th century wrote about the impact of a network's size on the nature of the interactions among its members. Simmel studied social units even as small as two and three (called *dyads* and *triads*) and considered them to be social groupings that can teach us a lot about how groups are structured and affect people. Simmel demonstrated, for example, that when a network expands from two to three, relationships in the network are changed most critically, for alliances and collusions become possible. The nature of the network can be altered by the number of people in it and by its form or structure even more than by its content or the specific nature of the activity people in it engage in (1908/1950).

More modern analyses of networking have contributed much to the understanding of how social networking operates online. In his study of what has been called the *small-world phenomenon*, psychologist Stanley Milgram asked people to forward a letter intended for a certain person to someone whom they thought would most likely know that person. He found that it took on average only five or six forwards for most letters to travel to their destinations—a finding that has given rise to the phrase "six degrees of separation" (Milgram, 1967). Network researchers Duncan Watts and Steven Strogatz (1998) have applied this concept to different kinds of networks with much the same results, concluding that most of our human-created networks are very well connected and interconnected (see also Boase & Wellman, 2006).

Barry Wellman, along with many of his students and coauthors, has pioneered the study of how digital social networks connect us both locally and globally (see, e.g., Boase & Wellman, 2006; Hampton & Wellman, 1999, 2003; Quan-Haase & Wellman, 2002; Wang & Wellman, 2010; Wellman & Tindall, 1993). Social networks predate the internet, web, and social media, of course; connections and pathways between people have existed for as long as people have exchanged resources with one another, but newer technologies have enabled new modes of creation and possibilities for their use.

In what Lee Rainie and Barry Wellman have termed *networked individualism*, people strategically operate, switch among, and use their social networks as needed. "Networked individuals have partial membership in multiple networks and rely less on permanent memberships in settled groups," they explain. "Technologies such as the internet and mobile phones help people manage a larger, more diverse set of relationships. . . . The new media is the new neighborhood" (2012, pp. 12–13). Again, we see the metaphor of the community/neighborhood invoked to explain how modern networks operate and also how they *feel* to their users, and how people use the internet and the web to build and grow these networks.

The strength of the ties and communities that connect people in high-tech societies is frequently questioned. In fact, both strong and weak ties—and everything in between—are found in online networks (Brenner, 2013; Chayko, 2008; Hampton, Goulet, Marlow, & Rainie, 2012; Hampton, Goulet, Rainie, & Purcell, 2011; Haythornthwaite, 2005; Ling & Stald, 2010; Rainie & Wellman, 2012; Wang & Wellman, 2010). The closest of relationships are built and sustained via digital technology, but more fleeting, ephemeral ties are in evidence as well. Most individuals' social networks contain hundreds of social ties that are weak, strong, and in between and that are both face-to-face and digitally enabled (Caughey, 1984; Chayko, 2008; Hampton et al., 2011; Preece, 2000).

Even so-called "weak" social ties, it is important to note, have great utility. As sociologist Mark Granovetter has established (1973), weak ties bring into contact people who might otherwise have no way to know of one another at all, thereby opening up pathways which eventually provide *all* members of one social network with access to *all* the members of a second network. Novel information and social capital move along these pathways from one set of people to another (Bakshy, Rosenn, Marlow, & Adamic, 2012; Haythornthwaite, 2005). Communities are dense with these crisscrossing pathways and networks, and they provide numerous opportunities for people to become connected online and offline—and therefore for societies to become more cohesive. In essence, networks help to "stitch" societies together, and because they are so plentiful, digitally enabled networks do quite a bit of this stitching.[1]

creating digital environments

People build their social spaces and environments as they communicate with one another. Shared symbols, such as language, images, sounds, gestures, and avatars, help people envision, build, communicate about, and understand the meanings of these spaces. Symbolic representations of other people (thoughts of them, images, photos) remind us of others when they are not physically with us so that we can continue to bond with them, even in their absence.

Members of groups create and use symbols constantly: Sports teams and schools have slogans, logos, and representative colors; friends and families have favorite foods, nicknames, and catchphrases; and religions and nations grant great importance to icons, statues, pictures, and documents. These symbols, in effect, stand in for people and groups because a group is "too complex a reality" to be retained in the mind (Durkheim, 1912/1965, p. 252). Most modern individuals are part of many groups that cannot all remain in our minds all the time. So the symbol—like a flag or a logo—is "treated as if it were this reality itself" (p. 252). It brings the group into the minds of its members whenever it is seen or deployed and does it so reliably that it inspires the same powerful feelings as the group does. It can even be treated *as* the group.

This is why people can become so intensely emotional at the performance of a symbolic gesture like flag burning or flag saluting or the playing of a religious or national anthem. Flags and anthems bring to mind the reality of a nation or group so concretely and powerfully that they bring the reality of the group to the fore. The burning of a flag, for example, can feel like the actual destruction of the nation. Of course, whether we are face-to-face or online, we can never interact with an entire nation or even the entirety of a large group, but because the symbol stands in for it, we are still able to *feel* our sense of belonging to that nation or group—we can feel and appreciate its complex reality. We can feel community with others in the group even though the group is not, and may never be, physically gathered in one place at the same time.

Symbols, therefore, are critical to helping people to express and experience the reality of their digital worlds. Along with metaphors, they also help people explain their worlds and evaluate the comparability of items within them. This helps people determine their "place" in these worlds. Digital phenomena can be compared to books (Facebook), clouds (the nonphysical space where so much data are stored), streams (a flow of or mode for the delivery of data), bulletin boards (online discussion spaces), and town squares or forums (the Foursquare app, online message forums, etc.). Even the web and the net are metaphors. Look for the many examples of this online—of physically separated people using metaphors that suggest physical objects or spaces. Metaphors and symbols help the individual imagine and envision things, people, and places that are otherwise abstract or invisible, and they also help groups of people envision them similarly.

However, metaphors are limiting as well, for they represent assumptions that constrain us from thinking about things differently. For example, thinking about data as being collected and stored in a seemingly airlike, remote "cloud" may prevent people from investigating exactly how their data are being stored and secured, and at whose hands. The casual use of metaphors, therefore, can hinder more precise understandings of digital and informational phenomena and their impacts (see Hwang & Levy, 2015).

A digital space called a *platform* is a computerized framework on which an application can run. Platforms can be blogging sites like Blogger and WordPress; social media sites like Facebook, Twitter, and Instagram; video-streaming sites like Netflix, Hulu, and YouTube; or audio sites like iTunes and Spotify. While platforms are initially designed from the top down, they are also shaped from the bottom up, each taking on a style, logic, and grammar—or vernacular—all its own. For example, the Twitter *hashtag* (or # symbol) was developed by users rather than being "designed-in" (Bruns & Burgess, 2011). In *hashtagging*, the # symbol is followed by a word or phrase, allowing people to mark a topic or a moment in a digital environment and then identify and find others using the same word or phrase. Hashtagging has spread to other platforms, such as Facebook and Instagram, and is even used in face-to-face conversation, sometimes accompanied by a gesture intended to replicate the symbol.

Hashtags have real power to help people become grouped together in social media environments. They facilitate the gathering of people in online spaces for information exchange and "Twitter chats," and the communication and curation of information at conferences and other events. They are also used rhetorically in at least five distinct ways: to emphasize, critique, rally people together, identify characteristics of the writer, and iterate internet memes. Like other cultural artifacts, *memes*—representations of pop culture that can take the shape of a text, video, or photo with words that are often jointly created and remixed by multiple individuals—can evoke such a sharp or emotional response that they can spread widely and quickly through digital networks and be said to go *viral* (Bruns & Burgess, 2011; Daer, Hoffman, & Goodman, 2014; Milner, 2013; Zittrain, 2014). Memes have become extremely popular ways for *subcultures* (smaller groups within a larger culture) to share and enjoy ideas in common and to cohere as a group, cementing, in effect, a subcultural identity as a grouping of people who appreciate and understand the meme's meaning and implications. Even when a meme is "contested" and members of a group disagree as to its meaning, the resulting conversation (or struggle to resolve the conflict) can produce shared knowledge and cultural capital that can bond members together (Nissenbaum & Shifman, 2017).

In all these ways, digital spaces and the activities that take place in them are collaboratively envisioned and created. They are shaped and reshaped, individually and jointly, again and again, as people enter and exit these spaces and come to feel a sense of one another as truly *there*. In the process, digital environments are given form, texture, contour, depth, and detail—in short, *reality*.

reality, presence, and proximity

Digital life is, simply, real life. The reality of living with technology, especially in computerized/digital form, is sometimes described as an *augmented reality* (Jurgenson, 2012a), which means that digital technology has enhanced, or augmented, the environment to a significant extent. For people who live in technology-intensive societies, this happens all the time. But the truth is that even before the age of computerization, life has been augmented by technology.

From the earliest of times, human beings have created tools that would enable them to build shelters, use fire, colonize the natural world, transmit information to one another, and defend their territories—in short, to do whatever it took to survive. As we saw in Chapter 2, the invention of spoken and then written languages allowed people to make greater sense of the raw phenomena they encountered every day and to communicate in increasingly more abstract and complex ways across time and space. People have always used tools and technologies to build and augment their societies. In modern societies, all kinds of ICTs enable the transmission of concepts and ideas.

Online experiences, and the social connections and environments created with the assistance of digital technologies, are a critical component of modern techno-social life in which people's responses are genuine, meaningful, and often profound. When we are online, our brains and bodies think and feel and act. We may experience bodily fatigue or pain, worry or be delighted, make a friend or become involved in an altercation, strengthen a relationship or destroy one. What a person does online has an influence on the rest of one's life because it is *a part of* that life, not a separate thing. It is important, then, to think about and describe this environment in ways that highlight its realness—for example, *not* to call the face-to-face realm IRL (which means "in real life" and wrongly promotes the idea that the face-to-face sphere is more real than the digital).

In my interviews with people who find and form connections over the internet, I heard many descriptions of how unexpectedly deep and authentic these connections could become. For example, as a member of an online group dedicated to religion told me,

> I didn't come (to this online group) looking for friendship, and am surprised at how some of the regular posters have become real people to me. Some of them just have a very personal way of expressing themselves that I've come to recognize, and sometimes, to like very much. This has nothing to do with spelling or mental brilliance or even depth of faith, for that matter. I think what draws me to some people here is their authenticity and their willingness to be imperfect. But even the ones I don't especially like have touched my heart to the extent that I sometimes worry about them and wish I could reach through the computer and help them, somehow. In fact, now that I think about it, it is amazing how real some of these distant, unseen, frequently anonymous message board posters have become. But, of course, they *are* real! (Chayko, 2002, p. 114)

The authentic and deeply personal nature of the connections and communities that are formed in digital spaces has been a common theme throughout my research.

People also told me that they felt that they could get to know very well even those individuals whom they encountered exclusively online, absent any face-to-face interaction. In response to my request for a description of the "personal" nature of the online relationship, one young woman mused,

> How can it be personal? It *feels* like it is. If people said, "Oh, gee, do you know so and so?" I would say yes. I wouldn't say, "Oh well, I met him once." I'd say, "Oh yes, I know him." (Chayko, 2002, p. 86)

Because online social connections are so often experienced as absolutely real and deeply personal, it is but a next step to perceive digitally encountered others to be *present.*

The internet and digital media facilitate the perception and experience of proximity and presence in ways that transcend the physical. When connecting online, those with whom we connect are often perceived to be "really there." This sense that the other is "really there" is called *social presence*. According to the social presence theory advanced by communication scholars John Short, Ederyn Williams, and Bruce Christie, a communication medium can provides its users several ways to become aware of one another's presence. They can know one another's qualities, characteristics, and inner states and begin to perceive and experience one another as socially present (Short, Williams, & Christie, 1976). This theory, which predated the internet and digital media, has since been updated to explain the variety of ways that people can use these technologies to be cognitively present to one another even as they are physically distant (see Chayko, 2002).

Feeling the nearness or presence of others across distances has been called *perceived proximity* (O'Leary, Wilson, & Metiu, 2014) and, when electronic media facilitates the connection, *electronic propinquity* (Korzenny, 1978; Walther & Barazova, 2008). In a large-scale international study, professors of business Michael O'Leary, Jeanne Wilson, and Anca Metiu found that colleagues working hundreds of miles apart from one another communicated as often, on average, as colleagues who were located in the same office. Additionally, colleagues separated by distance felt the same level of shared identity and sense of cognitive and affective closeness as those who worked together in the same location. Individuals at work, the researchers determined, can form strong bonds despite being separated by large distances.

Similar effects have been found when popular culture is the mediating element among physically separated people. Sharing common interests in a television show, movie, or type of music can bring about a strong sense of shared identity and community among devotees. They, too, can come to feel that they inhabit a social world with one another. Cultural products and franchises that can inspire such involvement among users have an excellent chance of popular success. Communication and media professor Henry Jenkins calls this "the art of world making" (2006, p. 21; for more on this, see Chapter 9).

With the advent of digital and mobile technology, however, members of any group or "world" can enjoy *ambient copresence*—an ongoing but background awareness of the presence or nearness of others (Ito & Okabe, 2005, p. 264; see also Chayko, 2008, 2014; Gray et al., 2003; Quan-Haase & Wellman, 2002). Portable devices allow users to keep their channels to one another open nearly all the time if desired, checking in on one another often and even leaving "away messages." These short, frequent updates convey that one is "there" (see Park & Sundar, 2015). It is becoming common for groups of people (especially younger people) to stay in near-constant contact with one another this way via group chats, texts, and tweets (see Chayko, 2008).

Social media and blogs do much to enable a sense of presence among dispersed users. They allow the presentation of experiences and stories neatly and simply. They provide opportunities for individuals to share ideas, enter a conversation, and gain a sense of the presence of others in the conversation or group. Core members of social media and blogging communities, the most active participants in the group, are most likely to welcome new members or to monitor and enforce (formally or informally) the rules and norms of the group. Having had a stake in it the longest, they tend to take on the responsibility for safeguarding and communicating the group's collective memory and identity. But even those who lurk in the group or participate less actively help to shape it and can have their presence sensed (Chayko, 2008).

Often, ambient copresence takes place in spaces defined either formally or informally as online "hangouts"—the kind of spaces in which people can spend unstructured time with few (or no) obligations and responsibilities. Over 70% of U.S. adult internet users go online at least occasionally just to pass the time or to have fun (Rainie, 2011). They may pass the time leisurely, lurking or hanging out on a social media platform like Facebook or Twitter, checking out a discussion board, visiting a chat room, playing a game, reading a blog, spending time in a Google hangout, or some combination of these. It is possible to spend large amounts of time in such spaces, entire days and nights, just hanging out, checking out what others are doing and saying—not necessarily interacting with them but still sensing others' presence in an ambient way, feeling a sense of perceived proximity and community with them. "I just like being there," one woman told me, describing her affinity for an online hangout, "and I don't know why" (Chayko, 2008, p. 30).

Sociologist Ray Oldenburg calls these kinds of hangouts *third spaces* (1989). They are places other than homes and workplaces—the first and second spaces—in which people spend time and relax, usually without a fixed agenda. While Oldenburg focuses on casual offline places, such as coffee shops, pubs, beauty shops, and the like, the concept is quite useful to also describe the kinds of informal online spaces in which people simply hang out. And such spaces are plentiful.

Hangouts, both physical and digital, are important because they provide a space for people to spend unstructured time in the company of others. They permit individuals to engage different aspects of their lives and identities than they do at work and at home. By spending time with those who are like-minded, simply experiencing a sense of shared identity and culture, individuals can feel known and accepted.

Presence in third spaces is optional and voluntary, and there are no requirements. In them, people can get to know one another (or not) in a low-obligation, low-pressure way. Spending time in third spaces can help people relieve everyday stresses while they make contacts and feel a sense of community.

Being around others in this kind of environment can help people relax since the kinds of obligations that exist at work and at home are absent. They can also make the individual feel part of the larger society, part of the culture, connected to others.

Lurking or participating minimally, or lightly, in third spaces can provide the opportunity to be part of a larger dialogue, to gain a sense of others and their conversations. It also provides that all-important, life-affirming feeling of being "plugged into" or integrated into a society (we discuss this in greater depth in Chapter 9). Because it is so critical for people to feel connected in this way, it is generally healthy to spend some time in third spaces, so these spaces can be seen as good or "healthy" for the society as a whole. Spending too much time in them, though, can certainly represent or lead to an unhealthy escape from offline responsibilities.

Sometimes, to be sure, people do not feel the nearness of others when they are online. They feel solitary, alone. But more often, they feel proximal and connected, part of meaningful social worlds. And, as it turns out, the brain is wired to consider these social worlds to be fully and completely real.

reality and the brain

The mind and body are intricately connected. They affect one another continuously, as can be seen in physical illness that derives from psychological disturbance, or in mental confusion that results from physical fatigue. Our minds and bodies "talk to" and inform one another all the time. They are a unit, finely meshed (Chayko, 2008, p. 41; Goleman, 2006).

The brain considers both digital and physical forms of connectedness equally real. Mental images that correspond to all kind of experiences—whether physical or digital in nature—are recorded in the same part of the brain. The same exact cognitive processes are used to encode, process, and retrieve these images, whether they originated in physical experience or in mental experience. This is how we can sometimes be unsure whether something in our past actually happened or whether we simply imagined that it occurred. As brains store both physical and mental phenomena in the same way, in the same place, they "code" physical and mental phenomena as equally real (though, like all body parts, brains are also imperfect and fallible; see Chayko, 2002; Neimark, 1995).

Human beings can respond to both digital and physical phenomena in similar ways as well. Once an event has occurred—whether in physical or sociomental space—it becomes interpreted and assigned meaning. Realness—or degrees of realness—can be assigned to any event. Individuals can also identify different types or spheres of reality as being meaningful and consequential. These realities—which include the "reality of everyday life," dreams, fantasies, games, fiction, religious experience, erotic experience, and even drug-induced states—each carry their own norms, rules, and logics and can feel entirely (if temporarily) real (see Berger & Luckmann, 1967; Caughey, 1984; Davis, 1983; James, 1890/1983; Schutz, 1973). "We live not in one reality but in two (at least)," sociologist Murray Davis notes of everyday life, "and we continually alternate between them, often against our will" (1983, p. 10).

Furthermore, the brain and body often respond to mediated and digital events in the same way that they would respond to those that take place face-to-face. When watching TV or a movie, reading a book, listening to music, or using social media, it is common to become so cognitively and emotionally engaged in the event that the body responds as if the event were unmediated. The brain's cognitive and perceptual systems prepare the body for the situations that are confronted, and, physiologically, the body and brain respond. We cry, we laugh, we sweat, we cheer, we move our bodies (Bellur & Sundar, 2010; Reeves & Nass, 1996). We can even come to feel that we are developing a kind of relationship with our technologies (see "The Human–Machine Connection" in Chapter 10).

Some people claim that digital environments are rife with deception and hence less real than offline spaces—that the relative anonymity found in many digital spaces breeds deceit, falsity, and danger. Indeed, deception is a possible outcome of digital tech use, given that face-to-face accountability is diminished. Other possible negative outcomes include nasty or hurtful verbal exchanges, harassment, the causing of physical harm, stalking, identity theft, drug sales and trafficking, and a greater availability of pornography and sexually oriented material. It is worth remembering, though, that these behaviors exist in physical space as well—albeit in different ways, with different social dynamics and outcomes.

Deception and secrecy are common in the physical world and so would be expected to exist digitally as well (see Baym, 2010). People lie to one another frequently—multiple times nearly every day, by some estimates (DePaulo, 2004; Feldman, Forrest, & Happ, 2002; on secrecy, see also Nippert-Eng, 2010). This kind of behavior occurs online and offline. But conscious, deliberate attempts to deceive others online and the taking on of different identities do not occur to the extent that many worry about (Baym, 2010). When gender switching takes place, for example, it is usually a role-playing or game-playing experiment rather than an act of deliberate deceit. The majority of those online do not undertake experiments in which they take on a different gender identity, and most of those who do abandon the practice (Roberts & Parks, 1999; see also Martey,

Stromer-Galley, Banks, Wu, & Consalvo, 2014). For the most part, when people interact online, they do so as themselves, carrying with them their identities, personal values, and standards (see Chapter 6).

In Western society, the mental realm tends to be stigmatized relative to the physical, so people often do not consider mental phenomena to be as consequential as the physical. The mental is still often seen as not *really* real—mental illness, for example, is less well understood than physical illness; it may not even be covered by some insurance plans because it is not considered "real" illness. When people say that something is "all in your mind," it is implied that something authentic is absent. But this is a false and even dangerous bias that minimizes or discounts people's lived experiences.

It simply isn't helpful to think of digital, mental activity as a species separate from, outside of, or less than real life—not when real life (whatever that is) is drenched in cognitive activity. It is a false dichotomy. The mental *is* real, and it is all around us, not just in our heads. And the physical and the mental are inextricably enmeshed. As a result, online experiences can be as richly emotional and deeply intimate as those that directly emerge in face-to-face interaction.

emotionality and intimacy

It is common for time spent online to have an intimate, emotionally rich dynamic. Intimacies and emotions are exchanged profusely and nearly instantaneously online. In fact, they serve as a kind of "glue" for the relationships that form there. This "emotional glue" is especially important in the absence of the "physical glue" that face-to-face interaction can provide.

Digital environments and the experiences created in them can be extremely, perhaps surprisingly, intimate. As social creatures who desire interpersonal closeness, human beings are highly creative in finding and forging intimacy, including in digital settings. While a wide variety of types of relationships can form online, spanning the spectrum of human intimacy, even the most fleeting of relationships can be highly intimate when those involved disclose a great deal about themselves and feel that they have come to understand much about the other person as well. It is this kind of personal disclosure and understanding and the positive progression of a relationship (even if it does not turn out to be especially long term) that render it intimate and meaningful. Short-term relationships can be highly intimate, just as they can be offline.

The human need and desire to form intimate relationships is so strong that it happens all the time online, often without great difficulty. Mobile and social media play a big part in this. Since many people take cell phones with them wherever they go, they can use small bits of time to check in on others and/or provide updates, whether by Facebook or Twitter or some other social media platform. Interestingly, this is how intimacy tends to develop face-to-face as well—in the small, everyday moments of connection as much as in grand gestures and experiences. And with a device with which to connect and network always at one's side, it has never been easier to remain in constant contact with others, even a large number of others, and to find that intimacy has developed, sometimes quite unexpectedly and swiftly (see Chayko, 2002, 2008; Fortunati, 2002; Fox, 2001).

The emotions that arise in digital environments are those that sociality inspires in all of its forms. Feelings of warmth, belonging, intimacy, even excitement are commonly generated online. Fear, anger, and disgust are elicited as well. A surge of emotion often arises when two or more people feel that they "click," whether online or offline (Baker, 2005; Chayko, 2008). This feeling can be so strong and satisfying that to obtain it can be central to people's desire to use social media (Chayko, 2008; Chmiel et al., 2011).

I have termed these emotional surges *the rush of human engagement* because they are generated in and by the human engagement so often sought and found online. In my research, many described it exactly that way—as a "charge" or a "rush." People told me of crying real tears when learning of a tragedy online, experiencing a surge of excitement upon getting good news or receiving just the right text at the right time, becoming angered or enraged when a negative comment was placed on their blog, or becoming downright giddy when an online exchange became flirtatious or romantic. These waves of emotion can provide "a rush that I really can't explain," as one online connector described it to me (Chayko, 2008, p. 77). According to another,

> It's great when you find somebody that loves the book that you love. The feeling is kind of "Oh, wow!" Or "Oh, me too!" . . . I think it's cool. I think it's neat. And I like those kind of connections. And I have even tried to sort of cultivate them. . . . ["Can you describe these connections for me?" I asked.] Oh, they're definitely bonds. (Chayko, 2002, p. 70)

In short,

> Sometimes when I get back to my room I just move the mouse and go to my favorite site and check my profile, and it's like someone has left me gold or something! (Chayko, 2008, p. 62)

This rush of excitement can be similar to the rush one gets from drugs, sex, gambling, chocolate, and other things that activate the pleasure centers in the brain (for more on how this works, see Chapter 7).

MIT internet scholar Sherry Turkle claims that people sometimes turn to information and communication technology when they *want* to feel something. They use the technology as a kind of conduit for emotion and use it to express love, hate, fear, rage—basically any mood imaginable. People also go online to moderate or to try to control their moods and emotions (see Chayko, 2008). At the same time, media companies may be trying to influence our emotions as well, whether by using algorithms to ensure that we see certain kinds of postings in our social media timelines (as occurred in the famously controversial Facebook "emotion contagion" experiment) or by encouraging us to "emote," albeit in a "nicely packaged" way (Polgar, 2017). "When these technologies have a power over our affect, or emotional life, you have to ask who is doing the emoting," suggests professor of philosophy Evan Selinger. "The more that Facebook can trigger certain emotions, and if we're unclear that they're being triggered in a rather contrived way, then to some sense we are outsourcing or delegating some of our emotional life without being fully conscious with how that process of delegation is working" (in Polgar, 2017).

Emotional responses in technology use are, therefore, fraught with complication. Of course, all human interactions are complex, messy, unpredictable, and fraught with risk. Examples abound of sad, unfortunate, even fatal outcomes of digitally influenced emotional responses—for example, relationships that have ended at the suggestion of online infidelity or lives that have ended when online bullying or public embarrassment became too much to take. Events that take place in a digital environment have profound consequences for people and are, again, undeniably real.

so . . . what about physicality?

It is sometimes hard to understand how community, social presence, emotionality, and intimacy can be experienced when physical cues are absent or diminished in digital environments. If we can't see someone's face (which is often the case online) or touch a hand or meet up for a date, can we really become intimately connected? As it turns out, people are quite creative when it comes to forming social connections and building social environments in which they do not physically interact or even see one another.

It seems strange to some that connections can form without the full benefit of external cues—without tactile, or in some cases, visual and aural information.

Communication researcher Joseph Walther (1996), among others, has theorized exactly how people make sense of (and make social connections in) *cues filtered out* situations. He argues in what has been called the social information processing theory that people who use their other senses and their limitless creativity to adapt their interactions accordingly and even without physicality can find out enough about one another to forge connections and potential intimacy.

People can learn quite a lot about others even if they only communicate textually. "Even with nothing but text, we can still tell a great deal about people from the language they use—their vocabulary, their grammar, their style," language and communication researcher Crispin Thurlow and his colleagues have found. "Besides, if we can't actually see social cues like age, sex and looks, we can always just ask. . . . This kind of direct request would seem pretty rude in [face-to-face] communication but it's considered acceptable in [computer-mediated communication]" (Thurlow, Lengel, & Tomic, 2004, p. 53; see also Baker, 2005). There are many ways to gather information about one another online, as we discuss in Chapter 6. People provide clues to their personalities in their nicknames, avatars, writing style, and in the design of their platforms and sites. In fact, when individuals go online with an eye toward possibly making a social connection, these kinds of fact-finding activities are among the first things they do.

Individuals can actually get to know one another *better* when their initial contacts are digital as opposed to face-to-face. They can like one another more and even gain a more accurate view of one another when visual cues are absent or reduced (Baker, 2005; McKenna, Green, & Gleason, 2002). Some people find the physical body to be a distraction and that in its absence they are better able to form honest, authentic relationships. "When we talk to someone in person," says psychologist Katelyn McKenna, "we pay attention to their subtle body language and facial cues that let us know how we are coming across. This fosters reticence in fully expressing our thoughts and feelings" (as quoted in Chayko, 2008, p. 46). Thoughts and feelings may be more easily, comfortably, and authentically shared when physicality is absent.

Some people communicate more freely about themselves in the absence of the physical. Put another way, the physical presence of a body can distract from the effort to get to know another person. Closeness, involvement, even attraction can be enhanced when people are not in one another's physical presence (Chayko, 2008; Hian, Chuan, Trevor, & Detenber, 2004; Hu, Wood, Smith, & Westbrook, 2004; Nowak, Watt, & Walther, 2005; Walther, 1996). A relationship can grow strong and intense even more quickly than when the interactants have met face-to-face. In fact, online relationships can be even *more* intimate and personal than those conducted primarily face-to-face. Joseph Walther calls such relationships *hyperpersonal* (1997).

When people are in contact without being able to see or touch one another, they can become *disinhibited* (Suler, 2004; see also McKenna et al., 2002). Their inhibitions can be lowered and their behavior can become a bit (or a lot) more outgoing or daring. Disinhibition can be even more pronounced if individuals do not share their names or personal details online and are anonymous to one another. They may find themselves behaving differently than they would face-to-face—perhaps sharing personal information more quickly, even ill-advisedly, perhaps becoming thoughtlessly negative or nasty, perhaps becoming spontaneous, impulsive, wild.

Darkness, too, favors disinhibition. For many, face-to-face intimacies are more easily shared in darkness, especially late at night, than in the midday sun. They may feel less embarrassed, less self-conscious, than they ordinarily might. They may behave more freely and "open" themselves up more quickly, more intensely. Even in face-to-face copresence, some individuals avert their eyes when discussing something extremely personal and emotional or when they do not wish to be visually confrontational (Suler, 2004; Thurlow et al., 2004). In fact, people who meet in a darkened room tend to disclose more personal information to one another and even to like one another more than those who meet initially in the "light of day" (Gergen, Gergen, & Barton, 1973; McKenna, Green, & Gleason, 2002).

There are certain similarities to meeting in the dark and online. Reduced physical cues can replicate the openness and intrigue of darkness and nighttime. The absence of a physical presence can contribute to an environment in which information and intimacies are more easily shared. This can promote closeness and social connectedness.

Furthermore, digital and mobile media allow people to connect at odd times of the day or night and in odd places. This, too, is conducive to the development of intimacy. It is common to prefer to be in a private, out-of-the-way setting when sharing something very personal or private. There is something about finding someone else online in the middle of the night and reaching out to him or her that makes the moment a bit out of the ordinary and imbues it with specialness. This is similar to the "meeting on the train" phenomenon, in which people confide secrets to a total stranger whom they do not expect to ever see again simply because the setting lends itself to the sharing of intimacies. The repercussions of such sharing may seem lower or be temporarily ignored (McKenna et al., 2002).

Technologies are continually being developed that approximate or reintroduce visual and sensory elements of the face-to-face experience to online or mobile connecting. The sharing of photos and videos has exploded in popularity on social media. But some still prefer the greater anonymity and clarity of text-based exchanges, especially for use in the early stages of relationships. Some shy away from using webcams in internet dating, psychologist Jeff Gavin has found, because they prefer to delay seeing their partners face-to-face. "There is something special about text-based relationships," he says (ScienceDaily.com, 2005).

Many of those whom I interviewed agreed. This thoughtful perspective came from a member of an intellectually rich and engaged online community:

> It could even be argued that we are engaging on a deeper level than we would be able to if we were face-to-face. A lot of things get lost and misconstrued in oral arguments. With this, everything is in writing. One often edits and rephrases for clarity. Putting things down in writing is far different than just blurting something aloud. Many posts only come after much reflection and a sorting out of thoughts. So although we miss the tones and facial expressions of the people with whom we are communicating, it could be argued that we are still communicating on a more profound level. (Chayko, 2002, p. 122)

Many people told me that there was something uniquely valuable and intimate about getting to know a person in a nonphysical sense before (or instead of) sharing physical space with them.

At a certain point, of course, to enjoy certain satisfactions people must meet face-to-face to share the full range of sensory experiences with one another—touch, smell, taste, physical nearness, bodily contact. Personal accountability is generally enhanced as well when people are face-to-face with one another. One concern about nonphysical connectedness can be put to rest, though, and that is the worry that internet-enabled relationships will somehow replace or substitute for face-to-face relationships. Rather, the online and offline tend to intersect and mesh in people's everyday lives and be experienced as a blended whole.

the intersection of the online and the offline

It is tempting, and quite common, to assume that what we do online happens at the expense of or displaces the offline (as detailed and critiqued by Boase &

Wellman, 2006; Rainie & Wellman, 2012; Tufekci, 2010, 2012; and Wang & Wellman, 2010). Research paints a very different picture of how people use digital communication technology, however. Certainly, some people who are lonely gravitate toward the internet (Amichai-Hamburger & Ben-Artzi, 2003), and some become so immersed in their online connectedness that their well-being suffers (LaRose, Eastin, & Gregg, 2001; Morgan & Cotten, 2003). This is not the norm, however.

Most people use online connectedness to build, bolster, and give new dimension to face-to-face interactions and communities. They choose their online friends from among their offline contacts and use both mediated and face-to-face means to sustain all their relationships. As we explore in depth in Chapter 6, it is common for groups and relationships to exist in spaces that encompass both the online and the offline (see Ellison et al., 2009; Hampton et al., 2011; Haythornthwaite & Kendall, 2010; Rainie & Wellman, 2012). Online activities fulfill a wide range of needs, gratifications, and desires and are experienced as part of, not separate from, one's lived experience (see Baym, 1995, 2000, 2010; Jurgenson, 2012a, 2012c; Katz, Haas, & Gurevitch, 1997; Kayany, Wotring, & Forrest, 1996; Walther, 1996, 1997).

One's lived reality with technology is generally experienced as a blending, a mixture, of the online and the offline, rather than as one or the other (Baym 2010; Beer, 2008; Cerulo & Ruane, 1998; Floridi, 2007; Jurgenson, 2012c; Kendall, 2010). We do not tend to separate our lives into online and offline—or experience things as either digital or face-to-face. Social media theorist Nathan Jurgenson calls this separation *digital dualism*, and, as he and other thinkers have noted, it is both an artificial and unnecessary separation of realms that are actually enmeshed (2012c). While qualities and characteristics of the online and offline realms are surely different—a smile given or received in physical space is not at all the same thing as encountering an emoticon online, for example—the realms in which these experiences occur are not in opposition to one another. They are simply different aspects of lived experience that swirl around and intersect with one another, coagulating, in a sense, to become, simply, our realities—our lives.

Just as using new technological devices or platforms is usually confusing or clunky at first but becomes easier with time, digital technology tends to be integrated and folded into the everyday life of people in tech-rich communities and societies. This can happen so seamlessly that people can forget about or ignore the technology that has mediated the experience and simply focus on the experience itself (see Floridi, 2007; Rainie, 2006; Thomas, 2006). In doing so, they gradually adapt to those new technologies that become part of their everyday lives and become used to the way that their lives have become impacted and augmented by technology (Jurgenson, 2012c).

To consider the online and offline wholly separate spheres and engage in digital dualism is to also ignore or minimize their high degree of interpenetration. "It is because social media augments our offline lives (rather than replaces them) that research shows that Facebook users have more offline contacts, are more civically engaged, etc.," Jurgenson argues, for "the online and offline are not separate spheres and thus are not zero-sum" (2012c). Indeed, offline activity fuels online content and expression; many individuals now spend significant time and energy considering how they may document online what may be happening in their lives offline (Jurgenson, 2012a; see also Ess, 2011). It should also be kept in mind that face-to-face interaction is not always inherently satisfying or best suited to every task (Calhoun, 1986). Obtaining and sharing information, resources, and certain kinds of support are often accomplished more effectively online than offline.

Those who have grown up immersed in the internet and digital media use may see the online and offline as melding seamlessly. Youth may be ushering in an era in which distinctions between the online and offline, and the real and the unreal, are becoming deeply blurred, if not obliterated. The worlds of young technology users bleed together, information technology professional Charles Grantham observes. "It is pretty useless to draw borders around different spheres of life for them" (as quoted in Rainie, 2006; see also Baym, 2000, 2010; Cerulo & Ruane, 1998; Ess, 2011; Ito et al., 2010; Thomas, 2006; Wilson & Atkinson, 2005).

Digital environments are so fully enmeshed with the physical world that one need not even be online to feel the impact. Even when spending time offline, perhaps enjoying a quiet, tech-free day in a natural setting, people can be influenced by their use of the internet and digital media. They may decide that they will document the experience with a photo (or several) that they plan to share later, mentally construct a status update they will later post on social media about the offline experience, or perhaps send a quick text message. Jurgenson calls this viewing the world with a "Facebook Eye"—thinking about how lived experience might translate to a future post, tweet, or update (2012a).

This kind of activity is common in a society rich in technology. Technology can be so deeply integrated with so many aspects of life that it is almost as though the tech has seeped inside the person, cyborg-style. And indeed to a certain extent, due to its frequent use, the tech *has* seeped in—mentally. The online–offline enmeshment is cognitive as much as it is experiential. In a tech-rich society, it may be difficult at times to truly "log off," for the brain may remain "logged on."

Because so many in technology-rich societies spend so much time and energy in digital environments, conceptualizing this experience is critical to understanding modern social life. As we have seen in this chapter, research on the experience and environments in which techno-social life takes place comes from numerous fields of study. I encourage you to bring *your* field of study and your everyday understandings and knowledge to bear on all of this. In your experience, how are digital environments evolving and changing and influencing social connectedness?

To make sure that our view on this is not myopic, though, we turn next to the topic of digital sharing and surveillance. It has become a norm to share information in digital spaces—often as widely as possible—even as companies and governments peek in on and collect and even sell this information. We shall see how these practices affect people's ability to be private, to form relationships, and to have control over their lives so we can better understand and protect ourselves in superconnected, techno-social environments.

note

1. Portions excerpted from Chayko (2014).

4 SHARING AND SURVEILLANCE

sharing and prosuming in a participatory culture

Many internet and digital media users make and share stories, postings, photos, videos, comments, music, memes, and musings, exchanging a wide variety of types of information, often with great frequency. They consider it enjoyable and creative—a big part of the online experience. The result is a *participatory culture* in which members of the public take active part in the creation and consumption of their cultural products and are expected to share them freely and widely (see Bruns, 2008; Jenkins, 2006, 2009).

A participatory culture is also an economy in which content, goods, time, effort, and money are, to one degree or another, shared, exchanged, and spent. This kind of sharing economy transcends the internet. Companies such as Uber and Airbnb have devised ways for such products as cars and vacation homes to be shared or rented instead of purchased. Digital sites and apps may seem free to visit or use, but a bounty of personal information is generally provided during such visits. Even as the iRobot "Roomba" is used to vacuum a floor, information about the items in that person's house (and their mapped locations) is being collected and could theoretically be shared and sold; imagine ads for armchairs following you across the internet simply because your Roomba has detected that you do not own one (Astor, 2017)!

As people contribute information to websites, blogs, and social media networks, they tell others a great deal about themselves and make quite a bit of personal information public without being compensated in return. Such data, in the aggregate, can make organizations and corporations very wealthy. The word *sharing*, then, ignores the extent to which doing so disproportionately benefits the more powerful among us. Still, content is created and spreads in abundance in digital spaces.

We should not assume that people always desire to share their information, however. Sometimes they limit the disclosure of personal information. They may want to reduce the potential for information to be made public, avoid possible interpersonal conflicts, protect their self-interests, or enhance their own images. "Individuals often make strategic choices to limit or restrict information," organizational communication researcher Jennifer Gibbs and her coauthors have established. "Choices to share or not to share knowledge in social media applications are likely to be influenced by such concerns" (Gibbs, Rozaidi, & Eisenberg, 2013, p. 104). Widespread public sharing is not everyone's goal, all the time.

Different kinds of content are often created and shared by different groups of people. According to internet researcher Grant Blank, political content is most often created by society's "elites," while social and entertainment content is often created by "non-elites." Online content, then, is not only different in type but may reflect differences in the backgrounds and perspectives of its creators (Blank, 2013).

In tech-rich societies, so many people produce and consume content so frequently that it has become normative to do so. People (or *makers*) design and make personalized technological products, and they consume that of others. Often teaching themselves how to do it, people use social media and blogging platforms, tools available on the internet, and open source software to produce all kinds of content. It is then shared, consumed, critiqued, and sometimes appropriated and remixed by others (see Benkler, 2014).

It has also become common to express one's creativity by remixing and reconfiguring existing content, including music and video. In this *remix culture*, materials are taken from the pieces of existing texts, whether it is legally permissible to do so or not, and new versions are created. As these new texts are then frequently remixed by others, the processes of production and consumption become merged. The practice became normative due to "implicit permissions, coupled with a background culture of open sharing and rising rhetoric of openness," notes network and legal scholar Yochai Benkler (2014, p. 296). Producing, consuming, and remixing content online has become a defining feature of modern technological life that has resulted in new ways of thinking about what should be legal or illegal, paid or unpaid, public or private. It has, media researcher Aram Sinnreich says, rendered our whole culture "configurable" (2010).

In true postmodern fashion, a combo word has popped up to capture the blurring of production and consumption into a cyclical, sometimes simultaneous, process. Introduced by Alvin Toffler (1980) and since repurposed by sociologists George Ritzer and Nathan Jurgenson (2010), this act is now frequently called *prosuming* or *prosumption*, and the people who do so are known as *prosumers* (see also Ritzer, Dean, & Jurgenson, 2012). The activity is also sometimes called *produsage* (see Bruns, 2008). Combo words like *prosuming* are not just a convenient shorthand but, as with *techno-social*, are also a representation of how fully two entities have fused.

Prosumption has become part of the business model of many companies. To produce as much as possible, as cost-effectively as possible, has long been a primary business goal. Companies are highly motivated to increase the efficiency of the production, distribution, and consumption of goods and services so as to generate as much profit as possible. In the First Industrial Revolution of the mid-1800s, factories were a primary site of production; in the Second Industrial Revolution of the early 1900s, assembly lines added a layer of efficiency. Production processes in many ways define eras and societies.

As the expectation of efficiency in mass production became accelerated in modern technological cultures, it became apparent that if consumers were to participate in the production of goods or services (unpaid, for free!) the profit margin of a business would be significantly enhanced. The company would no longer need to hire as many workers. After a time, consumers might not even expect to have certain tasks performed by waged—or even human—employees.

In many industries, including those developed around internet and digital technology, this is exactly what has happened. Customers willingly participate in the production of the product or service, even as they consume and sometimes pay for the experience. Grocers, for example, once filled customers' orders at food markets, fetching their items and providing fresh-cut meats. Supermarkets now require customers to select their own items and fill their own orders, and, correspondingly, there are now far fewer grocers and butchers to be found. Some restaurants now require customers to work cafeteria-style to obtain their own orders and clean their tables afterward (Ritzer et al., 2012). Such companies can then employ fewer people, and at a lower wage, since the work to be done by those employees that remain is regimented and easy to train people to do. This, in turn, makes those workers more easily replaceable and (seemingly justifiably, to the management) they are paid less, due to the rote work they are doing. This increases company profits even more, although it depresses the incomes of many employees.

Computerized technology permits the automation of many consumer behaviors that used to require the human touch. Whether one is shopping, banking, or trying to contact someone at a business by phone, it can be difficult if not impossible to find a human being to be of assistance when making transactions or discussing pertinent issues. Rather, consumers are expected to accept responsibility for the tasks involved and to spend time and energy figuring out what to do and how to do it. As companies develop the technological expertise to automate more and more of their online product, consumers have no choice but to accept the setup—or, if they do not accept it, to be left out, especially since it is often impossible to find anyone to complain to about it! Consumers then become like unwitting, unpaid producers—de facto employees—for these companies. They are expected to do much of the company's work for it, and for free.

Classical sociological theorist Karl Marx has theorized at length that regimented, low-paid work like this is exploitive and can become highly alienating for workers as it cuts them off from more creative, more fully human ways of living (Marx, 1844/2012, 1887). Individuals can spend so much time and energy earning low wages in relatively demeaning environments that they end up spending their whole lives making other people rich and feeling alienated from the products they spend so much time producing but do not even get to use. Inevitably, Marx claimed, workers would become alienated from other people and from their own selves, unable to see that they are part of a system designed for profit and not for their well-being—a system that will never operate for their benefit. Marx's views have remained controversial even in the modern era, as people debate whether the economic system he endorsed—communism—would reduce inequalities or create other socioeconomic and political problems.

As internet users began to create, configure, consume, and spread all kinds of content on the web, user-created, often unpaid (or poorly paid) content became the foundation of many websites and web companies. Social media platforms, such as Facebook, Twitter, Instagram, Wikipedia, YouTube, and a host of blogs and other sharing sites, rely heavily if not entirely on individuals producing content for public consumption and thus engaging in *digital labor*. And to the extent that this content is intended to produce or influence the emotional states of others, it can be called *affective labor* as well. Thinking of online media use in this way represents a major shift away from models of understanding media audiences as passive consumers (a model that was becoming outdated anyway) to those in which users are highly active and constantly producing while consuming. They are prosumers and, in effect, digital, often affective laborers, producing and consuming a mountain of content that, collectively, is always on the increase.

Why do people create and in effect give away for free so much of their own time, creativity, and labor? To a certain extent, they may be exhibiting *false consciousness*—they may not realize that to do so benefits the more powerful in society more than they themselves benefit. They may accept without critique the narratives of those of higher socioeconomic status that state that sharing one's information is good and that to fail to share freely is to be left out. Descriptions of the financial benefit to media corporations are generally omitted in the "sharing is good" narratives.

On the other hand, there *is* much to be personally gained by laboring to make digital products, creating content, remixing music and video, and the like. It can be a highly creative, expressive, fun activity. In the prosumption process, social connections, networks, and communities can be created and joined, support may be provided, and the "rush of human engagement" can be felt. It can even be a political statement or an act of resistance against a culture or company that prohibits or discourages such individual creativity (Sinnreich, 2010). It is the norm in a modern high-tech society, and when something is a norm, more and more people do it in order to feel fully a part of the culture, to not feel left out. They do not feel that they can opt out. Yet as makers continually produce, consume, and create, they can be exploited in ways that may not be immediately apparent to them.

Individuals pay for the digitized experiences in which they take part by contributing their labor and data. This happens even as they simply click around the web, communicating and sharing information with one another. Collectively, a ubiquitous yet largely invisible economy is shaped that "doesn't look, feel, or smell like labor at all," says media theorist Trebor Scholz. "This digital labor is much akin to those less visible, unsung forms of traditional women's labor such as child care, housework, and surrogacy" (2012, p. 2; see also Andrejevic, 2012). In other words, its invisibility can serve as a kind of smokescreen—or trap.

Nearly everything one communicates or shares online is appropriated, commodified, and sold to companies that want to know more about you, usually so they can target advertising to you. This is the trade-off for the ostensibly "free" internet (which is not really free, anyway—the costs of technology and access are passed along in the form of advertising and higher-priced goods, in addition to hardware and access charges). Many are unaware of these costs and trade-offs, however. And it is impossible to totally opt out of the system (see Vertesi, 2014). To obtain needed information, to create and share, to work, to purchase things, to socialize—to do all these things online requires making public one's behavior and content.

There are both advantages and disadvantages to prosumption, as there are to nearly all techno-social phenomena. New business opportunities are indeed available; the internet has made it easier to set up and publicize small "shops" and online venues in which a wide range of things can be made, promoted, and sold. Opportunities to make and remix content, sometimes collaboratively, can be fun and expressive and fulfilling on many levels. But to monetize something is to change its nature and the dynamics that surround it—and internet content is constantly, if invisibly, monetized. "What happens to the culture of digital media if—like most media before it, printing press and radio and TV included—it ends up in the hands of a few powerful interests?" wonders social media researcher Bonnie Stewart, who has written two successful blogs. "The . . . reconfiguration of cultural practices and power relations involved makes navigating the path to becoming a producer as well as a consumer an increasingly challenging one" (2012).

"Media cartels and government agencies are seeking to reimpose the regime of the broadcast era," opines pioneering technology author and critic Harold Rheingold. In such a regime, he states, "the customers of technology will be deprived of the power to create and left only with the power to consume" (Rheingold, 2002). Battles over copyright, file-sharing, and other intellectual property issues threaten the openness and neutrality of the web. For the internet to remain a space in which production and consumption of content and enterprise can flow widely, prosumers will need to resist the ways that powerful, entrenched business interests seek to shape and control the technology and business models of the internet and digital media and, indeed, the content and users of the web themselves (Rheingold, 2002).

crowdsourcing

In a digital environment, with the assistance of social media, physically separated people prosume content not just individually but also together. Large numbers of people can now easily gather together online to participate in shared digital activities. In groups—sometimes very large groups—people can collaborate in telling a story, solving a problem, compiling and editing information, funding a project, or doing almost any group-oriented activity that can be imagined.

When several or more people take on or share a task in a distributed but collective manner, physically separated from one another, the activity is called *crowdsourcing* (or, when the task is explicitly oriented toward raising money, *crowdfunding*). Derived from the concept of outsourcing, crowdsourcing exists when tasks or activities are taken on by, or "outsourced" to, a number of people. Crowdsourcing and crowdfunding are activities that represent the collective response and action of a group. They do not necessarily reflect a formal or explicit charge or requirement (see Korthaus & Dai, 2015).

Some say that crowdsourcing returns to the masses a certain level of power. With the ability to find one another in social networks, share information, and contact members of other groups and networks, individuals are given a voice, a platform from which to speak. There is power in numbers, and there is power in digital networks. Then again, as Marx explained (1887), the owner of any organization has so much economic power that it eclipses that of its workers, unless, as Marx suggested, people resist and revolt against the owners and question and reject even the very concept of ownership.

In many groups, a certain collective energy emerges that transcends that of the individual (Durkheim, 1912/1965). This energy can be positive and represent a kind of collective wisdom, sometimes called *collective intelligence*. It can also be negative, when a group turns unruly or destructive. Georg Simmel called the latter "the superiority of the individual over the mass" (1908/1950), describing how in groups, especially large ones, people often revert to the "least common denominator" and behave less thoughtfully, more crudely.

Certainly, we see both positive and negative group behavior online. We reap the benefits that crowdsourced knowledge and crowdfunded charitable efforts bring about, even as we see strings of cruel comments and threats made online as well. Crowdsourcing can be best understood as a combination of these extreme viewpoints. It is an excellent way to gather and filter the resources of a group, but it remains prone to the problems that can be experienced in groups—problems that anonymity can intensify (Flanagin, Hocevar, & Samahito, 2014; Hmielowski, Hutchens, & Cicchirillo, 2014; Rowe, 2015).

Because the sum of the contributions of a group so often exceeds the contributions that any one or a few people could produce, crowdsourcing can yield astonishing innovation. Wikipedia, perhaps the ultimate example of crowdsourcing, is not a perfect or unbiased repository of information, but it is an intricate record of the ongoing information-gathering activities of a very large group of people—tens of millions of them, primarily males with strong skills in digital literacy (Hargittai & Shaw, 2015). With its sheer number and volume of topics, as well as its ability to be constantly updated, it has changed, probably forever, what people think of as an encyclopedia. In the same way, sites such as Change.org have the potential to alter what people think of as a petition. Once solely distributed through face-to-face and door-to-door activity, petitions that could potentially drive major social change can now be initiated, signed, and presented online.

Other sites feature group comments and ratings on items or services. This kind of collective feedback can be more helpful in assisting prospective buyers to make a decision than a single opinion because it is more likely that numerous individuals' biases will be collapsed within the overall "average" of the crowd's opinion. It has become so popular to comment on and rate items online that this feature is now widely enabled on news stories, entertainment features, items for sale, and so on. Commenting is a satisfying and motivating activity for people who enjoy being part of—and perhaps achieving status in—groups that serve as online information pools (Flanagin et al., 2014).

There is always a possibility that off-topic, nasty, threatening, or abusive postings will result when crowdsourced comments are invited. This generally occurs when respondents are anonymous, the activity is unmoderated, and a range of response types are permitted and are perceived by the community as acceptable (Hmielowski et al., 2014; Rowe, 2015). Some people choose to comment harshly or use the comments section of a site as a personal soapbox or to sell things. But crowdsourcing is also a way to gather in the aggregate potentially more fair and unbiased responses to an issue or task than a single individual (or small group) might provide. While some individuals, called *trolls*, may "hijack" a thread and provide extreme, irrelevant responses in an attempt to pull focus away from the thread's original intent, many people are motivated to contribute usefully to the group and take such tasks seriously (Flanagin et al., 2014).

Sometimes the crowdsourced task is to raise money. At this writing, several websites, including Kickstarter.com, serve as a place where individuals who want to raise money for a project, charity, or other activity can appeal to those who might be interested in helping a project thrive. Those who want to kickstart a project post a description of it, along with possible rewards that donors may receive for funding the project at different levels. If enough people kick in, the project is a "go." Many people, contributing very small amounts of money each, can make a real difference, especially in the lives of those who have very little. Kiva.org, for example, is a site where people collectively fund small loans or grants earmarked for individuals who are in great need of the money. Some live in very poor, remote areas of the world and yet can be "found" and substantially aided by relatively small cash infusions to help provide them (or their community) with such necessities as water or sanitation or to help them set up small businesses and generate income for themselves over time. This process is called *microfunding*, and it is another example of the good that can be done by crowdsourcing a project.

Sometimes goods, skills, or time are crowdsourced instead of money. Some communities have set up so-called freecycling days in which people trade or recycle unwanted items in a kind of giant swap meet. Groups have set up bartering systems in which people trade their expertise in one area for someone else's expertise in another area. In such cases, a centralized system of credits can keep track of who does what so that, for example, someone can provide someone else in the community with an hour of guitar lessons in exchange for something like an hour of plumbing or lawn mowing, which might be provided by a different member of the community. For his 2012 film *Fixing the Future*, David Brancaccio of National Public Radio traveled across the United States to observe how these kinds of systems—local business alliances, community banking, and work co-ops—actually work. He noted that in addition to providing a crowdsourced kind of clearinghouse for expertise and talents to be exchanged, they can bring a community closer together by inviting interaction and conversation at all points in the process. Similar to the idea of community gardening (the crowdsourcing of a garden), when people collaborate it is likely that new connections will follow and community will be upheld.

It is difficult to imagine collaborations like these finding widespread success without the use of the internet and computerized and mobile media to coordinate and publicize the efforts. Interestingly, what often happens when crowdsourced activities are organized via the internet is that face-to-face interaction in the community increases. This is in keeping with the finding that use of the internet is positively correlated with face-to-face interaction—a key finding in the literature on digital social connectedness that is discussed in depth in Chapter 7 (see Chayko, 2014). Keep in mind, though, that no social scientific finding occurs every single time, all the time. Sociological research uncovers and reports trends and patterns but cannot speak to the reasons why a particular individual might act in the way that he or she does except to consider how and why that individual might relate to a general, overall pattern.

As an expression of the desire to share things on the internet, crowdsourcing has become an increasingly common, popular way to share knowledge and resources online. As the web and social media invite discussion, commentary, interpersonal response, and evaluation, they give groups a venue, a space in which to emerge. In the process, these groups can gain power: a means to raise money and awareness, and a voice to speak back to the mighty (Korthaus & Dai, 2015).

liking and following—and being liked and followed

Are people exploited when they share content and data for free on the web, as Marx might have predicted? Do they become alienated from one another—less able to appreciate the humanity in themselves and others? Or has digital technology changed the contours of the modern world such that the beneficial outcomes of internet and digital media use outweigh the harms?

We take part in a different type of economy, one not predicated solely on finances, when we are online. In this economy, sometimes called the *attention economy*, "attention is the real currency," business and management professors Thomas Davenport and John Beck explain (2002, p. 3). In an atmosphere in which the paying of attention is relatively scarce and much desired, attention can take on some of the attributes of a monetary instrument. "Those who don't have it want it," Davenport and Beck continue. "Even those who have it want more. . . . People work to preserve and extend what they already have" (2002, p. 3).

Online attention can take the shape of a simple glance at a photo or a more active step: a like, a follow, a share, a comment. But attention is also a two-way street. In exchange for accumulating likes and follows, it is generally expected that one will like and follow in return, though not necessarily in an even one-to-one exchange. It has become social media etiquette to provide attention to others in exchange for their attention and to prove that you have done so by liking, favoriting, retweeting, or following the other account. Proof that one has the attention of others can be measured in the number of likes or comments a post receives on Facebook, in the number of retweets or followers attracted on Twitter, and so on. When relationships transacted on social media prove to be one-way, or lack reciprocity, unfriending or unfollowing can result (Zevallos, 2011; see Abidin, 2014).

This is, indeed, a kind of economy, and it is one that has come to matter to many of us. Attention is attracted as something shared is acknowledged online. A kind of compensation follows in the form of likes, follows, and comments. More tangible rewards like social connections, jobs, and money can even follow. Other rewards are intangible but can be profound in their impact—approval, confidence, happiness, the feeling that one is special or even loved. Conversely, if their contributions are ignored, people can feel hurt, rejected, or left out. Again, we see deeply human needs and desires expressed in digital environments.

Attention online is subject to increasing returns. That is, the more one has of it, the easier it is to get more. The most well-known celebrities attract attention nearly constantly; in fact, they are followed by photographers called paparazzi. There is an appetite or market for information about them and thus more and more such information is generated all the time. They continually receive attention (and likes and follows) almost no matter what they do. To succeed in such an economy, it helps to create or remix attention-getting content and then to rapidly capitalize on bursts of attention as soon as they occur, sometimes by including hashtags that will help content be seen or by engaging with and following social media influencers in the hope that they will follow back and engage in turn. This is why one can see the same attention-getting topics mentioned repeatedly, over and over again, and the same people (i.e., Donald Trump) referenced repeatedly in the mass and digital media (Davenport & Beck, 2002).

ownership of online content

It has always been a little tricky to discern who owns what when it comes to people's ideas, or, as it is sometimes called, their *intellectual property.* Credit, and in some cases payment, can only be given to a person if it can be demonstrated that what he or she is writing or saying has been actually devised by that person. It's a complex issue that has been made even more complicated in the age of digital media.

Thoughts, words, and longer creative works have always been to some extent amalgamations of the contributions of a number of people. We generally think in the way that we have been taught to do so by those groups that have shaped us, sociologist of knowledge Karl Mannheim explains. "Only in a limited sense does the single individual create out of himself the mode of speech and of thought that we attribute to him," Mannheim observed. "He speaks the language of his group; he thinks in the manner his group thinks" (1929/1960, p. 4).

Individuals have no choice, for example, but to use the language of the groups of which they are a part in forming their thoughts. They also have no choice as to the groups into which they are born and the ways of looking at the world that these groups bestow on their members. People have more choices later on, but thoughts and expressions and even emotions are still largely unconscious processes that result from the assimilation of the symbols, norms, values, and culture of a group. The ways in which individuals arrange their thoughts and ideas can be said to be their own, but even that is influenced heavily by those around them.

People cannot claim others' specific writings and works as their own, however. This is an overreach of personal power. *Copyright* laws regulate intellectual property so that people can be credited for and in some cases paid for their creative work. The concept of copyright actually appears in the U.S. Constitution in Article 1, Section 8, Clause 8, which guarantees Americans exclusive right to their own writings and discoveries, at least for limited periods of time. While general concepts and thoughts (and, interestingly, titles of works) cannot be copyrighted or therefore "owned," specific intellectual contributions are legally protected. But it is very difficult to isolate and quantify such specifics, especially in the modern media environment.

The sharing economy has complicated copyright matters. Lots of information on the internet and digital media is prosumed, crowdsourced, and remixed—created collaboratively by producers and consumers alike, sometimes in large batches. It can be hard to attribute to a specific author information that has been shared or reconfigured in a digital context. Pieces of information can be digitally cut and pasted and spread without attribution from one place to the next. They can be distributed widely via such avenues as tweets, memes, wikis, and blog comments. Some view these processes as not substantially different from the ebb and flow of everyday conversational exchanges, while others view them as something in between formal published works and communal "talk." Either way, they are very difficult to regulate.

Additionally, a *culture of free* has arisen with regard to the internet and digital media use. Napster, a free music-sharing program launched in 1999 by 18-year-old tech entrepreneur Shawn Fanning, was an immediate, explosive internet phenomenon. For two years, users of the program could upload music from their own libraries and then pass it along to others for free through peer-to-peer file sharing. But artists were not paid for their musical compositions in this system, and music companies fought back. They filed lawsuits against Fanning, Napster, and even some of the program's users who stored the music files on their own computers. In 2001, courts ruled that Napster had violated copyright laws and shut it down.

Other file-sharing services have come and gone since, and iTunes, and later Spotify, Pandora, and other music streaming services, have provided models by which music can be both shared and paid for (albeit in different ways). "One thing was certain, though," tech writer Clyde Haberman declared. "The culture of free was not going away" (2014). An environment of open information sharing had proved wildly popular among media users. Individuals began to expect to find free or low-cost music, information, and all kinds of services on the internet. And owners of media and technology businesses, unsurprisingly, resisted, and continue to resist, the idea.

Technology had proved capable of providing all kinds of means for people to share, remix, and contribute content via the internet and social media. Media corporations and music companies, in turn, saw their profits and very existence threatened. Rather than adapt to the new environment, they dug in their heels and chose to fight, even to prosecute, these media makers, citing copyright laws that preceded the development of the new practices that the internet and digital media inspired and made possible. The result has been what Aram Sinnreich calls a "piracy crusade" (2013) that can cause harm not only to individuals and small business but to privacy, free speech, and democracy itself, for the widespread shaping of technology is essential for democracy (Volti, 2014, p. 17; see also Benkler, 2014).

Plagiarism—the theft of ideas through their incorrect or incomplete attribution or unauthorized spreading—is also on the rise, especially when the internet is used (Birch, 2011). Students, teachers, writers, media creators, and business professionals alike struggle with when, whether, and how a piece of information should rightly be attributed to someone. Sometimes it is difficult if not impossible to determine where an idea originated. Other times, ambiguity is used as a kind of screen behind which these inquiries fail to take place. This has become such a thorny, tangled issue that some have argued that copyright laws developed in a predigital age may need to be changed or abolished lest they quash creativity and innovation (see Benkler, 2014; Lessig, 2008; and Sinnreich, 2013).

To acknowledge this, a nonprofit organization named Creative Commons was developed in 2001 by law professor Lawrence Lessig and his collaborators to give people and organizations flexibility in terms of how much control they would like to have over copyright (Plotkin, 2002). Creative Commons licenses permit creators to waive some of their copyright rights and state this clearly. It has been credited with expanding the *public domain* in which creative works can be freely produced, consumed, distributed, and remixed or repurposed at will. Critics, however, are concerned that thinking about copyright in this way may lead to abuses of the system and changes in copyright law that could result in artists not being properly compensated for their work.

It is certainly possible that in the future copyright laws may have limited power or change form radically, and plagiarism may be dramatically recast. For the time being, the onus is on those who quote or paraphrase written work to try to track down the origin of the intellectual property and cite it properly, even if the origin is a tweet, a post on Facebook, a video, a wiki, a blog post or comment, or the spoken word. This ensures that the content creator can receive full credit for it and allows readers to know that written work is accurately and legitimately sourced and more likely to be credible and reputable.

the power to disseminate and publish information

A constant flow of prosumed content, shared widely in various formats, has wrought many changes in the distribution and publication of information. At one time, if someone wanted to distribute printed information, he or she would generally have to hand copy it. As of the mid-21st century, one would have to mimeograph or photocopy paper pages, which could quickly get expensive. Still, pamphlets, newsletters, and zines (small-market, often underground and alternative, magazines) were produced in these ways and distributed by hand or by mail. Larger production and distribution projects have generally required a publisher—someone to evaluate a work's print-worthiness and then take on the task of producing and sometimes promoting it. Until fairly recently, there was no way to produce and access written work on any kind of large scale without going through the publishing industry, which had enormous power over what would be mass produced and consumed.

Similarly, the services of formal businesses were once required for the wide production and distribution of audio and video products to take place. Musicians and filmmakers could record and produce their work independently, but it would be quite costly to purchase the needed equipment and technology to do so, especially if one was looking to achieve a high-quality result. And it was even more difficult to make such products available to others, let alone distribute them widely. There was no such thing as downloading music or streaming to an appropriate device; the MP3 files that would allow audio streaming were only invented in 1991, and the first MP3 players were not available until late 1997 (McCormick, 2009).

All of this changed when internet, digital, and mobile media technologies, platforms, and apps became widespread. Now, due to the ability to produce and distribute multimedia content to a potentially wide audience, text, audio, and video are in the hands of everyday users. Many of these platforms (social media, blogs, websites, music-making and video-sharing sites) are do-it-yourself in nature, and the means of production are free or inexpensive and relatively easy to understand and use. Not everyone has an equivalent ability to do this—some people are better at it or have more resources and capital than others. But the possibilities for engaging in and sharing these kinds of creative activities as an independent artist and entrepreneur now exist and are plentiful.

Even books can be produced and distributed more easily and at a much lower cost than was once the case. Technologies that permit a book to be produced, distributed, and consumed electronically (as e-books) are now available. Self-publishing is relatively inexpensive and yields ready access to one's work, even leading in some cases to lucrative traditional publishing contracts. Again, though, this is not equally easy for all to do, and it is not a feasible alternative to more formalized modes of production for all.

Publishing and music industries have been deeply affected by all of this, as have all industries related to the making of creative works, including journalism. As it is no longer necessary to turn to a large company for production and distribution, in many cases these industries have seen their power, profits, and very existence threatened or diminished. The industries themselves are no longer seen by many as essential. Still, they can assist writers, artists, and musicians in many ways, helping them create a professional, reputable product and promoting their work in ways that can be a challenge for even the most resourceful independent producer.

With these internet-inspired changes, there has been a rise in open source publishing. As costs to produce a magazine or newspaper are reduced because much of the product is distributed online, those costs no longer need to be passed along to the consumer. Due in part to Creative Commons licensing and technological advancements that permit the easy and inexpensive construction and publication of web-based content, publishing has become open to independent writers and contributors.

It is now free or inexpensive to publish material on the internet on many different platforms via open source publishing that provides open access to the product. This is hailed by many as a positive step in allowing individuals to create, publish, and find an audience for their works. It is less popular, of course, among those who tout the many services provided by traditional companies that can ensure a more professional product, such as extensive copyediting and copyright approvals, fact-checking, slick production, widespread promotion, and so forth. Professional journalism and news dissemination have changed dramatically as untrained citizens have begun to take on many of these roles and can share and publish information on social media without a "gatekeeper" (for more on this, see Chapters 5 and 8). Open source publishing is also responsible for diminished profits for many companies and is unpopular with them for that reason as well. The battle between traditional and newer publishing models will surely be fought for some time to come.

accuracy, inaccuracy, and the rise and transmission of "fake" news and information

As individuals and organizations take advantage of the increasingly open architecture of the internet to shared and spread information freely, there has been in an uptick in the transmission of inaccurate or "fake" news, facts, and information. A news story is considered to be *fake news* when it has been deliberately written to spread misinformation and lies; essentially, the story is an intentional hoax.

Open publishing platforms have made it possible to create websites and social media accounts that look like, or mimic, credible news sites, but are not. They are not operated by trained journalists but by those who seek to spread information that looks official and, perhaps, to perpetrate falsehoods. It is possible to duplicate such sites and social media accounts widely through the use of bots and algorithms that systematically share (and even create) misinformation in ways that make it look very real. It can become difficult or impossible to tell what is a legitimate news site, which information and stories are accurate and fact-based, and which are merely *propaganda*—intended to represent a biased, possibly extreme point of view. And it is already in many cases impossible to tell whether photos or videos have been altered so as to convey some edited version of reality.

Some consider fake news to be simply information with which they disagree. Others claim that we can no longer regulate truth in an era where fake news spreads so easily and that we therefore live in a "post-truth" society. These are both dangerous ways to look at an issue which is critical to the health of a society, particularly one premised on democracy. Facts matter. They are the cornerstone of free, civil debate and essential for intelligent decision-making on the individual, communal, and societal levels. It is a problem threatening freedom and democracy when it is difficult, if not impossible, to get to the bottom of whether certain information is factual or not.

The representation of an opinion as "the truth," while often protected by the First Amendment on free speech, leads to the polarization of differing points of view, generally in the political sphere. People are more likely to become enmeshed within *echo chambers*, listening to and believing only those who agree with them and closing their minds to ideas that do not confirm what they already believe to be true (this is known as confirmation bias). Social media, and Facebook and Twitter in particular, are increasingly called out for encouraging the development of echo chambers on their platforms (though, as we have seen, Mark Zuckerberg may now be taking greater responsibility for the content hosted and spread on Facebook). Those who manage these platforms and sites have sometimes responded by claiming that they cannot be held responsible for the rhetoric of those who use the platforms. Others point out that much (though not all) of this speech may be protected under the First Amendment. Facebook, at least, is responding by employing more human fact-checkers to ensure that bots do not place inaccurate information on the site too easily and to also monitor the rise of cruel and hateful speech and harassment on the platform. And Germany has enacted a law requiring social media companies like Facebook, Twitter, and Google to remove content that is illegal in Germany, such as Nazi symbols (Eddy & Scott, 2017).

News organizations who desire to provide equal time to various points of view may at times unwittingly provide space or airtime to fake or unchecked news stories. While an impulse toward balance in the presentation of points of view is understandable, many think that this should not be prioritized over accuracy. "Don't seek balance, seek accuracy," warns feminist legend Gloria Steinem (Media Mentoring, 2017), lest a *false equivalency* be set up between two or more points of view that are given equal time and legitimacy in their presentation, but are not equally accurate.

The rise and spread of fake news is a major problem, particularly in democracies that depend on their media representatives to speak for the people and hold governments accountable. Fake news and information cannot be combated by organizations that privilege balance over accuracy, decline to take responsibility for the speech that occurs in their spaces, or refuse to fact-check the texts they present and stories they tell. In a world in which citizen journalism is becoming increasingly common (as we will discuss in Chapter 5), we must all take on these roles and the responsibility to ensure accuracy. We must not accept the veracity of what we see online at face value, and we should beware of conversational patterns that result in polarization of the extremes and the spread of fake news. Such conversational "battles," rife with negativity, are only becoming more common in the digital age. They can inhibit the spread of accurate news and information and prevent people from coming to understand one another and forge the commonalities that are so necessary for a strong, cohesive society.

Ideally, we should respond to the very real problem of the spread of inaccuracy and fake news by holding an ever more rigorous standard for the speech that we utter and spread. We must gain, and employ, the tools that have served journalists and social science researchers so well for so many years: requiring multiple sources before writing or sharing a story, checking and double-checking facts, and assessing the accuracy and credibility of information before sharing it. If we are all citizen journalists as we share stories on social media platforms, then we should look to the disciplines of journalism and the social sciences to act in ways that uphold truth, accuracy, and understanding.

vertical, or asymmetrical, surveillance

As people become increasingly available and visible to one another in digital contexts, online *surveillance* has become a constant reality. Online surveillance occurs when someone uses the internet to track or monitor someone else's behavior. Individuals, organizations, and governments subtly (and not-so-subtly) observe people's presence online (Holtzman, 2006; Lyon, 2007; Marwick, 2012; Nippert-Eng, 2010; Nissenbaum, 2009; O'Harrow, 2006; Raab & Mason, 2004; Solove, 2004). Personal information collected through this process is routinely mined, gathered, shared, and sold for purposes that range from commercial to political to legal.

Surveillance is considered asymmetrical or "vertical" when a strong hierarchical power structure is involved, as when governments or corporations seek to influence, manage, protect, or direct the behavior of a population (Lyon, 2007, p. 14; Marwick, 2012, p. 381; Tokunaga, 2011). In many instances, the people being watched may not know they are being surveilled or that the activity is pervasive and ongoing. As the power structure is asymmetrical and does not favor them, they may not feel that they have the means to resist such surveillance.

Governments often assume considerable latitude to view or investigate the behavior of individuals in ways that some citizens feel encroach upon their freedom. Tasked with protection of the populace, those in power often claim that this charge justifies the surveillance. While the Electronic Communications Privacy Act of 1986 extended the prohibition of government wiretaps from phone lines to also include computers, 2001's PATRIOT Act, enacted in the wake of the September 11 terrorist attacks, greatly reduced these protections in the name of national security, exposing citizens to warrantless wiretaps and the seizing of such data as phone records. The Foreign Intelligence Surveillance Act of 2008 extended the ability of the U.S. government to perform warrantless wiretaps in foreign nations. While these laws will surely be debated and amended over time, the question must be asked and continually revisited: When do these kinds of activities shift from being appropriately protective to becoming undemocratically intrusive and a betrayal of civil rights?

Digital technology is intrinsic to the act of modern surveillance. Data related to online behaviors and preferences are persistently tracked when people are online. Habits and behaviors are discerned, and individuals' preferences and lifestyles are profiled. A phone can be wiretapped or can transfer information remotely even when turned off, acting as a microphone and transmitting conversations that take place within its vicinity. GPS systems can track people's locations as well and in some cases have been placed in people's cars without their knowledge and even without a warrant (Claburn, 2009).

Surveillance can also be positive. Surveillance can assist in the rescue of people stranded or lost, as locations can often be remotely tracked via one's smartphone. It can prompt the suggestion of new information or the introduction of new people into one's life. And information tracked and compiled via surveillance can help people fend off intrusions, attacks, or crimes and make them safer. In 2017, a New Mexico man was arrested for alleged domestic violence when the Amazon virtual assistant "Alexa" detected a cry for help and contacted the police department (Miller, 2017). While this is a rather intriguing example of positive surveillance and practical, digitally facilitated assistance, I think we can all imagine examples of the opposite scenario as well, in which Alexa reads a situation incorrectly and makes it worse!

When individuals go online, they leave data traces (called *cookies*) that disclose exactly which sites they have visited, for how long, and, in many cases, for what purpose. From these traces, it is easy to determine a lot about people's identities and lifestyles. People also disclose a lot about themselves in postings, emails, and text messages, nearly all of which are traceable and archivable. It is important to keep in mind that such information, like inappropriate language or depicted activities, can be used against you in a variety of ways. By some estimates, nearly 80% of companies monitor employees' email, internet, or phone use, even just intermittently or with the use of an automated program. In 2017, 70% of employers used social media and internet searches to screen candidates before hiring—a rise of 60% from 2016, which suggests that this may be an increasing trend. And at this writing, about a third of college admissions officers check social media accounts before deciding whether to offer a prospective student admission (Career Builder, 2017; Ribitzky, 2017; Somers, 2017). It is becoming more and more common to hear of or even know someone who has lost a job, been arrested, or been declined an opportunity due to social media (mis)use.

Some organizations specialize in finding or "mining for" bits of personal information and using them to make inferences about what people are like and what they might like to buy or do or even *be*. This is called *data mining*, and it is happening nearly constantly whenever we are online. In data mining, information is extracted ("mined") from a larger body of information in order to uncover details or patterns about the behavior of a person or organization. This can have troubling privacy implications because much of this happens without a person's explicit permission or even his or her conscious realization. At times, permission to do this may have been obtained, but this often occurs in the process of accepting fairly complex *terms of agreements*, which people may not read or understand or which may keep changing.

Some companies exist solely to do this kind of data mining, aggregation, and analysis. In other cases, media organizations such as Facebook and Google mine, collect, and aggregate data as people use their products and sell this information to advertisers and to data mining firms that collect it in huge databases (see Marwick, 2012, p. 1). At times, governments and law enforcement may request this information directly from the social media organizations. In recent years, "the collection, aggregation, and utilization of personal data for targeted advertisement have become an accepted social norm" (Young & Quan-Haase, 2013).

Search engines, which people use to locate information on the internet, allow data mining to happen rather efficiently. Google is, by far, the most popular search engine; it is used in over 65% of web searches. Other search engines include, in descending order of use, China's Baidu, Yahoo, Russia's Yandex, and

Microsoft, which are used, at this writing, in fewer than 10% of searches. Search engines sort through, filter, organize, and display information to the searcher by using algorithms. These algorithms consist of sets of digitized instructions programmed into computerized systems that can result in the recognition of patterns and the mining and gathering of data on that basis. The results can influence what an online search yields, what users are exposed to when they surf the net, and what information is displayed in social media feeds.

At the same time that it produces results for the user, Google also stores, caches, and archives large portions of web content as the web is being searched. It sells to companies the ability to improve their standings in search results. Apple, Microsoft, Facebook, Yahoo, and other major tech companies also allow the data that flows in and through their platforms to be mined and in some cases participate in the mining. As a result, nearly everything that is done on the internet is tracked, analyzed, stored, and then used for a variety of purposes (Chen, Pavlov, Berkhin, Seetharaman, & Meltzer, 2009; Cobb, 2012; Sengupta, 2012).

Once mined and discovered, information can be used in a number of ways by law enforcement agencies, governments, hackers, employers and future employers, and corporations. Credit can be denied to you because you have been profiled as someone unlikely to be able to purchase something. Advertisements are targeted to you because you have been identified as someone who is likely to make that purchase. You are placed in a niche (say, as a "socially liberal organic eater," or a "single city struggler"), and ads that are customized to appeal to you follow you around the internet from page to page. Advertisers now have tremendous power to influence people's internet experiences (Turow, 2013).

In order to use many of the services that take place online, data must be provided. Personal information is truly a "new form of currency" (Madden, Cortesi, Gasser, Lenhart, & Duggan, 2012). But because time spent on the internet is so often engaging and involving, this is an easy thing to forget. And many people, certainly including the youngest digital tech users, do not know that when they are online they are subject to surveillance. Those whom I interviewed for my portable communities research had mixed, varied responses to being surveilled while online:

> It has made me vulnerable, yet more protective . . . I personally think that the advantages that a cell phone brings in convenience and safety far outweigh what I am giving up in terms of privacy. (Chayko, 2008, pp. 137, 139)

Ever-more intrusive digital surveillance technologies are being developed and deployed at a rapid pace. The technology now exists to implant chips under the skin that can track people's locations and send information about them to others. Small as a grain of rice, these chips can store all kinds of data and allow the government or an employer to track the whereabouts and other characteristics of the individual who has been "chipped," with both positive and negative effects. Implantable chips can store lifesaving medical information, help find kidnapped or other missing people, and identify bodies in the case of tragedies.

A few companies have begun to require some employees, such as those who have high levels of security clearance, to be chipped. In 2017, more than 50 employees of the Wisconsin software company Three Square Market began chipping employees, implanting the tiny chips between the thumb and forefinger, allowing employees to enter the workplace, log onto their computers, and order food (Rosenthal, 2017). While the chips are currently voluntary, it will be interesting to see whether employees who opt not to get them feel sufficiently disadvantaged by inconvenience (or peer pressure?) that they opt for them over time. Additionally, a beach club in Barcelona, Spain, has chipped partygoers so that they can "breeze past bouncers and entrance lines, magically open doors to VIP lounges, and pay for drinks without cash or credit cards" (Lewan, 2007). It is a realistic worry that implanted chips will permit employers, the government, or anyone in power to track people's whereabouts and what they are doing and to gather highly personal information in an intrusive and even illegal manner (Hilden, 2002). One might also consider how difficult they may be to remove.

Increasingly, individuals are subject to surveillance by remotely piloted flying machines called *drones.* These aircrafts, which can be small or large, are used for purposes that range from recreation to video recording to warfare, and, increasingly, they are used for surveillance. Drones can be equipped with cameras and electromagnetic sensors that can detect objects behind physical barriers and thus can perform surveillance functions discreetly, without the involvement of a human pilot. In many circumstances, it is impossible to know whether a drone is flying overhead at any given time and whether it may be gathering information on what you or others are doing behind closed doors.

As with algorithms and the remote use of smartphones and GPS technology, surveillance can occur invisibly and in situations in which it may not be expected. Surveillance can invade as easily and as subtly as it can protect, and as it intrudes further and further into spaces once thought of as private and impenetrable, such as the human body or the personal residence, we are challenged to consider its benefits and costs.

How individuals and societies respond to vertical surveillance—whether they accept or resist it—will shape their futures in critical ways. Several organizations advocate for digital civil rights on an ongoing basis. The Electronic Frontier

Foundation has fought for internet civil liberties since 1990, working to defend those whose use of technology is attacked in ways considered unfair and undemocratic. In 1994, the Center for Democracy and Technology was established with the aim of influencing national policy regarding such issues as free expression and privacy. The Free Software Foundation, founded in 1985, supports the creation, distribution, and modification of free computer software. This aim is shared by many in the open source movement who encourage, invent, and make possible ways for ideas and information to be shared and accessed freely and openly without costs or undue complications that would exclude many from participation. As a result of these efforts and many like them, it is now possible for people to be aware of and in some cases challenge surveillance activities on the internet or even to surveil those doing the surveillance.

horizontal, or social, surveillance

Social media sites are designed so that people can easily see what others are up to. Users follow news feeds or timelines and get to know a lot about one another. They may feel that they have much in common with their fellow posters and even feel that they are getting to know them fairly well. To peek in on others as they go about their everyday lives and post about it online is a common occurrence, serving "the essential purpose . . . of seeing and being seen," says sociologist and social network expert Duncan Watts (as quoted in Cassidy, 2006, p. 54).

This behavior is sometimes described as gazing, creeping, voyeurism, or, at its criminal extreme, stalking, but it really is another kind of surveillance. Rather than surveillance coming from someone more powerful, this kind of surveillance is more "horizontal." In the words of sociologist Alice Marwick, it is *social surveillance,* and it has become an ordinary and expected aspect of the online experience. As one of Marwick's interviewees put it, to look at what others are doing online is "not really weird for anyone anymore" (2012, pp. 378–379).

Online communities are characterized both by watching and by a high awareness of being watched, Marwick points out (2012, p. 379). People generally know that their content may be seen and that they are effectively being watched when they are on social media sites. They consider being watched part of the experience. They may (or may not) tailor the content they post to certain audiences or particular others they believe will see it, thereby shaping it with the knowledge that social surveillance will take place.

Some consider the experience of watching others online less an act of surveillance and more an indicator of emotional involvement. For longtime blogger Rebecca Blood, it is real emotion, not cheap voyeuristic glances, that tend to be exchanged when people blog. "There may be some people who follow blogs to 'watch,' but there are many others who really come to care about the lives of the bloggers," she says. "Many times, readers will come to a blog to read about a subject they are interested in, and slowly become invested in the everyday life of the writer, as it is revealed in bits and pieces over weeks and months" (as quoted in Chayko, 2008, p. 177). For even when one is merely lurking online, he or she can be engaging with others in a deep and meaningful way.

The experience of social surveillance—of presenting and viewing information—is a bit different from vertical surveillance, as it is an exchange of information among people with relatively equivalent levels of power. Inequalities are not absent in social surveillance, of course. People do not have equal power in their relationships, and these dynamics are seen in their interactions both online and offline. Power differences related to race, class, gender, age, sexual orientation, and other kinds of social statuses are also seen in these relationships, playing out in ways that reflect their offline dynamics.

Perhaps the biggest difference in horizontal versus vertical surveillance is in the amount, type, and expectation of reciprocity in the relationships. People often produce content with the desire that it will be seen, liked, commented upon favorably, and maybe even inspire others' content. Thus, people are performing a kind of active surveillance of one another, consuming and commenting on one another's content and paying continued attention to one another as they create and live in the attention economy. All this activity results in the ongoing formation of social connections, networks, and communities, which helps to maintain and cement interpersonal relationships and bring people closer together. At the same time, social asymmetries and inequalities are also highlighted.

In an environment in which people are expected to be almost always available to one another, they can become prone to checking up on one another more often. Friends and partners, romantic or otherwise, can technologically keep an eye on one another, and parents can monitor their children. It is even possible to purchase spyware software that can be secretly installed on a computer and inform the installer of every move and keystroke. The ethics of this are tangled and complex. Should parents surveil their children in an effort to keep them safe, and, if so, to what extent? Is this ever acceptable among adults, and, if so, when? How much checking up on one another is too much—suffocating, unfair, illegal? Are we creating societies in which people have become so accustomed to surveillance, both horizontal and vertical, that personal privacy has become dispensable? To what extent is privacy something to be protected, to be valued?

As with vertical surveillance, my interview subjects were divided on their responses to social surveillance and privacy. They ranged from the negative (i.e., the phone is a "leash")—

> Unfortunately, the cell phone feels like a leash. I feel trapped. "Where are you?" "What are you doing?" "When will you be back?" "Why didn't you call me, I would have loved to have joined you?"

—to the ambivalent (i.e., it is "a little odd")—

> Having your feelings and thoughts so easily scrutinized on a blog is a little odd to me. It is also odd that people can comment on anyone's journal entries . . . (this) feeds into the continual erosion of privacy . . . people's feelings and private matters are so easily accessed.

—to the positive (it's "fun"!)—

> It's fun to see what people are up to. I guess it makes me seem almost nosy, but I just like to see what people are doing. (Chayko, 2008, pp. 133, 137, 174)

Social surveillance can also lead to the complexities and misunderstandings that arise when very different audiences see one another's content and interact online. When one's social media audience consists of, say, both family and work colleagues, information may be inadvertently shared that would not be appropriate for both contexts, perhaps causing strife or trouble. Someone may complain about work, forgetting or failing to realize that the boss has the ability to see that complaint. A parent or future employer may see evidence of inappropriate behavior meant for the eyes of peers. When two or more audiences or publics coexisting on social media in effect "bleed into" one another or "collapse" such that it becomes difficult to keep them separate, it is called *context collapse* (Marwick & boyd, 2011).

Technology contributes to the blurring of the boundaries of all kinds of contexts, such as between *public* and *private* and between such formerly strictly demarcated categories as *work* and *off duty* (Nippert-Eng, 1996). Within these contexts are *social roles,* which are the expected behaviors that accompany *social statuses*—our positions in the various groups we are part of. For example, one of your social statuses may be that of a student. This can entail the following roles or behaviors: studying, going to class, maybe having fun on a Friday night with your friends. On social media, students may post content that relates to each of these behaviors, forgetting (or not knowing exactly how to navigate) the fact that different audiences may see all of the content. Teachers may see posts related to disliking a class. Parents may see posts about partying on a Friday night. Different audiences can see the same content online as different contexts overlap and collapse.

To share content online and on social media is to communicate with a number of audiences, some of which are known and some of which are unknown. One might use a different tone and posture with these different audiences when they are neatly separated into different physical spaces. This is harder to do online. One cannot know exactly who is out there viewing one's content at a particular time. Even if restrictions are placed on who may view what is posted through privacy settings, and even if audiences are kept carefully separate in different social circles, content can still be reposted, retweeted, accidentally forwarded, or simply seen over one's shoulder on a screen. There is no way to know exactly who may see information once it is digitized. And even though users may "sense their audience at a particular point in time," as boyd and Heer note, "they have no conception of who might have access to their expressions later" (2006).

As decisions are made that result in personal disclosures, sharing online can become a highly intricate, strategic activity. It allows people to share information widely and efficiently while forfeiting some control over what will happen to that information once shared and how those who see it may respond. But these are "normal parts of day-to-day life in communities that are highly connected through social media," Marwick points out (2012, p. 391). Additional opportunities for social connectedness and increased social capital can accrue in the sharing and networking that can accompany horizontal or social surveillance. A lack of privacy, exposure to harm, and continuously collapsing contexts can be among the negative results, representing some of the risks of living in a more open society.

privacy and obscurity

So the internet is not a private place; there are really no corners in which to hide. Everything can be potentially accessed and seen, many of life's contexts come into contact with one another, and it is difficult to ascertain who may or may not see content at any given time. For these reasons, it is best to be extremely careful when online. As noted earlier, many future employers and graduate schools check the social media profiles of prospective employees or students, looking for goodness of fit and possibly even objectionable content before making a hiring or admission decision. Whether we realize it or not, individuals leave a *digital footprint* when online and even when simply sending text messages. And this footprint never fully disappears.

It seems that the very nature of privacy has substantially, irreversibly changed. An individual cannot hope to be fully private when online; online spaces are public by default. Smartphones and cameras that might catch misdeeds proliferate. Vertical and horizontal surveillance are always present. Youth and teenagers are already altering their notions of privacy and may be at the forefront of a new way of conceptualizing what public and private spaces are (boyd, 2014; Marwick, 2014).

Many people are also becoming aware of the importance of developing specific strategies to address their privacy needs. Such strategies include limiting profile options, untagging and removing photographs, and refusing friendship requests from strangers (Young & Quan-Haase, 2013). While such strategies help to protect one's data in interpersonal situations, they are less useful when guarding against institutional or vertical surveillance. To try to keep one's data private can begin to feel like fighting a losing battle.

It is healthy to have places to retreat sometimes and to feel that what one is doing is private. It helps an individual feel safe and free. It provides a measure of autonomy. Tech ethics scholars Woodrow Hartzog and Evan Selinger say that such private, safe spaces are becoming harder to find because individuals' data are no longer easy to obscure, to keep disaggregated and hidden (2013). The vast amount of data that can serve to identify aspects of an individual's life—address, employment info, interests, credit score, purchasing patterns, and the like—used to be difficult to aggregate, or gather in one place. If a person wanted to obtain a fairly obscure piece of information about another person (let alone many such pieces of information)—say, a comment one may have once made related to a hot-button social issue like race relations or war—it would have been fairly difficult to find. Individuals could be reasonably sure that if someone wanted to locate and gather such information, perhaps to be used against them, it would be very difficult—perhaps impossible—to do.

In modern tech-intensive societies, information is no longer easily obscured. Data mining processes help organizations gather and categorize info and comments that an individual may have made over many years. Comments, posts, and bits of information that might otherwise seem incidental can be (and regularly are) technologically retrieved and pieced together. A detailed profile of an individual, consisting of his or her purported characteristics, interests, habits, behaviors, and so on, comes into shape. It has become much more difficult to find spaces in which data are not being gathered and aspects of the self can remain obscured, hidden, or private.

Companies that mine and sell people's data have developed extremely sophisticated ways to piece together and aggregate information. Algorithms are used to procure and digest this information and to place people into categories based on the patterns that emerge. This kind of profiling can have a significant impact on a person's life. People may be provided—or denied—jobs, credit, or other opportunities based entirely on algorithms that make predictions about them based on how they or how other people with similar characteristics have behaved in the past. *Algorithmic profiling*, or predicting the behavior of individuals based on their own aggregated data and that of others perceived to be like them in some way, has become big business.

It is easy to forget that this kind of institutional vertical surveillance is happening when we are online (Young & Quan-Haase, 2013). Certainly, many internet and digital media users are unaware that this happens at all. Our computers and smartphones often feel as if they are part of personal, private, intimate environments. This is not surprising, as we use them in our homes and in the most intimate of spaces, even keeping them in our purses and pockets. It is easy to become overly casual and relaxed when we are online, to say and do things that we might not want preserved forever. It is also common for children or younger people not to take into account the impact of their actions on their "future selves" when participating in online activity. To do so would require a maturity they often do not possess.

If people want to preserve their rights and live in free, open societies, attention to these issues must be paid. Civil rights and freedoms are not always evident or protected in digital spaces. They must be articulated and fought for whenever and wherever they are threatened, in both digital and physical spaces. The techno-social environment is always changing. New technologies are always being invented, and their impacts must be carefully considered.

It is always helpful to be aware of power differentials when examining (and *living*) techno-social life, whether in digital or face-to-face environments. In the next chapter, we examine technology-related inequalities and impacts as they exist globally. We look closely at how individuals and societies across the globe are impacted by the internet and digital media and speak back to power, and we explore some ways of living that are very different from our own.

5

GLOBAL IMPACTS AND INEQUALITIES

globalization and technology

The world can, in many ways, be seen as a single, interconnected society. This is called *globalization*, and it has been made possible by innovations in transportation technology (such as highways, cars, railways, and air travel) and information and communication technology (such as the internet and digital, social, and mobile media). As communication and transportation technologies have spread and diffused globally throughout the last couple of centuries, though certainly not to every corner of every nation, commercial and social transactions that involve two or more nations increasingly take place.

As a result, a global marketplace for products like energy, cars, electronics, and entertainment has developed. Sometimes this results in the *outsourcing* of jobs and opportunities, in which a job or job type that originated in one country becomes relocated to another, where it can likely be performed more cheaply. The growth of global internet and mobile communication networks has made it possible and economically feasible for some jobs, such as customer service and even sales, to be performed far away from the company's home area, sometimes in another country and sometimes without the customer even knowing. The outsourcing of jobs is a highly controversial practice. Some say that to keep jobs in the home country is the best way to keep the economy of that country strong. Others say that when business profits are enhanced by outsourcing jobs, the nation as a whole is strengthened because companies are more profitable and can contribute to the national economy.

It is always useful to consider who can benefit and profit from a technology once it is introduced and undergoes the process of diffusion. Doing so reveals much about the power dynamics and values of the societies that will use the technology and how people in those societies will live and regard one another. Groups of people rarely have equal political or social power, and the introduction of technology into a society can exacerbate these differences. People do not benefit equally from the affordances or opportunities that technology can provide. People are not all in the same position to access it, learn about it, use it, or even to invent it in the first place.

To determine who has the power to create, understand, and use technology can be highly instructive in exploring at a fundamental level the components of techno-social life. Power differences can be examined at all levels: from the interpersonal–relational to the global–political. As people invent, disseminate, adopt, critique, improve, and reinvent uses for the internet and digital media, power is expressed, claimed, and deployed. Patterns of social inequality are reinforced and reproduced, and they can be altered as well.

stratification and inequality

Groups and social units can be differentiated from one another in many ways. People, and the groups and units to which they can be said to belong, can vary on a number of characteristics—age, race, ethnicity (people who share a common heritage or ancestry), gender, sexual orientation, socioeconomic status, intellectual or physical ability, occupation or occupational type, religious beliefs, political or national affiliation, and so on. Every society contains inequalities that arise on the basis of these social characteristics. Societies are often metaphorically divided into layers or tiers (upper class, middle class, working class, the poor) that form a hierarchy, or ranking. The process by which these layers are collectively determined and these divisions (and subdivisions) are collectively formed is called *social stratification*, and the societies are said to be *stratified* (another metaphor, derived from the layers found inside a rock or a tree, which are called *strata*).

People who occupy the same rank or position in a stratified social system tend to have certain things in common, such as perspectives on the world, attitudes, and beliefs. They may also share dispositions toward, comfort with, access to, competency or literacy in, and ways of approaching and using technology. This can be a factor in their having a shared level of social power. People's attitude toward and use of technology affects many other elements of their lives, including their wealth, careers, relationships and family lives, and cultural activities and choices. All of this both results from and creates further social divisions or stratification because so many aspects of life are related to one's technology use.

The difference or gap in the ways that groups access and use technology is often called the *digital divide*. A wide and deep divide separates those who have access to digital technology (and can afford to buy and use and even create it) from those who lack this access and knowledge (see van Dijk, 2005). A digital divide has many dimensions, including the means to produce digital technology (Hargittai & Walejko, 2008); participate in digital activities (DiMaggio, 2014; Schradie, 2011, 2012); and be considered digitally literate (Napoli & Obar, 2013). You can learn a lot about a group or society by examining which technologies are prominent in it and who is included and excluded from their use.

Nations vary widely in their ability to leverage computerized technologies for increased global competitiveness and to enhance the well-being and prosperity of their citizens. According to the World Economic Forum's *Global Information Technology Report* (Baller, Dutta, & Lanvin, 2016), seven of the 10 countries that rank highest in this regard are European, including Finland, Sweden, the Netherlands, Switzerland, the United Kingdom, and Luxembourg. The non-European nations in the top 10 are Singapore (1), the United States (5), and Japan (10). These advanced, high-income economies lead the way globally in providing the optimal regulatory, business, and social environments for networked readiness, use, and performance. In general, richer countries (in terms of gross domestic product per capita) have more internet users among the adult population than poorer nations (Baller et al., 2016; Dutta et al., 2015).

Many European nations, including France, Belgium, Slovenia, and the Czech Republic, are improving their networked readiness, as are three of the former Soviet Republics, Estonia, Latvia, and Lithuania. Particularly strong contrasts are apparent in the Caribbean, Middle East, North Africa, and Asia, where the economies of countries like Chile, Bahrain, the United Arab Emirates, Malaysia, and China are more digitally competitive than those of, for example, Haiti, Kuwait, Mauritania, and India. Steady improvements in the digital infrastructure and readiness of countries like Costa Rica, El Salvador, and Bolivia are encouraging. But the trend is reversed in sub-Saharan Africa and South/Southeast Asia, where digital advancements are slow and inconsistent and the overall standard of living is shockingly low (Baller et al., 2016; Dutta et al., 2015; Pew Research Center, 2015, 2016).

Internet access rates, which are closely linked to national income, vary considerably across emerging and developing nations. Two thirds or more of people in Chile (76%), Russia (73%), and Venezuela (67%) have internet and/or smartphone access, while less than half in South Africa (42%) and the Philippines (40%) do. Rates are climbing in the Middle East—Israel is at 86%, Palestinian territories at 72%, and Jordan at 67%. In Ethiopia and Uganda, however, the rate is close to 10% (Pew Research Center, 2016).

When the rate of internet penetration is low, the abilities of these citizens and their countries to benefit in a global economy is reduced. Individuals are at a significant disadvantage for economic attainment and for improving the quality of their lives. Education, employment, and access to health care are all seriously hindered. The gap between these individuals and those who are more reliably connected to the internet—with all the affordances that access and connectivity provides—becomes ever harder to cross (DiMaggio, 2014; McKinsey & Company, 2014).

Cell phone ownership is much more common than internet service in emerging and developing nations. Between 45% and 75% of the citizens in most emergent nations own or share a cell phone. But smartphones—and the mobile access to the internet that they make possible in some locations—are not nearly as common as conventional cell phones. Only 24% of adults in developing nations say they own a phone that can access the internet and digital applications. In comparison, at this writing, 77% of American adults own a smartphone that can access the internet (Pew Research Center, 2015, 2016; Smith, 2017).

The uneven diffusion and adoption of internet and digital technologies can only be overcome at the larger, structural level. Some countries, such as those listed earlier (and poor or rural areas of many other countries), have severely underdeveloped digital communication infrastructure and little or no internet network access or mobile internet coverage. Underfunded, with limited resources of all kinds, these nations may not even have an ICT strategy to address these issues. In addition, electricity and sufficient roads and means of transportation tend to be scarce in these areas.

Low income and standard of living is also a barrier to digital connectedness. In poorer areas, even if internet access were available, it would be difficult for people to afford. The devices and hardware needed to become connected would also be relatively expensive. When there is high unemployment and underemployment and people do not make enough money to cover basic necessities, they are essentially "locked out" from using the internet.

Lack of education is another barrier to internet and digital access. People with limited or no relevant education may not have the skills required to use digital technologies, especially in ways that transcend the rudimentary. For many, a low level of language literacy—difficulty in reading and writing—is a factor as well.

Political and governmental control over the internet and digital media also impacts the ability of citizens to access and use them. In much of the world, political control over the media is expressed by repressive legislation (Saudi Arabia, Zimbabwe); public ownership, licensing, and regulation (China, Syria, Morocco); vigilantism (Russia); or the collusion of private media owners with the government (Latin America). China, Syria, and Russia use internet service providers to filter out critical or dissident websites (Curran, 2012). Turkey has passed a law to censor online content and expand digital surveillance. In Azerbaijan, internet use is not heavily filtered but is so heavily monitored that dissidents are punished and arrested; as a result, social media has been rather effectively demonized and squelched (Kendzior & Pearce, 2012). Such nations as Egypt, Iran, and Libya have overtly "shut down" the internet at times in an attempt to halt the use of social media, often when citizens protest the restrictiveness of these regimes (as in 2011's Arab Spring protests). As we shall see later in this chapter, though, social media offers opportunities to push back against some of this control. Social media users can be quite creative and persistent in working around these internet shutdowns and in organizing to protest such restrictions and inequalities (Curran, 2012; Tufekci, 2014).

Finally, there is simply less incentive for some to become digitally connected than for others. Whether for cultural, social, or personal reasons, some people do not feel compelled to go online. They may be unaware of the internet's affordances, skeptical of the security of their information, fear a loss of privacy, or consider it cost-prohibitive. They may not know many others who are digitally connected (or may not want to)! They may be among the cyberasocial who have difficulty conceiving of and making connections online (Tufekci, 2010). They may be making a personal or political statement against what media researcher Laura Portwood-Stacer (2012) calls the "powerful, normative force of media consumer culture"—refusing to use Facebook, for example, as an act of resistance (which, she then points out, may be considered by others merely an attempt to act cool by being different). In short, some individuals simply may not feel the need to use particular forms of digital media or may not find it relevant to the way they live their lives (see Annafari, Axelsson, & Bohlin, 2013). Additionally, many others use these technologies but do so in a rather limited fashion for these same reasons.

It is important to keep in mind that while ICTs are critical for the economic and social well-being of a nation and its people, they can only contribute to substantial, stable transformation when people have the means and motivation to adopt and actually use them. When a nation does make a commitment to bring affordable internet access and equipment to large portions of the population, socioeconomically disadvantaged communities and their members can benefit greatly. When mobile phones and data plans were first made accessible and affordable to youth in urban India, for example, these first-generation digital media users swiftly negotiated the hurdles to using the tech. Computer scientist and researcher Neha Kumar noted how they used the internet (and, especially, Facebook) as a "tool for self-empowerment," which led to their becoming "legitimate members of a global community" (2014). When those who are homeless own smartphones that can access the internet, at least three quarters of them tend to use that phone for texting and voice calls daily (though the internet less often), providing a means for them to connect to health and medical information and, potentially, to chart paths out of poverty (Rhoades, Wenzel, Rice, Winetrobe, & Henwood, 2017).

Factors that limit the reach and scope of internet and digital technology are associated with and influence one another. This makes it a challenge for global and local digital differences to be ameliorated (see Dutta et al., 2015; McKinsey & Company, 2014). ICTs are "vectors of economic and social transformation," Dutta, Geiger, and Lanvin remind us. "By improving access to services, enhancing connectivity, creating business and employment opportunities, and changing the ways people communicate, interact, and engage among themselves and with their governments, ICTs can transform our world" (2015, p. xv).

cultural divides

While the spread and use of ICTs can help bring about meaningful change, inequalities and differences within a society can also limit and undermine many of their benefits. In addition to economic divides, nations and societies often evidence cultural divides. Their members can be stratified based on the ways that they produce, consume, and experience culture.

Recall that culture consists of the material (art, music, books) and mental (norms and values) products of a group. These products are rarely consumed similarly and understood the same way by all members of a group, especially in a large, diverse society. Instead, divisions between those who understand and enjoy things one way and those who prefer things another way constantly emerge, sometimes vying for people's attention and interest. These divisions can become quite contentious, as when fights break out at sporting events among people rooting for opposing teams, or when people with different beliefs clash.

The internet and digital media can contribute to the development of common understandings by providing a window on different aspects of culture or points of view. People can use the technologies to "dig deeper into the policy issues before them, to learn more about their worlds, and to enjoy an unprecedented wealth of aesthetic experience," says sociologist of culture Paul DiMaggio. He warns, though, that "it is unclear just how many people this potential will benefit" (2014, pp. 390–391). Those who are already engaged in politics and the arts may gain the fullest benefit from internet-accessed culture, while others may face barriers in locating or accessing cultural products.

On the other hand, internet use can impede the development of shared understandings. Many people choose to focus their attentions on issues with which they are already familiar and communicate with those who feel the same way they do (Hampton, Rainie, Lu, Dwyer, Shin, & Purcell, 2015). Depending on how individuals decide to use the technology, existing cultural inequalities can simply be deepened (DiMaggio, 2014, pp. 390–391). This can lead to a mirroring and extension of the same kinds of prejudices and discrimination that exist in physical space.

Prejudice is an attitude—the prejudging of people based on their membership in some group, social unit, or category without taking individual characteristics into account—and it is usually thought of in a negative sense (that is, to be prejudiced is a bad thing). While prejudice can lead to negative or harmful outcomes, a certain amount of prejudice occurs because it is impossible to learn everything there is to know about everyone with whom we come into contact individually. It is common, therefore, to categorize or group people into types, with some qualities and characteristics assumed on this basis. While this simply reflects the human need for order and understanding, it can result in negative prejudicial views nonetheless. And when prejudice results in discrimination, the stakes are raised.

Discrimination is a behavior—the unfair treatment of people based on their membership in a group, social unit, or category. It occurs when actions are taken, often on the basis of prejudices, that are unfair or harmful, such as paying people less or abusing them simply because they are members of a certain group. Members of disempowered or nondominant groups in particular have experienced discrimination in numerous forms for many years. Social history influences the ways that groups and members of groups continue to interact, online and offline.

Because the internet and digital media bring people into frequent contact with one another, prejudice and discrimination occur online just as they do face-to-face. When women and racial and sexual minorities are harassed and abused, for example (for more on this, see Chapters 6 and 7), it is generally *because* they are members of these categories. Harassment serves as an exertion of power to assert dominance, frighten, and punish those who have been historically disempowered—to keep them "in their place." It is also aimed at people who defy rigid racial, gendered, and sexuality "rules" and boundaries. LGBT youth, for example, experience online bullying at three times the rate of their straight peers (Chemaly, 2014; Citron, 2014).

It is important to keep in mind that these categories and divisions are *social constructions* in the first place; they do not represent the natural order, or the way things have to be, but are a continuation of past attitudes and practices that have emerged as people in their cultures and societies have made certain decisions and taken certain actions. These decisions and actions, however, can be changed or reconfigured over time. We do not have to think and act in the same ways that we have seen people think and act in the past. We can create new meanings and representations for age, gender, race, sexual orientation, physical and intellectual ability, and so on, and we can think about and treat one another differently as a result. We can even, to some extent—if we are highly creative and in solidarity with one another—try to dispense with some social divisions.

It may be helpful to think less in terms of a *divide*, which indicates a rather restrictive, either/or way of thinking, and more in terms of a *spectrum* of ways that people use and are affected by technology. A spectrum can better depict the complexity of a situation. For example, income level and level of education are often correlated with digital connectedness; the more income or education a person has, the more likely he or she is to be digitally connected (McKinsey & Company, 2014). But income and education are not either/or variables; people do not either "have" or "not have" income or education. They are a matter of amount or degree. Using a scale or spectrum to help us model or think about technology use, we can look at the many levels and increments in which income, education, technology use, and power can be distributed. It may be a more flexible way to examine these multifaceted issues than to try to force them into the model of the either/or divide.

The internet and digital technology provide spaces in which people can learn more about one another and their common interests, even their common humanity. But they are not always used toward that end. While digital technologies can be used to help build a world in which differences are not so pronounced, inequity in the way that power is distributed and exercised can bring about many troubling outcomes.

hacking, danger, crime, and war

With the growth of newer, more open ways for people to prosume, crowdsource, and disseminate information has come a rise in the ability of people to cross digital boundaries, both for good and for harm. Nations, organizations, and all kinds of entities have digital as well as physical borders—systems intended to provide technological access to those who belong to the group and to exclude those who do not. From the macro (large scale) to the micro (small scale) to the meso (in between) levels of society, it is increasingly a challenge to maintain these boundaries, keep outsiders from intruding, and otherwise prevent the often quite serious problems that can arise in a more open system.

Outsiders can attempt to penetrate a computerized system by hacking into it. *Hacking* is the manipulation of the programming codes that tell computers exactly what to do and is also often the term used to describe the manipulation or inappropriate release of the information that is obtained in this way. Hacking can be done both legally and illegally, and for positive and negative purposes. The term also sometimes refers to creative, upstart, usually independent, and somewhat subversive forms of computer programming, content creation, and information dissemination (see Castells, 2000, 2001; Markoff, 2005; Rainie & Wellman, 2012). Hacking in this sense is a thriving culture that actively encourages creative approaches to programming and other digital innovation and the unfettered sharing of that which is produced and accessed. Some of these approaches are outside the boundaries of current laws, some are within them and clearly noncriminal, and some exist at the borderline and require a society to consider how open it wants its information to be.

Certainly, when digital spaces are hacked into and information is rerouted or repurposed (or destroyed or made unintelligible, as by a computer virus), breaches of security, even terrorism, can occur. These are unambiguous crimes and can occur on the smallest and largest of scales. In the increasingly common crime of *phishing*, usernames and passwords are stolen when individuals are tricked into providing them to thieves impersonating legitimate entities. This information can then be used for a number of destructive purposes, including theft of funds and identities. Large information systems can also be destroyed or disabled by intrusions and viruses introduced by hackers. Monetary systems, power grids, websites, personal information, and basically anything that is gathered, organized, and stored via computer can be affected when digital security is compromised. This is called *computer crime* or *cybercrime*.

Large-scale cyberattacks can take two forms: information attacks and infrastructure attacks (Volti, 2014, p. 315). In the former, personal information can be retrieved, made public, and used to harm or embarrass or generate fear. In the latter, critical services can be disabled. Messages can be sent out under the ISP name of another organization, websites can be defaced, money and information can be stolen, sabotage can take place, threats can be made. Large data breaches, such as those in which the personal information (including Social Security numbers) of up to 143 million Americans was exposed when credit bureau Equifax was hacked in 2017 and the personal information of 83 million J. P. Morgan Chase customers was stolen in 2014, are becoming more common. Sony Pictures' computers were hacked in 2014, which resulted in numerous leaks of data and included a threat of even larger-scale disruption attached to the upcoming release of the movie *The Interview*, which was temporarily shelved. In 2015, international hackers stole as much as a billion dollars from over 100 banks in 30 countries (see Davis, 2015). Nearly all the major internet companies have experienced large-scale hacking. Such incidents are not only becoming more common, but their reach and impact is expanding, often across international borders. To guard against these attacks as best as possible, companies must make serious and often expensive cybersecurity investments.

Some politically motivated attacks rise to the level of *cyberwarfare*. These can include attacks on populations, such as the sabotage of water systems, health communications, transportation, the electric power grid, military systems, financial networks, and the stock market. Terrorist operations now routinely coordinate their efforts via the internet, digital media, and mobile phones, even using mobile phones to detonate bombs. A nation or group's ability to launch a cyberattack can be seen as "a continuation of a high-tech arms race that has been going on since the invention of gunpowder," says sociologist Rudi Volti (2014, p. 316). When internet or digital technology is used to make threats and create widespread fear in a society, it is called *cyberterrorism*.

Cyber defense is now a critical component of government operations. The United States currently has a head of cybersecurity that coordinates government, military, and intelligence efforts and a cybercommand unit that centralizes its cyber defense efforts. Social media is a key element of the unit's intelligence-gathering methods. In some cases, the same digital technologies that terrorist or enemy groups use to amass resources are used to gather evidence against them (Kjuka, 2013).

Individuals can also be harmed by hurtful and hostile online behaviors. Comments that are derogatory or offensive and are perceived as such by the victim constitute harassment (see Chapter 7 for more on harassment). When such activity is deliberate, repeated, and hostile, it can be considered *cyberbullying*. While we often think of cyberbullying as taking place among children, adults can be cyberbullied as well. A credible threat of physical harm constitutes *cyberstalking*. Most U.S. states have laws on the books to protect citizens from these crimes, which range from misdemeanors to felonies. Except for Australia and Japan, most other countries do not have laws against cyberharassment (for more on cyberstalking and cyberharassment, see NCSL, 2013).

Other crimes against individuals include identity fraud, theft, internet scams and spam, drug trafficking, exposing children to pornographic images, sexual predation, and kidnapping. These range in degrees of seriousness as well. Dangers to children in the internet and digital age are not as plentiful as they may seem, however. For example, crimes against children, including sex crimes and criminal victimization, have actually fallen since the introduction of the internet. Assaults and sexual predation between strangers who meet online are but a small proportion of stranger crimes overall (Baym, 2010, pp. 42–43; Cassell & Cramer, 2007; Clark, 2013). Crimes and harm that involve tech use are not specifically caused by the technology (recall the fallacy of technological determinism). Dangerous or criminal acts can certainly be made more visible by computerization and the internet, but, as we have seen, these acts need not be blamed on the technology per se (Baym, 2010; boyd, 2006, 2007; Clark, 2013), and they are sometimes hidden within the "dark web" as well (see Chapter 2). It is worth keeping in mind that many of the crimes discussed here existed in the pre-internet era as well.

It is important to consider exactly how accessible and open computer systems should be—how various kinds of information should be accessed and who should do the accessing. Such conversations would indicate much about what a society and a nation values. Organizations and governments have legitimate reasons for keeping certain information out of the hands of the general population for safety and security purposes. On the other hand, if useful information that could help people or that rightly belongs to them remains out of their reach, it should not be surprising that some might attempt to obtain that information via hacking.

This was a scenario demonstrated most heartbreakingly by tech innovator, activist, and co-developer of the social media platform Reddit, Aaron Swartz. In late 2010 and early 2011, he decided to use MIT computers to download numerous academic articles from the online repository JSTOR. The repository kept the articles behind a *paywall*, which means that they could only be shared widely at a cost. Swartz wanted to "free" this information and make a statement that it should not have been behind a paywall in the first place. Federal charges alleging a number of computer crimes were filed against Swartz. He felt maligned and persecuted. Faced with an almost certain prison sentence, in January 2013 he took his own life (see Associated Press [AP], 2013; Schwartz, 2013).

Swartz's partner and family felt certain that his death was caused in large part by a "criminal justice system rife with intimidation and prosecutorial overreach" (AP, 2013). They remained firm in their conviction that "decisions made by officials in the Massachusetts U.S. Attorney's office and at MIT contributed to his death" (AP, 2013). Swartz remains a hero to many for doing, as the international nonprofit digital rights organization the Electronic Frontier Foundation has stated, "more than almost anyone to make the Internet a thriving ecosystem for open knowledge, and to keep it that way" (AP, 2013). As hacking of all types continues to take place, the tension between openness and ownership of information will continue to be tested. Hopefully, Swartz's sad outcome will not be repeated, but there is no easy resolution to this tension in sight.

finding solutions, bridging divides

Social problems always resist easy solutions. They generally result from a complex tangle of factors that contribute to their development and complexity and complicate their resolution. Given their widespread use and international scope, internet and digital technologies are integrated and implicated in all global and societal problems, such as poverty, crime, war, violence, destruction, racism, sexism, ageism, ableism, and homophobia.

More, or more sophisticated, internet and digital media use will not be sufficient to bridge these divisions, but it is clear that long-term investments in and strategies for global ICT development will help bring better living conditions and encourage prosperity. National policies and legislation must recognize the need for these investments, but this is a global concern and must be understood as an international initiative. The strengthening of each unit is necessary to strengthen the whole, and in this case, the whole is the globe—the whole world.

In addition, it is critical that individuals in all countries, rich and poor, have the means to become reliably connected to the internet and digital technology. This requires addressing issues of infrastructure, employment, education, and health care at a local and global level. It also requires literacy at the macro and micro levels as to how digital networks can be used and leveraged to meet outcomes. This represents an investment that goes well beyond the economic.

International networks and connectedness are the key not just to growth but to *equitable and inclusive* growth. Governments can support these networks by ensuring a robust and modern regulatory environment, consistent across geographies and technologies (Dutta et al., 2015, p. xvii). At present, the creation of such a cross-cultural international environment has not kept pace with technological development.

ICTs have substantial global importance in the area of health care and education. Interestingly, the most effective use of educational technology may not be getting the technology into the hands of the learners but into the hands of their teachers. When resources are directed to projects that facilitate teacher development, the impact on the education of children can be sustainable over a long period of time.

To bridge divides successfully and empower the world's citizens, technological growth and development must be inclusive. Three key components of inclusive growth are education, jobs, and well-being. Digital technology can be "an enabler, a catalyst, and a propelling force for all three," Dutta, Geiger, and Lanvin explain:

> Now that we can process huge volumes of data, and now that we have enough affordable processing capacity, we can build the holistic models that allow us to ask previously unimaginable questions, and we can answer those that were not previously answerable. This development makes truly inclusive growth a genuine possibility for the first time in history. (2015, p. xviii)

National and international policies and laws to support such initiatives and aid in the safe, widespread growth of ICTs, however, are in their infancy. And policies and laws are all the more critical when the stakes include securing people's safety, well-being, and full inclusion in the modern world. At this writing, comprehensive cybersecurity legislation has failed to pass in the United States because of privacy and due process concerns (Davis, 2015). More informal protocols have been established, such as the Internet Governance Forum (IGF), a space for nonbinding discussion, sponsored by the United Nations in 2005. But strong, coordinated national and international leadership has yet to coalesce, so increasingly, individuals and groups are using digital networks to empower themselves to bring about solutions and change and to bridge differences and divides.

speaking back to power: social organization, movements, and activism

Since social problems, inequalities, and power dynamics have an impact on individuals and their social worlds, those individuals may find that they want to do something to alter the balance of these dynamics. You may find this to be true of yourself—the more you learn about an issue, the more you become concerned. You may want to help shape a world that will be more open and fair and free. You may want to contribute to the public conversation about the pros and cons of techno-social life, to speak out against data mining and surveillance, to have a greater voice in a political dialogue. Or if this is not your style, you may at least want others to have such a voice and, perhaps, to provide support for them in your own way. In the modern world, there are a number of ways to do this—for people to use technology to speak back to power.

It may seem difficult or impossible to actually change the balance of power, and for sure, this is why some people do not try. But the internet and digital media can facilitate new forms of social organization that make this not only possible but very, very doable. It is now possible to speak directly to politicians, business owners, or leaders of all kinds of organizations via a Twitter account or a blog, for example. Of course, they may or may not get the message, make the change you request, or even reply. But at the very least, social networks open up pathways by which messages can more easily be sent to those who are in power. Even if recipients do not respond individually or even see every single message, tens or hundreds or thousands of such messages may have a collective influence.

The internet and digital media also enable people to reach out to one another and organize their actions so that as a group they might make a greater difference. People who seek information on social network sites are more likely to be politically active, both online and offline (Gil de Zúñiga, Jung, & Valenzuela, 2012). And, interestingly, people who are drawn into mobilization efforts via social media tend to be those who would otherwise not have been active (Vissers & Stolle, 2014). Just as important, social media helps people see themselves as a collective or as a class—as a set of people who have much in common and need one another to improve their conditions. Media "suture(s) social relations across a fragmented working class," report mediated social movement researchers Todd Wolfson and Peter Funke, who have studied how a network of Philadelphia organizations called the Media Mobilizing Project uses radio, video, and the internet to empower local poor and working people. Media, they found, "knits and thickens class identity" (Wolfson & Funke, 2013).

The most successful media-influenced social movements combine online and offline interactions. Potential activists can find one another online, discuss their common cause, recruit interested others, and make plans to meet in person. Efforts to bring about change can gain much widespread steam and publicity online as people solidify their stances, organize groups and rallies, and publicize their efforts. Most politically active students are active both online and offline (Vissers & Stolle, 2014).

Social media has been instrumental in helping to inspire, jump-start, spread the word about, and sustain a number of movements. The Women's March, Social Science March, and other protests that coalesced in response to Donald Trump's election in 2016 and inauguration in 2017 were organized largely on social media. They had been influenced by the Occupy Wall Street movement in 2011, which protested income and social inequality ("We are the 99%!" was the most well-known of its slogans), and the other Occupy movements that followed all organized and publicized in large part on social media. In January 2011, protesters took to the streets in Egypt for 11 days to call for the resignation of Hosni Mubarek, and they did not cease until he left power. The Arab Spring protests in the Middle East and North Africa in 2011 have also been called Facebook or Twitter revolutions, as those platforms played such a large role in the events. Protesters in Tunisia and Spain in 2011 also used social media quite effectively to demand change in their political systems and in social and economic inequality. In 2014, the deaths of Michael Brown in Ferguson, Missouri, and Eric Garner in New York City at the hands of police resulted in numerous, massive protests that were organized and documented on Facebook and other social media worldwide. Hashtags such as #BlackLivesMatter and #ICantBreathe sprang up on Twitter. In 2017, the hashtag #TakeAKnee sparked debate as to whether it was appropriate to "take a knee" during the national anthem preceding National Football League (and other) events in protest and widespread action. Numerous rallies were held in support of free speech following the 2015 murders of 12 journalists who worked at the French satirical newspaper *Charlie Hebdo*, and the hashtag #JeSuisCharlie set a new record for the most tweeted hashtag. Social media helped to bring about all of these movements, even in conditions in which money was scarce, conditions were poor, and people were afraid.

Social media platforms are often looked to as a kind of lifeline by people who suffer under repressive regimes. Those same authoritarian governments often fear the power of the internet and social media and may attempt to filter it, monitor it, curtail its use, or even shut it down. But increased access to one another and to resources and social capital have enhanced the importance of social media in people's lives and proven especially indispensable in places where people have minimal rights or freedom. When Turkey blocked access to Twitter in early 2014 right before a crucial election, users fashioned highly creative work-arounds and found their way onto Twitter, exchanging more tweets the day after the ban than the day before. Even under difficult conditions—perhaps *especially* under them—the power of social media to help individuals gather and fight for their rights has become apparent and has become a primary affordance of social media (Guillén & Suárez, 2005, p. 687; Tufekci, 2014).

Digitally influenced social movements have the best opportunity for sustained success when they operate on both the local and global levels (this is called *glocalization*). When multiple networks become activated at the local community level and the message is spread as widely as possible (often with photo and video accompaniment), social movements have the best chance to attain enough legitimacy and authority to have global reach. While many digital movements pride themselves on being leaderless and decentralized, the development of strong leaders is generally of great advantage in sustaining change over the long term (Polk, 2014). It is also advisable for networks to meet face-to-face and consider goals and strategies carefully, over time, to enhance their chances for sustaining success.

Contrary to fears that political and civic engagement is dead or dying in modern life, it remains very much alive (see Chayko, 2014). Social media, as we have seen, routinely and widely prompts face-to-face interaction and encourages political participation. Online deliberation of controversial political and social issues is less widespread, though. Many people shy away from discussing hot-button ideas online, especially with those whose beliefs differ from theirs (Hampton et al., 2015). Of course, some people also shy away from political activism, both online and offline. Reaching out to others on social media is not the same as doing so face-to-face, and it can induce what has been called *slacktivism* or *hashtag activism*—the substitution of talking about doing something (especially on social media) for actually doing something face-to-face. But as we have seen, using social media to organize an effort can be quite productive, and the most effective movements blend both online and offline efforts.

The internet, and social media in particular, gives people a platform and outlet for the expression of all kinds of views. Unsurprisingly, people with the strongest political or ideological views (e.g., the most liberal Democrats or the most conservative Republicans) are most likely to share them. Estimates indicate that about two thirds of American social media users have used a social media platform to do at least one of the following civic or political activities: encourage people to vote; post, repost, promote, or indicate agreement with political concerns; take political or social action or join a political group; or follow an elected official or candidate (Rainie & Wellman, 2012).

The internet and digital media provide literally countless opportunities for the politically inclined (or curious!) to become active in causes that matter to them. Digital activism is having a huge impact on politics, governing, and civic and social involvement, opening up tremendous opportunities to find a place among digitally enabled political and social movements or even to start one's own. How will the internet and digital media assist *you* in making an imprint on the world around you and perhaps changing the balance and use of power?

the rise of citizen journalism

Many people now choose to make their imprint on the world by using social media and blogs to spread and comment on the news and to take on tasks previously performed by professional journalists. Gathering and disseminating newsworthy information to a large number of people once required the coordinated efforts of trained professionals in organizations both small (local newspapers) and large (the wire services, such as the Associated Press and United Press International). These organizations had tremendous control over production processes. They even decided what *was* newsworthy, a standard that has changed over the years (for example, in the 1930s and 1940s, large news organizations agreed—somewhat tacitly—not to reveal President Franklin D. Roosevelt's polio to the nation, a collusion that would be practically unthinkable today).

Today, most anyone with internet and digital media access can post on social media sites or on individual blogs content that will become the "news of the day." These *citizen journalists* essentially produce and spread this information without a "gatekeeper" to oversee its accuracy. At the same time, many news organizations have begun to incorporate the work of citizen journalists into their own professional products. The result is another permeation of digital boundaries: the blurring of the difference between "legitimate" and "amateur" news items and outlets.

Citizen journalists and other content producers often remix and repurpose available information into new, different configurations. Internet-based technologies and social media are perfectly suited to these practices, as copies of web pages and files can be made, searched, and remixed from multiple sources at minimal cost (Lessig, 2008; Martin, 2014). Media aggregation and reuse ventures proliferate on the internet and have become big business. Aggregators assemble a range of news sources in an easily digestible, summary form (Martin, 2014). They *curate* these sources, carefully selecting, arranging, and formatting them. Some also offer their point of view. Many people now turn to Twitter or Facebook for up-to-date information on news events or even for breaking news rather than (or alongside) more traditional media outlets like newspapers, television, radio, and the wire services.

Citizen journalism can provide a voice for people in societies in which the mass media are not independent of the state or where freedom of the press is limited. In such areas, citizens have special motivation to use social media to share and stay abreast of the news. In China, for example, where the media are state controlled, mobile telephony is the least regulated media space. Texting and social media therefore provide opportunities for citizens to inform and be informed about current events (Wei, Lo, Xu, Chen, & Zhang, 2014).

Of course, most citizen journalists have not been trained in professional journalistic techniques. They are not, for example, required to obtain multiple credible sources verifying the accuracy of an item before publishing it, and they may not be concerned about the pitfalls of plagiarism. They may not verify the veracity of the information they claim as factual. Professional news organizations have such standards. They are incorrect sometimes, too—they may be in a hurry to be fast (or first) getting a story out and rely on sources that may be wrong or absent, or they may be more interested in the attention-getting (and financially lucrative) aspects of a story than the facts. But information provided by professional journalists and news organizations is generally considered to have the edge in accuracy and believability over that of citizen journalists or bloggers.

This is not always the case, though. The competition for an audience among newsmakers sometimes results in the making of critical errors that sully, if not denigrate, the product itself, which is, to a large extent, the *facts*—the truth. In the process, the reputation of the news outlet itself can be seriously compromised. A decline in a news organization's reputation for fairness and accuracy can benefit the independent journalist or citizen journalist, who can then appear to the general public as just as, if not more, trustworthy. Although independent and citizen journalists also make errors, unique and important contributions to a story's overall coverage can surface through their coverage of an event. Taken together with news provided by traditional news organizations, a more complete story can be told.

The desire for an audience has also led to the practice among both professional and citizen journalists and organizations of making the news seem as interesting as possible in an attempt to attract more viewers or readers. This has led to a fairly high general level of sensationalism in which news stories are written and produced so as to catch and hold the eye of the audience member. When style is favored over substance in conveying information, as it sometimes is, factual accuracy can suffer. When professional organizations fall prey to this, it opens the door for newer upstarts to be quite competitive if not more successful in terms of communicating information in a newsworthy manner. And as we saw in Chapter 4, the door is also opened for "fake" or inaccurate news and information to spread more easily and widely.

Independent and citizen journalism represents a voice for "the people," an opportunity for them—us—to be heard, to gather, and to make a difference. It lets us see some of the power traditionally held by governments and news organizations being expressed by members of the public. It can potentially represent and lead to a real shift in the balance of global power.

To determine who has power and how that power is being exercised can be highly instructive in understanding the dynamics of any group or society. To go one step further and then try to improve the conditions around you—to challenge the status quo—can be even more informative and empowering and can contribute to real social change. The key to not feeling overwhelmed by the number of challenges to be faced is to decide which issues have the most meaning for you and about which you feel passionate enough to take the first steps. Then, find others who feel similarly. The internet and digital media, especially social media, can be indispensable in this effort.

Do not be surprised if, along the way, you find yourself changed as well. In the next chapter, we look at issues of self and identity construction in digital spaces. We'll discover how the self is shaped throughout one's lifetime and how the internet and digital media influence the fascinating process of techno-socialization.

6 TECHNO-SOCIALIZATION AND THE SELF

socialization, self, and identity

As we go through life, we learn the ways of society and how to participate in it. At the same time, many of our personal qualities and characteristics come into being. Sociologists consider the individual *self* to develop as part of the same process by which one becomes a member of society. This process is called *socialization*, and it can be thought of as two sides of the same coin: As we begin to shape our personhood (the self) out of the raw matter of infancy, we learn the ways of society (socialization) and become participants in it.

The internet and digital media can play a large part in socialization and the development of the self, for this process takes place as we interact with others. For many people who live in tech-rich communities and societies, plenty of interaction occurs online. *Techno-socialization* takes place as people engage with those whom they know online, face-to-face, and in both contexts.

There are differences between self and *identity*. Your self is your personhood—literally, the person that you are, physically, psychologically, and socially. The self can be further thought about in terms of an *actual self* or *empirical self* (one's most enduring traits—see James, 1890/1983); an *ideal self* (the type of person one would like to be); and an *ought self* or *possible selves* (the types of attributes that might be possessed someday—see Higgins, 1987; Markus & Nurius, 1986). Your identity comprises your personal qualities and characteristics—what you are *like*. This includes your internal self-definition—preferences, values, beliefs, interests. Though there is a definite distinction between self and identity, for our purposes we consider them to be similar and roughly interchangeable.

Self and identity are shaped and transformed in interaction with others. When we learn about the world and how others operate within it, much of this knowledge is incorporated into our identities. Gradually, our qualities and characteristics—physical, psychological, emotional—develop and change. This is an ongoing process, continuing until the day we die.

We also learn about society's norms, values, and cultural products and processes as we undergo socialization. For those who are digitally connected to others, these processes take on fascinating dimensions. The internet and digital media provide countless opportunities for people to observe and learn about others, many of whom will come to influence their socialization in different ways. On the internet, individuals are encountered and met and befriended, and a stream of potential aspects of self and identity are explored. People compare themselves to others, learn new norms and values, and grow as individuals and as members of society.

Additionally, mobile phones, so often carried on or near the physical body, can be seen a part of the body and the self. According to business and marketing professor Russell Belk's extended self theory (1998), objects and possessions can become viewed as part of the self when individuals are able to exercise power and control over them in much the same way as they control the actions of an arm or a leg. Mobile technologies increasingly function as "an extension of our physical selves—an umbilical cord, anchoring the information society's digital infrastructure to our very bodies" (Harkin, 2003, p. 16; see Clayton, Leshner, & Almond, 2015). In intriguing new ways, the internet and digital technologies permit experiments in identity development, selfhood, and socialization to take place constantly (Palfrey & Gasser, 2008).

development and performance of the self

Selves and identities develop in concert with other people. As the classical sociologist George Herbert Mead has theorized, self and identity are created in part by *taking the role of the other* (1934/2009). People "try on" the attitudes, behaviors, and even physical items (like clothes) of other people. They do this both with *specific others* (particular individuals looked to as role models, such as caregivers, siblings, friends, and even some who are not personally known) and with *generalized others* (groups of people who are observed, both close up and at a distance, and who represent a type of person or a way of life, such as groups of teachers, musicians, or football players).

As people are observed, and in some cases interacted with, it is common to consider what life would be like in their shoes, their reality. What traits or qualities do these others have, we might wonder? How are these qualities expressed? Would any of them "fit" as part of our identity, our life? This intriguing line of consideration begins in childhood, as children play games that involve pretending that they are other people (sometimes specific other people and sometimes generalized others, or types of people). This process continues throughout adulthood, as traits, attitudes, and interests are observed, considered, and tested out in terms of their potential "fit" with existing traits. These traits and attitudes then become gradually integrated into self and identity, or they are discarded. This process is repeated so often that some of these traits become permanently incorporated into one's personality, identity, and self. Bit by bit, piece by piece, people are always growing and changing, and selves and identities are always under construction.

Specific and generalized others are encountered face-to-face at home, in school, at work, and at play, but they are also encountered, all the time, via the internet and the media. Both mass and digital media expose individuals to many, many other people and provide a sense of who those others are. Groups of people who turn out to have a strong influence on the process of identity development are called *agents of socialization*. They include family and friendship groups with whom it is more common to share one's emotional and expressive life (these are also called *primary groups*) and groups encountered in more specialized, instrumental settings like school or the workplace (called *secondary groups*).

Nearly everywhere people turn in a technology-rich society, a person or a way of life can be encountered that inspires the individual's imagination. I have argued elsewhere that through using mass media like television and radio, legitimate primary groups are generated because these media enable us to get to know one another in a fundamental and personal way (Cerulo et al., 1992). This is even truer of digital media and internet use. As others encountered on the internet and digital media gain personal significance, they can become, in Tamotsu Shibutani's words, *reference groups*, to whom people compare themselves and from whom much can be learned (1955).

Individuals also develop their selves and identities by using those in their immediate vicinity as a kind of mirror to the self. They look carefully at people's reactions and responses when "trying on" a new behavior, characteristic, or preference. If something elicits a positive response, it is more likely to engender a sense of confidence, and such a quality is more likely to persist. If the response from others is negative, one's self-esteem may suffer, and the self may flounder. Charles Horton Cooley (1922/1964) called this process the *looking-glass self*, as other people become mirrors (or looking glasses) that help one see and examine oneself and develop aspects of self-image in response. Like taking the role of the other, it explains much about how socialization operates in day-to-day life.

There is a digital component to the looking-glass self as well. People can become aware of and develop perceptions of others' responses to them in the digital realm. Through interacting with others online, which increasingly happens at younger and younger ages, individuals begin to learn how they are perceived by others. "Others on the internet constitute a distinct 'looking glass' that produces a 'digital self,'" explains sociologist Shanyang Zhao (2005). This self, Zhao has found, can differ from the identity one puts forth offline, especially for teenagers who are actively shaping their identities. For all of us, though, identity develops and shifts and changes over time.

According to sociologist Erving Goffman (1959), we all "act out" many aspects of our lives. This means we are in many ways performers, putting on a kind of "show" wherever we go. We act the way we believe people taking on that role, that part, should act. When people become parents, for example, they act as they believe parents should act, which helps them develop into the kind of parents that they will be. The same idea holds in all of the roles that we play. The self develops in the playing of these parts, which makes the self "performed."

It may seem strange to think of social life as a show, but think of how you might behave if there were no audiences whatsoever for your behavior—if you lived entirely alone and did not encounter others on a daily basis. Would you bathe and groom yourself and dress as you usually do? Would you smile as often? Would you be physically and mentally healthy? What would you learn about? What aspects of your personality would develop? People are almost continually involved in what Goffman called *impression management* (1959). They try to convey certain perceptions or impressions of themselves, in the hope that others will see them in a desired light. This is a critical part of the process of socialization that helps individuals develop their selves.

It is sometimes said that when people are online they are in a sense performing for others—that they are not being authentic. To be sure, some people play rather freely with their identities online. But as Mead's, Cooley's, Shibutani's, and Goffman's (and certainly other) theories hold, this is a big part of how identity develops anyway. People imagine, play, perform. They try things out and see how others react. They act a bit differently in different settings. Aspects of the self change, gradually and sometimes imperceptibly, over time. There are almost unlimited opportunities to shape the self while online (Chayko, 2008).

Aspects of the self can fairly easily be experimented with in digital spaces. When interaction is text based, many social markers are invisible, and so gender, race, nationality, and age, among others, can be disguised or altered. People can play with identity online in ways that would be impossible offline, exploring different (or potential) aspects of their selves in the process. But this does not happen as often as one might think. Deeply ingrained social characteristics are difficult to disguise, especially over the long term. And mostly, people want to connect with others as themselves. They generally don't separate into entirely different, distinct identities, online or offline (Chayko, 2008, p. 169; Huffaker & Calvert, 2005; Kendall, 2002).

People do, though, "fix up" and edit words, photos, and interactions online so as to make them more positive, more flattering, more distinctive. (They frequently do the face-to-face equivalent of this offline as well.) Most, however, still want to make sure that their true or authentic selves are represented, both online and offline. As Nicole Ellison and her coauthors explain, "Pressures to highlight one's positive attributes are experienced in tandem with the need to present one's true (or authentic) self to others, especially in significant relationships" (2006, p. 417). Because people can control their self-presentational behavior online, they manage their impressions strategically and make decisions about what to self-disclose, and they do this both with known audiences and with strangers (Ellison, Heino, & Gibbs, 2006).

Digital tools provide a relatively controlled space in which to edit and express and explore the self. This is especially valuable when some aspect of face-to-face communication is difficult or challenging for the individual. Those whom I interviewed on this topic were nearly unanimous in praising this benefit of digital communication:

> Talking to my friends online has enabled me to open up as a person. Sometimes it's easier to talk online than in person because I am sometimes shy. For someone like me who has health issues and limitations . . . my listserv is always there to answer any questions and you also get to know many through their posts . . . . I find that I type things to my girlfriend that I would not normally say to her. At times that I am lonely or homesick I am able to easily chat with friends from home. (Chayko, 2008, pp. 172–173)

In the process of "opening up" online, various aspects of one's self can be expressed and discovered (Bargh, 2002; Bargh, McKenna, & Fitzsimons, 2002).

In the course of using the internet and digital media, people make frequent decisions that influence their self-development. They choose what they are going to share and with whom, and they choose the mode of expression, such as social media, word processing, or an app. Context collapse complicates matters as well (see Chapter 4), for choices must be made with regard to the audiences for these expressions. Who should be friended and followed and from which components of one's life? Who gets placed in which social circles? What information gets revealed to whom? What happens when others see postings not targeted for their eyes? Thinking about exactly how one's self will be revealed to others encourages the development of self and identity in interesting ways.

Some scholars conjecture that the different aspects of identity that are explored in different social circles online never quite merge together into a singular and unitary self. Rather, they argue, people cycle through a number of different and segmented selves online (Higgins, 1987; Kennedy, 2006; Markus & Kunda, 1986; Turkle, 1995). Feminist technology scholar Donna Haraway claims that the self is always partial, consisting of pieces or fragments, and that this is necessary so that we can understand different viewpoints (in Kennedy, 2006; see also Haraway, 1998). As cultural sociologist Stuart Hall sums up this position, the modern identity is "never singular but multiply constructed across different, often intersecting and antagonistic, discourses, practices and positions" (1996, p. 4).

Others, however, such as sociologists Lori Kendall (2002) and David Huffaker and Sandra Calvert (2005), find identity to be more singular. They point out that individuals are anchored in a single body and tend to speak with a single voice more or less consistently online, thus exhibiting a single identity. When alternate identities are assumed, as in a game, this is usually an experimental or playful activity; different avatars and identities, in this context, generally do not represent substantially different selves.

It may be most helpful, then, to think of the self as consisting of aspects, each of which can be explored and developed as we interact with others, rather than to think of it as consisting of distinct, different identities. Since there is no real line dividing online and offline, and since those spheres are best thought of as enmeshed (see Chapter 3), it makes most sense to think of the self that is created, performed, and exhibited online as a manifestation of the self that exists offline as well. In most healthy people, that self is fluid but unitary; there is one self with many aspects, many moods, many colors—not separate and distinct multiple selves (see James, 1890/1983, on the continuity of the self).

Georg Simmel (1908/1962) writes of how individuals are each situated within a complex "web" of diverse group affiliations. As they take on a large number of roles and identify, at least in part, with numerous groups, modern people may experience strain and conflict but also great flexibility in self-construction and expression. In the process, people can become more highly differentiated from one another, more different and specialized, than at any time in human history. In coordinating these diverse roles and expressing different aspects of ourselves in each group, the modern individual can become deeply complex and utterly unique. While this is an exciting, even freeing, proposal, it also presents a challenge: In creating a multifaceted self, one must find a way to bring these facets together (see Chayko, 2015).

Opportunities and challenges for the construction of the self abound in the modern technologized era. According to psychologist Kenneth Gergen (1991), the self becomes increasingly *saturated* as people become immersed in and dependent on relationships and as ways of being (attitudes, values, opinions, moralities, styles of relating) become more complex. The resulting *digital self* or *networked self* (Papacharissi, 2010; Zhao, 2005) is almost continually engaged with issues of self-presentation and identity negotiation. In a tech-rich environment, aspects of the self are frequently evaluated, updated, communicated, and expressed.

expression of the self

Human beings have a strong need for self-expression. Digital technologies, and social media in particular, are frequently used to create personal expressions of all kinds and to edit and manage these impressions as they are communicated to the wider world. In the process, developing and expressing the self can become a kind of project.

Digital media provides individuals with platforms and tools that can be used to express all kinds of ideas and impulses. Blogs and social media sites such as Facebook, Twitter, Pinterest, Instagram, Reddit, Snapchat, and Tumblr encourage personal expression and content creation through text, photos, videos, and so on. They also provide a platform for people to comment on and respond to what others share. This happens many times, over and over, all day, every day. In the process, individual selves are given opportunities to develop, groups and communities can form, and common understandings and common ground can develop.

Applications that support and encourage personal expression (and the sharing of such expressions) are increasingly free or inexpensive and relatively easy to use. To be able to personalize digital products and spaces is increasingly important to internet users (Tapscott, 2011). Portability and anonymity (or partial anonymity) encourage freedom of self-expression and, in some cases, as we have seen, boldness and disinhibition. Most people are less bound by physical restrictions online as compared to offline (though there are some who experience physical and perceptual difficulties that restrict digital access). Under these conditions, many individuals can feel more playful and free when they are online (see Fallows, 2006), which can translate to a sense of freedom when expressing the self.

People tend to produce and manage their online identities rather strategically and to evaluate others' identities just as strategically (see Rui & Stefanone, 2013). In ways ranging from calculating to inadvertent, they reveal information about themselves when online almost constantly (see Baym, 2010, p. 119; Ellison et al.,

2006). They provide clues in their content, behavior, linguistic and writing style, type and timing of messages, sites visited and contributed to, content liked and retweeted, choice of avatars and names, and even colors used—the list could go on and on indefinitely. With all this information, a profile of those encountered online begins to take shape. At the same time, a representation of one's own identity forms.

Online self-expression and representation takes both written and visual form. Emails, posts, status updates, blogs, and text messages allow us to document thoughts and feelings so we can remember and reflect on them later. In text messaging, a mode of communication whose popularity continually increases, dialogues can resemble an ongoing conversation that can extend into multiple directions. Emailing permits easier archiving of information shared and is considered more durable and appropriate for professional use. Social media and blog postings of all kinds provide a public platform for expressions that can range from deeply personal to strictly professional. Because these media are all so interactive, they allow users to "write themselves into being," for "to recognize [their] own existence in any meaningful way, [they] must be responded to" (boyd & Heer, 2006, p. 1; see also Bilton, 2013; Rettberg, 2014, p. 13).

In the late 1990s and early 2000s, webcam and video-sharing technologies became popular, beginning a shift in which people would increasingly communicate via visuals in addition to the written word (Senft, 2008). Since then, particularly from 2010 onward, video and photo image sharing has become a wildly popular mode of self-representation, expression, and documentation. Visuals know no language barrier, convey a great deal of information in an efficient and specific way, and, absent the costs of film development, are relatively inexpensive to share en masse. Some platforms and apps, such as YouTube, allow the easy uploading and sharing of videos. Others, such as Snapchat, allow photos and texts to quickly disappear once sent (although Snapchat does have the ability to archive its videos, and digital archives must always be considered potentially hackable).

With the technology to see and record one's image proliferating via cell and smartphones, the taking and sharing of *selfies* has become extremely popular. A selfie is a photo one takes of oneself that sends a message transmitting one's feelings and often inviting feedback and attention, generally in the form of "likes." Selfies have considerable cultural and personal significance. They can indicate, among other things, that a person has personally witnessed an event, is safely accounted for, wishes to document life in some way, has taken a stand on some issue of importance, or simply has a particular point of view (Hess, 2015; Koliska & Roberts, 2015; Lobinger & Brantner, 2015; Nemer & Freeman,

2015; Senft & Baym, 2015; Shaw, 2010; Tiidenberg, 2014). Contrary to popular belief, selfies do not seem to be associated with narcissism (Etgar & Amichai-Hamburger, 2017). Rather, they allow people to fulfill basic self-presentation needs in a manner that is often playful and semi-ironic, allowing some distancing from more narcissistic, overtly self-promotional motivations (Diefenbach & Christoforakos, 2017).

Selfies also confer authenticity. They provide evidence that one is present at an event or in a place, proof that one was really "there." Like all symbols, photos, and videos that can be digitally shared and spread, selfies can represent something meaningful about an individual or a group and in doing so can bring people together, solidifying a relationship or a community (Chayko, 2008; Senft & Baym, 2015).

Through representing, expressing, sharing, and documenting themselves on the internet—primarily on social media—individuals' identities constantly develop and socialization continually takes place. As these representations accumulate over time, stories—full-fledged narratives about experiences, perspectives, and lives—come into being. Social media lends itself to the act of storytelling, of constructing narratives about people and the lives they lead. According to sociologist Anthony Giddens, individuals create accounts of their lives and always have the "capacity to keep the story going." Giddens calls this the "ongoing story of the self" (1991, p. 56). When people view events as episodes in a larger story, they construct narratives that bring meaning and coherence to their lives. One's life and self can thus be better understood.

The telling and retelling of stories is critical to the establishment of groups as well. It gives a group definition and cohesion and creates solidarity among members. It also heightens social presence among the community members and supplies the detail and images that populate and shape the space that the group inhabits. The more detailed and resonant the story, the more personal these spaces can become and the more vividly the people in them can come to life (see Chayko, 2008, pp. 159–182 for more on self-expression and storytelling online).

For the digital tech user, "the social media deck is stacked in such a way as to make being 'a self'" relatively easy, claims media researcher Whitney Erin Boesel (2012). In fact, she explains, it is "easier and more rewarding than being a friend." While modern friendships often require reading, viewing, and responding to a flood of mediated content, the process of becoming a fully realized self benefits greatly from taking advantage of the many opportunities for online self-expression. On the other hand, technology critics like Nicholas

Carr (2011) respond, too much quick and superficial online expression lends itself to the construction of a self that is "flattened" and less interesting because it is developed in frequent short exchanges rather than longer, more in-depth interactions. The conversation as to how internet and digital media use impacts self and identity is one that will likely continue for some time, for self-expression will surely remain technologically mediated and publicly visible.

when identity is marginalized

People are not equally empowered to express aspects of themselves online without fear of harassment or danger, however. When a person or a group is marginalized or threatened in some way, identity and self development take on new dimensions. It is all too common to see discrimination occur on the basis of such social characteristics as race, ethnicity, gender, socioeconomic class, sexual orientation, age, physical and intellectual ability, and any of a number of other factors. This happens both online and offline and can strongly impact an individual's self-expression.

If the internet offers "a unique opportunity for self-expression," as psychologist John Bargh and his coauthors claim, "then we would expect a person to use it first and foremost to express those aspects of self that he or she has the strongest need to express" (2002, p. 34). An individual may form social connections online on the basis of characteristics that are not in the societal mainstream. People with nondominant backgrounds and lifestyles can discover unique avenues and spaces for self-expression and connection online that help them deal with offline challenges. They may find friends and communities that give them a feeling of safety or even use the technology to share information they might otherwise be reticent to share (Baker, 2005; Gajjala, 2004; Lin, 2006; Mehra, Merkel, & Bishop, 2004; Mitra, 2004, 2005), as did this interviewee of mine:

> After many secrets and lies, my parents finally confronted me about my sexuality in an email. I am a lesbian and had been in an abusive relationship. I had just not been able to find the words to talk with them. Finally, I got an email saying, "hey we know you are gay and it is okay," basically. I responded immediately from my own apartment with tears streaming down my cheeks, but I was so relieved it was finally out in the open. Eventually I would have told my parents, but it would not have happened so quickly and candidly. (Chayko, 2008, p. 52)

People who claim nonmainstream identities or identify with communities that are not in the majority may not feel comfortable with certain forms of communication. Whether online or off, it is important to take into account others' personal, social, and cultural circumstances when exchanging messages and connecting.

Sharing information and communicating via the internet and digital media is not always safe, and the dangers are not uniformly experienced. Low-income and disempowered individuals, particularly youth, are at increased risk for harm and harassment in public and private spaces, both online and in face-to-face situations. They are frequently surveilled by adults, peers, and institutions. They seek spaces that afford freedom of expression, interest-based communities, and privacy. When online, they may actively resist the ways mobile and social media are intended to be used and configured and create their own norms and carve out spaces in which they can feel comfortable—spaces that can be considered their own (Vickery, 2015). Of course, spatially separated members of dangerous or destructive groups can also use digital technology to find one another, gather digitally and physically, and cause harm (Carmichael, 2003; Glaser, Dixit, & Green, 2002, p. 22; Kjuka, 2013).

Those who have been targeted or harmed due to socially marginalized aspects of their identities can use the same digital technologies to find one another, rally, and support one another. In the process, their group identities can be bolstered and their individual identities strengthened and extended into new directions. For those who have experienced such struggles, this can be so supportive as to be lifesaving. When sociologist Douglas Schrock and his fellow researchers studied an online support group for transgendered and cross-dressing individuals, they found friendship, joy, and elation. Members had discovered a place where they could connect with one another, feel comfortable and safe, and share their stories with one another. Doing so "was very cleansing," one participant said. "I was amazed, it was like I broke through a shell. . . . It's almost like I had come home" (Schrock, Holden, & Reid, 2004, p. 66).

For people who have physical and/or perceptual difficulties accessing online content, the internet and digital media can feel like a closed club that they have difficulty entering. While technological advancements are making it easier for people with visual and aural impairments to access and use these technologies, for many it can still be difficult. When such barriers are overcome, the gains can be substantial, and independence can be increased (Akamatsu, Mayer, & Farrelly, 2006). Identities can be presented and expressed in environments where impairments are unknown, irrelevant, or supported by others. Those with disabilities can find and network with others in similar circumstances, gather needed information and resources, and express themselves more fully and spontaneously. For one group of disabled internet users in China, access to the online led to a significantly improved frequency and quality of social interaction and reduced barriers in both the physical and social environment (Guo, Bricout, & Huang, 2005).

For people who are part of disempowered groups, prejudice and discrimination are an ongoing concern. Diminished societal power offline translates to life online. But with the possibility to reach one another and create communities that may become safe spaces, opportunities to forge solidarity can be found and created. In some cases, barriers to interaction can be lifted, self-expression can be enhanced, and collective organization to improve status and circumstances can be enabled.

growing up online and offline

The process of becoming a self and a member of society is a lifelong process. Socialization actually begins long before birth. Those preparing for the birth of a baby likely have culturally influenced ideas as to how that child should be raised. The baby is brought into a world with preexisting norms and values related to social characteristics. The social climate into which a baby is born thus influences and may indeed determine quite a bit about his or her identity and *life chances*—a person's opportunities for *upward mobility* or improvement in social status, health, resources, and level of educational attainment.

Individuals are born with certain genetic, biological, and psychological predispositions as well. Some of the characteristics that seem to have a strong genetic component include extraversion (or its inverse, introversion or shyness), neuroticism, risk taking, and vulnerability to addictions (Kreek, Nielsen, Butelman, & LaForge, 2005; Viken, Rose, Kaprio, & Koskenvuo, 1994). Some people are born with challenging physical and/or mental conditions. In socialization, however, even those characteristics that have a biological component undergo shaping by environmental and life circumstances. Even one's gender, which usually has a clear biological component—genes, secondary sex characteristics, hormones—is fluid and flexible enough that some people feel it does not express their true selves, and they socially or surgically alter it over time. Growing up and developing a self and identity are complex processes that embrace the social, biological, and psychological.

Both mass and digital media are a major part of the everyday lives of most children in the developed world, and, as we have seen, cell phones are becoming more prominent and available for people's use even in less developed areas.

Through such activities as listening to recorded music and messages in the womb to watching TV and videos as babies to playing early games on iPads, the internet and mass and digital media serve as early agents of socialization. While parents and caregivers in technology-rich societies are often warned to limit young children's time in front of media "screens," and such use has more than doubled in the last decade, there is no one-size-fits-all recommendation as to how much screen time is acceptable for children. The ways in which children use smartphones, tablets, and computers must be taken into account—are they interacting, learning, and creating while online? To look merely at screen time, Blum-Ross and Livingstone find, is an outdated notion (2016). And along with family and friends, media provide a host of information about a culture and one's place in society and therefore serve as a primary group for people—a source of strong, close personal ties and a setting for socialization (Cerulo et al., 1992).

In the developed world, it is not uncommon for very young children to receive mobile phones from parents. Often, these parents may be concerned about potential emergencies and want their children to be able to reach them at a moment's notice. In some cases, they may not want it to appear that they or their children are on the wrong side of a digital divide (see Castells, Fernandez-Ardevol, Qiu, & Sey, 2004). According to some estimates, the average age at which children in technologically developed countries currently receive their first cell phone is approximately nine and is dropping. Some of these cell phones are not connected to the internet, but increasingly it is becoming a norm for children to receive phones at earlier and earlier ages (even in elementary school), and many of these phones are smartphones (Mascheroni & Olafsson, 2013).

Children who grow up with the internet and digital technology tend to become quite comfortable using them. Sometimes called *digital natives*, they have come of age in environments in which the internet and digital media are an ordinary part of people's lives. A technology-filled world may be the only world they know (Palfrey & Gasser, 2008; Prensky, 2001). Contrary to what some believe, this does not automatically make these children experts in the use of the devices, let alone in the consequences of their use. There is also no definitive word on how it will influence children long term to have spent so much time in front of screens. But it does tend to result in their having a certain comfort with digital technology and agility in using it. As with all populations, technology use by the young can have a range of effects, both beneficial and potentially hazardous, as identities, selves, and social connections are made and the early stages of the socialization process ensue.

In a pattern similar to that of older people, children tend to gravitate toward the social uses of their phones and computers. They use them to communicate and "hang out" with friends, play games that are often multiplayer games, surf the web, and listen to music. They use them to strengthen their friendships, often remaining in a state of constant connectedness or ambient copresence with their friends by checking in frequently with group texts and chats. Of course, as they connect with some they can alienate others, forming groups that exclude as well as include. As they do all these things online, they become socialized into the ways of a group or society and take on the roles and customs so critical to the development of identity.

They also use the technology to express themselves and, in so doing, develop their identities (Livingstone, 2009). They may customize the actual phones, computers, and tablets, as well as their cases. They spend a good deal of time and energy creating and editing social media profiles and avatars and using particular icons, ringtones, fonts, and so on that they feel represent them. They update profiles and pages fairly frequently, changing photos, deleting unpleasant comments, and altering friend and follower lists. They take, post, and share selfies liberally, sometimes adopting "sexy self-presentations" (van Oosten, Peter, & Boot, 2015). In short, they seem to recognize that much of what they do and see is an edited, sometimes playful version of the self. Still, they spend a great deal of time, energy, and often care in posting and responding to one another's posts. Doing so may represent and support the adolescent's struggle to create and sustain a unified self in the face of uncertain and shifting emotions, identifications, and demands (Livingstone, 2009, p. 103).

Young internet and digital media users are also fond of customizing and personalizing their language, creating abbreviations, shorthands, and symbol systems that differentiate them from adults and set apart their communities from those who do not share their system (Chayko, 2008, pp. 163–164). They may insert *emoticons* (text-created depictions of emotional states, such as smiles and frowns) and *emojis* (tiny icons and illustrations of all kinds of things) into messages via their devices to express themselves. Some worry that skills in formal writing and communication are being lost as children overuse or misuse these shorthand online languages, but at least one study has found that children that text more often score better on reading, writing, and spelling tests. This suggests that any writing may be better than no writing and that texting can help children practice language skills in an accessible, enjoyable way (Chayko, 2008; Psychology Today, 2007).

This is how communities and those in them develop distinct identities. Special words, nicknames, modes of speaking, symbols, clothing, colors, logos, and so on are used to create the group and form a kind of boundary around it that separates in-groups (those who understand the symbols and are "in the know") from out-groups (those who are not in the know). It is highly normative to live life as part of meaningful groups, and it makes sense that people would use the technology so frequently at their side to create and maintain these groups and to learn to do so from a young age. We will look at processes of friending and interpersonal relating further in Chapter 7.

Children, adolescents, and teens increasingly use the internet and digital media to create original content. At least one third of *all* American teens have created blogs or web pages; made original content in the form of artwork, stories, or videos; or remixed music or videos online (Lenhart & Madden, 2006; Lenhart, Purcell, Smith, & Zickuhr, 2010). Over 90% share and post photos regularly (Madden et al., 2013). They also use the internet to access health information, educational resources, and, increasingly, to view sexually explicit materials. Kids with mobile phones can often access such materials without adults' knowledge, though software and spyware intended to block such efforts (and even surveil the child) can be employed to thwart them.

As children become teenagers, the formation of their identities takes on new purpose and urgency. "Young people are engaged in struggles of identity formation," professor of education Angela Thomas notes. "They struggle for power, popularity, to define who they are, and to understand their sexuality. . . . This is reflected in their online worlds" (2006, p. 40). Both mass and digital media continue to be key agents of socialization for these children. As danah boyd (2014), who has studied the ways that younger people interact on social networking sites extensively, describes it,

> as teens transition from childhood, they try to understand how they fit into the larger world. They want to inhabit public spaces, but they also look to adults, including public figures, to understand what it means to be grown up. They watch their parents and other adults in their communities for models of adulthood. But they also track celebrities like Kanye West and Kim Kardashian to imagine the freedoms they would have if they were famous. For better or worse, media narratives also help construct broader narratives for how public life works. (pp. 18–19)

Growing up isn't easy, and finding and forming identity and a self can be challenging. The internet and digital media provide spaces and vehicles in which children and teens can begin to envision themselves as young adults and experiment with various freedoms (boyd, 2014, p. 19). They can try out and test who they are and who they want to be. They can also receive feedback—both positive and negative—and the social connections so critical to this process are formed and maintained.

Adolescents and teens spend so much time using digital technologies because that is where their friends are. The "spontaneous and enthusiastic adoption by children and young people of online opportunities for self-presentation and relationship construction is not technology driven," media researcher Sonia Livingstone reports. "Rather, what drives online and mobile communication is young people's strong desire to connect with peers anywhere, anytime" (2009, p. 92; see also boyd, 2014).

It can be difficult for adolescents and teens to find places to go where they can escape adult supervision and just hang out and have fun. A measure of freedom from authority is important in the development of maturity and identity—especially a sexual identity. But such spaces are not always plentiful or available offline, and they come with myriad rules. Young people are increasingly exposed to pornography online and increasingly decide to send and receive sexually-oriented texts and photos (sexting), but it should not be assumed that such behaviors are the cause of increased sexual activity or violent behavior. Exposure to sexual and pornographic images can result in uncomfortable, confused, upset feelings, but that may be associated with a lack of access to appropriate, high-quality sex education materials and explanations. There is, overall, a societal disinclination to see adolescents as needing to express and explore their sexuality, which tends to obscure the development of rational (and not panicked) responses to, and understanding of, such needs (Livingstone, 2017).

Free time is not plentiful for many teens in tech-intensive societies. Homework, after-school activities, and other events leave little unscheduled time. Spaces to just hang out with friends in can often be more easily created and accessed online than through face-to-face meetings. This is one of the real benefits for young people of mobile phone ownership; it can give them a sense of moving about more freely in more spaces (boyd, 2006, 2014). A social media space can be a "place to call their own" (boyd, 2014, p. 19), and they especially like to find or create their own such spaces—away from parents' and caregivers' eyes when possible. If they can't escape their parents' gaze, they may develop their own personalized ways of communicating with one another—through song lyrics or creative abbreviations, for example.

Children, adolescents, and teens—like all people—behave in digital spaces in ways that suit their needs, preferences, and lifestyles. Many younger computer users appreciate fast and fairly continuous contact with their friends and social networks and find that social media and text messaging accomplish this. They are often comfortable with and adept in blending digital and face-to-face contexts—incorporating technology into their everyday lives with ease, texting some friends while hanging out with others, and taking photos and posting updates to social media while physically with friends. Much as adults do, young people spend time online "because their friends are there and they are there to hang out with those friends," according to boyd (2006; see Lenhart & Madden, 2006; Madden et al., 2013).

Those who have grown up in tech-rich environments generally become rather comfortable with technology and are less likely to view the online and offline as separate contexts. "Where harried adults may try to reduce the interaction with the outer world," Rich Ling says, "younger people are comfortable increasing the amount of interaction, both online and offline" (2004, p. 111). They may even use what they learn online to improve their relationships offline. To have a wide and visible network of friends and followers can indicate to others (and to themselves) that they are popular, in demand, and, indeed, so connected as to be superconnected (see boyd, 2006, 2014; Ling, 2004; Miyata, Boase, Wellman, & Ikeda, 2005).

socialization never ends: socialization throughout adulthood

Identities continue to develop—sometimes dramatically, sometimes subtly—over the life span. Adults spend time in digital settings for many of the same reasons that children do—because their friends and other interesting people are there and because these connections are vital to the ongoing development of the self. Additionally, many people work and shop online and/or seek out, create, and share digital information, and much that they learn and observe in these contexts becomes incorporated into their lives and their identities.

In a tech-intensive society, people can become concerned with *self-branding*—the creation and dissemination of an identity using the internet and digital media. Personal brands may combine elements of one's professional and personal identities. To become known online can enhance opportunities and build and strengthen useful networks. Just as children and teens do, adults use social media platforms and profiles to continue to create and refine their identities and to understand their social worlds and the changes they may be going through. And, just like younger people, they are selective and strategic regarding how they edit and present their selves, adjusting the content they share depending on the audience (Marwick, 2014; Schwammlein & Wodzicki, 2012).

The changes that are encountered throughout one's life can be most pronounced when something in one's environment shifts radically, such as when one leaves home for the first time or changes jobs. People tend to try out new behaviors and norms when they take on new challenges because the structures that may have supported past identities are no longer there. In adulthood, the opportunities for identity construction and socialization are continual (Hormuth, 1990; Iyer, Jetten, & Tsivrikos, 2008; McCall & Simmons, 1978), and digital technology can provide a means to adapt to these changes, as it did for this person whom I interviewed:

> I recently moved 700 miles from home and (digital tech) has been a great way to keep in touch with friends and family. (Chayko, 2008, p. 90)

And according to another interviewee,

> Having email has made me feel more adventurous in where I live—it's not so scary to move thousands of miles every few years (which I've done) because I know I can stay close to everyone I know on a regular basis. (Chayko, 2008, p. 90)

Staying in touch with former friends and colleagues gains added significance as people age. Using the digital applications that seem most appropriate for different tasks, connections can be maintained and new aspects of identities can be pursued.

In growing older, one enters new phases in life. New roles arise, and existing roles (partner, spouse, parent, colleague) change form or disappear. Various skills and abilities are acquired and lost. And sometimes an individual may also feel that it is time to make a change—to develop new skills or characteristics because he or she simply feels a readiness or internal direction to do so. As these changes occur, the self can undergo transformation as well.

Socialization and identity development are, therefore, lifelong processes that are never quite done. The internet and mobile media provide countless opportunities for people to see what others are doing at any given time, to observe the roles others play, to use these others as mirrors for one's own self. As they did when they were children, adults continue to try on new roles. They continue to develop and "excavate" new aspects of the self over the course of their lifetime.

Numerous opportunities and choices for self-expression and representation arise online and can lead to the shaping of identity. Older adults frequently learn (or teach themselves) digital skills in the course of adopting a new interest or hobby (Riley, 2013). In order to pursue interests more fully, they may acquire information on the internet and can become involved in internet-based groups and relevant social media. Retired individuals may turn to the internet to rediscover an old interest that they may not have had time to explore prior to retirement (Riley, 2013). Internet and social media use in these years is often positively and enthusiastically embraced and tends to be associated with better mental health and enhanced social relationships (Mazur, Signorella, & Hough, 2018).

Sharing one's creative endeavors, talents, or points of view throughout one's lifetime, even into old age, can be highly satisfying and lead to personal growth and physical and psychological health (see Sass, 2014). As longtime blogger Rebecca Blood has observed, blogging can result in a heightened awareness of an individual's inner life that can lead to trust and confidence in one's own perspective and to the ongoing development of the self. It is a journey, Blood reports, of "self-discovery and intellectual self-reliance" (2002, p. 15). Women, in particular, seem to find blogging empowering, as it can represent an opportunity to exercise their agency and expand their communities (Stavrositu & Sundar, 2012).

Developing the self in multimedia public spaces is a complicated enterprise. Due to the complexity of context collapse, adults must grapple with the consequences of presenting various aspects of themselves to multiple audiences in different environments. As personal and professional reputations develop and are solidified, managing and controlling one's reputation in digital spaces can become a time-consuming priority. Professional identities must be tended to carefully, as a reputation honed over many years can be compromised by mistakes or inconsistencies that come to light via the internet and digital media. There are many examples of reputations and careers irreparably damaged or ruined by one errant or ill-advised posting, tweet, email, or text message.

The self that one creates and hones over time can be evaluated and assessed, both by oneself and by others, on a nearly constant basis. It is now possible to document daily life in a number of ways and, with the help of technology and various apps, to quantify or keep numerical track of these aspects of the self. This increasingly happens in the area of health and fitness; people may keep track of their weight on a regular (sometimes even daily) basis, track calories consumed or expended, and count minutes exercised and miles run. To use technology—often digital technology—to do so can help the individual control the process. By quantifying the effort and results, it becomes more likely that goals will be met. Keeping track of one's health is part of a larger trend toward *biomedicalization*, in which aspects of life previously outside the realm of medicine (such as alcoholism or stress) are considered to be health issues, and individuals are expected to take greater responsibility for them, often by using digital technology to do so (Clarke et al., 2010).

The *quantified self* movement is one in which people apply this practice to all kinds of aspects of their lives. Those interested in documenting or quantifying aspects of their lives and identities track and record data about themselves that they deem critical. This may be done via text, photos, or a computer program, and it can be done with reference to any number of characteristics: one's mood, level of stress, time spent working out, time spent studying, time spent doing any of a number of activities. The data are then interpreted as to what the findings mean for the development of the self.

Individuals can now capture and archive nearly everything about their lives. Lee Rainie and Barry Wellman call this "lifelogging" (2012, pp. 285–287). The internet and digital media have rendered much about modern lives potentially searchable. According to Bell and Gemmell (2009), the self-knowledge that can come from quantification and lifelogging can be extremely useful—even revelatory and life changing. Some share their journey of health management and self-development and join groups with others who do the same. Doing so can provide psychological benefits and social support and can contribute to the overall understanding of how the self might optimally develop. It can even inspire deeper reflection into some of the values that are at stake when one considers living in more quantified fashion—values such as autonomy, solidarity, and authenticity (Sharon, 2017).

On the other hand, as we have seen, any time that data becomes digitized, it can become mined and then hacked and potentially made publicly available. Problems that can follow can range from embarrassment to horizontal surveillance to harassment; jobs or relationships could conceivably be lost if health conditions or activities were outed. The long-term effects of having nearly every moment of one's life recorded—even if self-recorded—are difficult to predict.

It is apparent, though, that the construction of the self has become for many a deliberate and ongoing project. The internet and digital media enable this project in countless fascinating ways. As individuals continue to appropriate these technologies for personal, creative purposes, the self has the potential to become more complex and multifaceted (though still, generally, unified). To move smoothly and successfully among various aspects of the self requires a nimble, flexible mind.

As people create their selves and undergo techno-socialization, they develop connections and bonds and communities. Integrating into groups both large and small is a big part of the process of becoming socialized. In the next chapter, we examine the nature of the relationships and groupings that form in the process of using the internet and digital media. As we do, we will see exactly how superconnected our modern lives have become.

7 FRIENDING, DATING, AND RELATING

interactivity

Humans have a strong need for social connectedness and interaction. It is one of our deepest and strongest desires. Most individuals in high-tech societies are part of social networks that contain, collectively, hundreds of social ties that represent a variety of strengths (from weak to strong) and purposes (from instrumental to expressive; see Chayko, 2002).

A prime use of the internet and digital media is socializing—making new friends, reconnecting with old ones, and spending time with family both physically near and far away. As with physical places, individuals like to invite family, friends, coworkers, and acquaintances to join them in digital spaces. Because it is so easy to feel the presence of others online, it is common to spend time in social interaction with them there.

The internet and digital media thus facilitate and encourage social connectedness. Some social networking sites explicitly help individuals find and associate with one another, and many specialize and excel at this. Like email, texting, and speaking on the phone, these sites create a space for people to get to know one another and to potentially become involved in one another's lives. They also allow friends who know one another offline to stay in touch and maintain their friendships.

People exhibit extraordinary creativity in finding ways to interact and connect online. They develop and join groups of all kinds, from Facebook and Google groups to internet forums and bulletin boards. They invent ways to identify one another and form groups online, such as the hashtag, and invent platforms and apps that constantly reimagine the ways that people can interact.

With mobility, this kind of connectivity can take place almost constantly. Cell phones, tablets, and other mobile/portable media make it easy to reach out to others anytime, anywhere. As we shall see in Chapter 9, this inspires in some a compulsion to do just this. With a phone at one's side—always there, always on—social interaction can be nearly always enabled. It can be difficult to resist the temptation to check for messages, updates, and news.

Some worry that media-enabled communication and relationships will somehow replace or substitute for face-to-face relationships. But research has indicated precisely the opposite. In general, use of the internet tends to prompt—not substitute for—face-to-face interaction. It is very common to use the internet, cell phones, and mobile media to make dates to get together with others. Mobile phones even allow people to make plans on the go and are often used to do so. And along with social media, they are used to support and maintain relationships with faraway others—to keep bonds strong in between physical meetings and make those meetings far more likely (Chayko, 2014). Social interaction is well supported by the internet and digital media.

making digital connections

In internet and digital media use, individuals can easily become more aware of others and detect similarities and common interests, goals, and values. Such similarities and commonalities are critical to the development of social connectedness. Connections are made when people detect dissimilarities as well, but it is particularly easy to detect common interests online.

Both online and offline, people often act in ways that allow them to build what is called *common ground* with one another. People want to understand one another and to be understood; they want to see something of themselves in one another. In the process, they develop a common set of understandings—a common stock of knowledge—and may even feel that they are *like-minded.* This allows them to meaningfully interact and build social worlds together (Clark & Brennan, 1993). In general, the more people believe they are similar to another person, the more they like that person and the more they disclose about themselves. This makes social connections all the more likely to form. Of course, opposites attract as well, but usually there are still some underlying commonalities (Chayko, 2002).

Even if they never meet one another in person, people who meet online can come to feel that they really know one another well. They can feel unified by their common relation to an issue or idea; the like-mindedness that they may perceive to have developed can lead them to believe that they truly understand one another. Because digital social connectedness relies on shared interests and character qualities rather than physical (and perhaps more superficial) qualities, people in online relationships are often happier than their face-to-face counterparts, and their relationships are more durable (McKenna, Green, & Gleason, 2002).

While some find the making of a digital connection a curious way to begin or sustain a relationship, it actually has much in common with the process of developing face-to-face relationships. Both face-to-face and online, people are most likely to form connections when they assume others are similar to them in some way. It feels comforting to believe that friends and acquaintances are like us in basic, relevant ways. In seeking this kind of unity, we create it, and this actually helps launch the relationship.

Because this is a mental process, enabled by technology, it can even happen when one of the individuals involved is not alive. Deceased relatives and friends can be mourned in online spaces as well as in our own hearts, indefinitely. Just by encountering others digitally in stories, photos, or videos, we can come to feel extremely close to them. Even beloved fictional characters from books and movies (and any other mediated cultural offering) can feel very real, and we can feel quite connected to them (Chayko, 2002). In an absolutely authentic way, absent others can populate our worlds and we can feel connected to them.

As deeper connections are formed, it is common practice to project onto individuals the qualities we want them to have or believe that they should have. This is done in both face-to-face and digital relationships. As it turns out, the absence of visual cues can enhance this process of projection and thus encourage the progression of a relationship. Of course, as we will see later in the chapter, sometimes people want to bring a relationship begun in a digital space into physical space and to continue it face-to-face.

Early in a relationship, it is common to want to reduce the uncertainty inherent in being involved in something new and fraught with risk and to try to increase the predictability of the experience. One way to do this is to use the internet and digital media to track other people. Looking up content by and about the other person via Google or social media can accomplish this without seeming overtly intrusive or compromising fragile new relationships (Yang, Brown, & Braun, 2013). Of course, if discovered, this kind of tracking ("spying") can prove detrimental to a relationship. At an extreme, it can be considered "creeping."

As relationships progress, individuals may feel more comfortable sharing information with one another more directly. Younger people in particular may feel that they must follow rather strictly defined expectations as to how and when digital media should be used toward such ends. They may be most comfortable initially contacting newer acquaintances via Facebook or another social network site, allowing them to maintain a measure of distance but remain friendly (Choi, Kim, Sung, & Sohn, 2011; Ellison et al., 2007). Communication can then become a bit more personal, taking place over direct or instant messaging, and then, over time, can proceed to texting and phone calling. Violations of the sequence can undermine the development of relationships (Yang et al., 2013).

Such patterns—often very similar, in fact—are constructed and followed in the process of transacting most relationships. In relationship maintenance, various media are used in combination with one another—texting, telephoning, video chatting, exchanging messages on social media, and so on. The *polymedia* theory of interpersonal communication holds that individuals place great meaning on which media are used to communicate what, and make judgments on how media are being employed in the maintenance of relationships (see Madianou & Miller, 2011). For example, it is generally seen as more appropriate to break up with someone in person than electronically, especially the longer the relationship has been in effect. Media use is both practical and symbolic in modern relationships.

Digital technology, then, has enabled the process of people becoming aware of one another and then becoming and remaining connected to one another. These connections can become intimate, emotionally charged, meaningful, and reciprocal in nature. As we have already noted, communication technology scholar Joseph Walther finds that even without face-to-face interaction, people can become very close. In fact, he contends, strictly online relationships can be hyperpersonal and even more involving than those that develop face-to-face (Walther, 1997)—laden with intimacy, emotionality, and interpersonal attraction.

"chemistry" and synchronicity

Sometimes, two people feel a special attraction and an interpersonal spark, or "chemistry." They may feel a giddy kind of rush when together or thinking about one another. They may feel that they are on the same "wavelength"—somehow in sync with one another's thoughts and feelings. Sociological theorist Alfred Schutz called this the "tuning-in process" (1951), and he calls the feeling of forming a close social bond with another person "we feeling" (1951).

It is very possible to feel this way with others who have been encountered only on the internet and digital media. Indeed, it happens all the time. The internet and digital media use seem to specialize in fostering these kinds of feelings. "The moment [he] entered the [online] channel I was aware that he was different and special," said one woman who explored dating and romance online. She continued: "There is no explaining this" (Baker, 2005, p. 45). Sociologist Andrea Baker studied 89 couples that met online and found digital attractions very much in evidence among them. She determined that "chemistry" easily developed in digital settings and was as important to the development of a relationship online as it is offline.

Portable technology use lends itself to the establishment of digital attraction and online chemistry. Cell phones, tablets, laptops, and other portable devices can be used at odd hours, in odd places, any time of the day or night. Texting or "snapchatting" someone at a party at 2 a.m. is a different experience than doing so in the middle of the day at the office, just as having a personal conversation at a bar at 2 a.m. is a different experience than a midday chat on the street. As people in tech-rich societies now routinely bring portable devices to out-of-the-way places and use them at all hours, playful or flirtatious interactions are a common result, initiating that irresistible "rush of human engagement."

Not necessarily different from the kinds of feelings that can arise in face-to-face attraction, the "rush" that can be felt when people interact online in a particularly enjoyable way is often a by-product of the intensity of their engagement. One of my interviewees described it like this:

> One time I met a guy from Scotland online . . . we talked about anime and manga (Japanese comics translated to manga) and everything under the sun. It was crazy . . . it gave us a connection that we couldn't ever have had otherwise. I felt giddy like I was going on a date or something. It was surreal. (Chayko, 2008, p. 43)

It can be a heady experience, online and offline, to develop a strong attraction to someone else. And Baker confirms this kind of chemistry can "be present from the start" in online relationships (2005, p. 45).

It can also provide a general mood boost to spend time with those whom you like. While they also reported instances of feeling worse after spending time online, especially following hours of fairly sedentary use, my interview subjects overwhelmingly reported feeling happier and their moods enhanced after spending short-to-moderate periods of time online. This is often simply due to the positive effect that friends and family can have on an individual, especially when they might otherwise not be in contact. For example,

> If I'm tired or frustrated at work and a friend sends me a text message about going out somewhere I get excited and the day seems to go by somewhat quicker. It is uplifting

> getting comments or messages from friends who you would normally not get the chance to ever communicate with due to everyone's different lives and busy schedules. . . . It makes you feel like, hey, this person was thinking of me and you feel liked by others and that always puts a smile on my face. Checking my email and getting a funny joke or kind words can always lift my mood. I don't know anyone who during the course of a rough day at work doesn't appreciate a good joke or funny memory sent via text message. Thinking about it, though, I would assume that it can be used in a negative aspect as well, though I have not experienced this. (Chayko, 2008, pp. 56–57)

When people experience this kind of pleasure, neurochemicals like dopamine and norepinephrine flood the brain's pleasure centers. This creates a high that can resemble a drug or sugar high and can make the individual feel excited and alive. When the experience is new and novel, the pleasure can be even more highly charged. It becomes difficult to think rationally and logically; one wants to repeat the experience again and again.

Dopamine, a chemical and neurotransmitter released in the brain that is part of the reward system, fuels many human desires, including the desire to seek out new ideas and people. When these desires are gratified as quickly and easily as can happen in digital and social media settings, individuals can become enmeshed in a dopamine-induced loop in which rewards are readily produced. The brain is then immediately restimulated (perhaps by texts or tweets that are quickly returned or by a fast, immediate response in gaming), and the behavior is propelled forward. It becomes hard to stop. In addition, the unpredictability of when texts or responses will arrive stimulates the brain even more; this is called *variable* (or *intermittent) reinforcement*, and it helps to keep dopamine production high. Dopamine systems don't have satiety built in—our brains do not encourage these behaviors to stop. It becomes easy to crave more, more, more digital stimulation (Berridge & Robinson, 1998; Weinschank, 2012).

When a strongly rewarding behavior is repeated similarly in the brains of people connecting via the internet or other digital media and a social bond is formed in response, changes can actually occur in the brains of both people involved. Their brains become interlinked and then *synchronized*. They think *in tandem* with one another, becoming able to intuit one another's thoughts and feelings:

> Inter-brain neural linkages occur in all types of interpersonal interactions, even those that are fleeting,

> but are especially pronounced when people become very close. When this happens, people's thoughts and actions can become synchronized. This can take the form of our unconsciously mimicking of another's facial expressions and movements or of synchronizing our speech patterns to theirs. Online, a kind of textual synchronicity can develop whereby people gravitate toward a similar syntax. In human connectedness, as with many other social and natural phenomena, we constantly adjust and entrain to one another's rhythms and patterns, often in tacit, if unconscious, ways. This helps us to be brought experientially, if not physically, "together," and become firmly "linked" even if we are rarely, or never, physically copresent to one another. (Chayko, 2008, p. 28)

Our brains, our behaviors, and even inevitably our bodies can become literally reshaped as we form a close connection, whether online or offline. And all this can occur not only in pairs but in groups of people as well.

The phenomenon of temporal symmetry helps explain how this can happen even when people are not in physical contact. As sociologist Eviatar Zerubavel has explained (1981), when spatially separated people focus on the same things at the same time, their actions and thoughts become coordinated. This creates moments of bonding and togetherness. Perhaps the quintessential example of this is the impulse to celebrate the arrival of a new year by watching the ball drop, whether on television or in person. When this happens, people feel a unity in knowing that many others are doing the same thing at the same moment, and they feel socially connected, often quite strongly. Temporal symmetry can arise through the viewing of live events via television or internet livestream, listening to radio programs or concerts, celebrating holidays on the same days in much the same ways, posting and responding synchronously to one another online, and taking part in liveblogging, live Twitter chats, and group text messaging (see also Park & Sundar, 2015, on mobile tech-enabled synchrony).

Such behaviors, often facilitated by the internet and digital media, serve to synchronize people's internal rhythms. They allow stimuli to be similarly experienced and provide physically separated people with the means to go through an experience together. They also generate feelings of interpersonal similarity and deeper social bonds (Kaptein, Castaneda, Fernandez, & Nass, 2014). Temporally coordinated activities allow people to feel that they have been with or have met people even when the connection was not face-to-face. This creates a sense of "cognitive cohesion" (Cerulo, 1995, p. 13).

The closest and most intimate of relationships are created in these ways, both online and offline. The process of becoming so close that people's actions and brains are actually synchronized is the same process whether it is initiated through digital technology or face-to-face. At some point, many people who become close online want to meet offline to continue their relationship in person. Others do not, yet they still feel that they have become not only connected but also superconnected.

friendship—online and offline

Friendships develop and are maintained when people discover that they have things in common that matter to them. Relationships build just as much in the accumulation of small, everyday moments of connection as they do in grand gestures and experiences. Communication is a big part of the growth of a friendship, as people get to know one another through disclosing and exchanging their thoughts and feelings. By enabling interpersonal interaction and communication on a regular, frequent basis, the internet and digital media tend to facilitate friendships with great ease.

It is common practice for those who text and use social media to provide brief updates online and to view those of others. This reinforces and deepens their feelings of connectedness to one another. As we have seen, anonymity and invisibility can enhance feelings of connectedness and intimacy as well. Individuals can now share feelings and exchange information, even with a large number of others, on a nearly moment-to-moment basis. They can remain in touch with faraway friends and family members and reconnect more easily with friends from their past.

Though online and offline friendships are not qualitatively the same and the term *friend* does not necessarily mean the same thing in both domains, there are certainly similarities. Behaviors and attitudes generally considered critical to maintaining the bonds of friendship—self-disclosure, supportiveness, positive social interactions—take place and are important both online and offline. Many people do not hesitate to call those with whom they have become close in online and mobile communities their friends; in fact, the term *friend* has been recast as a verb to denote the practice of relating online.

Online friendship, like that which develops face-to-face, can be quite strategic in its formation and execution, albeit in different ways. danah boyd has noted that people friend others online for reasons that may include gaining access to one another's content, initiating reciprocation, looking popular, indicating one's identity and interests, and sometimes, simply, because it's easier to say yes when asked to accept a friend rather than no (2006; see also Boesel, 2012). Some grant friend status to build networks. Friending in this way may or may not lead to closer ties and friendships. Online and offline, there is no precise formula for the building of a friendship.

Relationships that exist solely online are an example of what Anthony Giddens calls *pure relationships*—bonds characterized less by traditional forms of commitment and more by the quest for personal satisfaction. Pure relationships, he states, can be deeply intimate and "above all a matter of emotional communication" (Giddens, 1992, p. 130). Friendships that develop online can become strong, bidirectional, and multidimensional. And they generally reinforce, rather than substitute for, face-to-face friendships.

A large body of research now indicates that the more people use the internet and digital media, the more social contact they have with their existing friends (Boase, Horrigan, Wellman, & Rainie, 2006; Hampton et al., 2011; Rainie & Wellman, 2012; Shklovski, Kraut, & Rainie, 2004; Wang & Wellman, 2010). Email, social media, and mobile phones provide easy, convenient, cost-effective means for people to remain in contact and to arrange dates to get together physically (Boase et al., 2006; Boase & Wellman, 2006; Rainie & Wellman, 2012). Internet users' social networks tend to be more diverse than those of non-internet users, allowing them to remain in contact with multiple social circles. Users of social media sites tend to have more close relationships than nonusers, with Facebook users in particular (and especially frequent Facebook users) more likely to have close connections and core confidants than those who do not use the site (Boase & Wellman, 2006; Hampton et al., 2011; Hampton et al., 2012; Rainie & Wellman, 2012; Wang & Wellman, 2010). Such relationships are generally sustained through a combination of online and offline interactions that can complement each other and even occur simultaneously (Hampton & Wellman, 2003; Polson, 2013; Rainie & Wellman, 2012).

People most often select their online friends from their face-to-face social circles (see boyd, 2014). Internet users tend to stay in better touch with their neighbors than non-internet users and to form more local ties (Boase et al., 2006; Hampton, 2007; Hampton et al., 2011; Hampton & Wellman, 2003; Lee & Lee, 2010; Wang & Wellman, 2010). People who use social network sites to learn more about people they know offline often feel more a part of their offline communities (Ellison et al., 2009) and are more likely to bring those whom they know face-to-face onto their online social networking sites (Ellison et al., 2007; Ofcom, 2008).

Long-distance friends and family also use social media and text messaging to stay in touch. This makes it more likely that they will remain socially tied over time and get together face-to-face in the future (Baym, Zhang, & Lin, 2004; Boase et al., 2006; Hampton et al., 2011; Rainie & Wellman, 2012). Additionally, connecting online permits a community to persist when its members can no longer meet in physical space or when the community no longer exists geographically (Haythornthwaite & Kendall, 2010; Lev-On, 2010; Shklovski, Burke, Kiesler, & Kraut, 2010).

Some relationships remain only online. Either their circumstances do not permit face-to-face meetings or the participants prefer to retain the element of distance in the relationship. People tend to bring online relationships into physical space when there is a strong reason to do so, such as a romantic or cultural connection (see Baker, 2005; Bastani, 2000; Kendall, 2002). While these *migratory friendships*, as Hua Wang and Barry Wellman call them, are less common than relationships that begin and remain online, once they "take" they are generally quite hardy and likely to survive, perhaps because it has become a norm to share intimacies and social support online (2010, p. 1157).[1]

It is now easy for networked individuals to move from one friend or friendship circle to another. They "switch fluidly from network to network, using their communication media to contact the social network needed for each moment" (Rheingold, 2002, p. 195). Those who establish multiple social ties and networks online make and juggle many social connections at once. Depending on how individuals define the word, some of these ties are certainly considered *friendships*.

With almost limitless opportunities for modern individuals to become connected, responsibility is placed on the shoulders of the individual—the "portal" for all this connectivity—to manage and coordinate these networks. This can involve considerable labor, such as posting updates, reading friends' posts, or indicating that you like or favorite their contributions, lest hurt feelings result (see Boesel, 2012). Online or offline, friendship is indeed a responsibility and requires effort and work (see Boesel, 2012; Rainie & Wellman, 2012).

Modern individuals must manage a great number of social ties and communities, both face-to-face and digital. As relationships both strong and weak continue to be made and maintained online, the traffic along digital social networks will only increase. While this introduces new complexities to the process of becoming and remaining a friend, it also brings new opportunities to find romance and love.

flirting, dating, romance, and sex

Relationships often take on a flirtatious, even romantic, quality in digital spaces. As we have seen, individuals may feel a bit more relaxed, open, and uninhibited online, where they can edit aspects of the self so as to appear exactly as they'd like. There is ambiguity in the use of text and even photos and videos; they invite and require interpretation—one needs to engage with them to find meaning in them. Because they are less about physical appearance or performance and can use fantasy rather easily, connections made online can easily become exciting, playful, and flirtatious. Digital tech users can probe shared interests and construct images of a shared romantic future ("imagined togetherness") tenuously and implicitly, thus "nourishing the excitement of romantic possibility" while postponing the disappointment and rejection that could ensue during face-to-face encounters (Mortensen, 2017).

The "rush" that can accompany online engagement in any form is of course evident when sex and romance are in the offing. People use their mobile phones to make connections at all times of the day and night and in all kinds of places, initiating the kind of giddy feelings that can arise when people connect in out-of-the-way places at odd times or get to know one another in any kind of close, personal way. As we have seen, anonymity and "darkness" can enhance this rush as well, as can the playfulness we often see online. As is true of the early stages of romantic and sexual behavior in any setting, this novelty, this playful uncertainty, can serve as an enhancement rather than a deterrent to the development of romantic and/or sexual relationships.

Sites explicitly designed to bring together people looking for dates, sex, or other kinds of romantic entanglements proliferate online. At least three of four internet users who are single and actively looking for a romantic partner have engaged in at least one romantically flavored activity online, such as searching for information about prospective dates and local singles scenes; flirting via email, text, or instant messaging; or visiting dating sites. Whether these dating sites are more or less successful than face-to-face meetings in helping people make successful matches is inconclusive (Madden & Lenhart, 2006; Smith & Duggan, 2013).

Approximately 15% of all internet users have visited dating websites, and a majority of them say they have had positive experiences. In addition, 41% of Americans know someone who has used online dating, and almost one third know someone who has met a long-term partner or spouse via online dating (Smith, 2016). About two thirds of those who visit dating websites have gone on a date with someone they have met there, and fully one fourth have entered long-term relationships or married someone they met online. People also commonly use social network sites such as Facebook to meet up and document romantic moments, trading messages and posting photos of themselves with those with whom they are romantically involved. Many people use the internet to flirt, research potential partners, and check up on old flames. About one fourth of internet users report taking part in such activities (Smith & Duggan, 2013).

After they have checked one another out online and perhaps had some direct contact, many who make an initial romantic connection digitally move their relationship offline (see Baker, 2005; ScienceDaily.com, 2005). As I have written,

> it turns out that these relationships may have a *better* chance of working out than when the couple has first met by more conventional means. This is because the often quite personal revelations that have been shared and understandings that have been reached online give the relationship a kind of "head start." Without external distractions, couples can share information and evaluate their compatibility in a more leisurely and perhaps thoughtful manner. In addition, those who take time getting to know one another online before they meet face-to-face tend to have more successful relationships than those who do not. Internet-initiated relationships, once taken offline, are more likely to survive than those initiated face to face. (Chayko, 2008, p. 99)

Sociologist Andrea Baker found that all the online couples she studied decided to continue their relationships offline after beginning their romances on the internet. She found that, on the whole, couples that had communicated over a longer period of time before they met face-to-face formed deeper and more permanent bonds than those whose communication did not last as long. Just as in face-to-face romances, moving slowly in online relationships and prolonging their initial stages improves their chances of success (Chayko, 2008, p. 99).

Sexual activity that involves the internet and digital media is ever-increasing (see Baker, 2005; Cooper, McLoughlin, & Campbell, 2000; Thurlow, Lengel, & Tomic, 2004; Whitty, 2005). Pornography is more widely available online than ever; by some estimates, 75% of American men and 40% of women download and view pornography (Albright, 2008). Sexual behavior online can take the form of sexually oriented conversations, phone sex, or cybersex—the exchange of erotic messages or fantasies while using a computerized device.

Sexting—the taking or sending of sexually explicit or suggestive photos or messages via texting or some other form of digital media—has increased in recent years, though it is by no means the practice of most adults (Lenhart & Duggan, 2014). Teens (aged 12–17) and adults (aged 18–29) alike who are involved with sexting are more likely to engage in sexual activity and to have unprotected sex than those who do not. This finding does not suggest that sexting leads to such behavior; it can certainly be the case that those who are sexually active and have unprotected sex are more likely to send and receive "sexts" than their nonsexting counterparts (Kosenko, Luurs, & Binder, 2017).

Cyber infidelity of partners and spouses is on the increase as well, especially if one considers the spectrum of ways in which people can be less than completely honest with one another in sexually oriented situations and the variety of ways that infidelity can be conceptualized, online and offline (see Boon, Watkins, & Sciban, 2014). Unsurprisingly, research indicates that people who are less satisfied in their current relationships, have more attachment anxiety, and are more ambivalent generally are more likely to engage in infidelity-related behaviors online (Aviram & Amichai-Hamburger, 2005; Ben-Ze'ev, 2004; McDaniel, Drouin, & Cravens, 2017; Whitty, 2005). To experience infidelity in a relationship in a digital space can bring about the same emotions and the same intensity as similar offline behaviors (Gabriels, Poels, & Braeckman, 2013). This can be attributed to the intimate, emotional, involving, and sometimes anonymous and escapist nature of the online experience.

In addition, some use digital technologies to do *sex work*—serving as models, dancers, actors, and participants in adult films or other sex-oriented professional settings. Relatively inexpensive access to media and technology has enhanced the ability of people to make money in this way. Increasingly, sex workers include people who are relatively class-privileged; while they may need the work, they may also be attracted to the interpersonal connections that can be made and may find these connections authentic and meaningful (Bernstein, 2007). Still, there is a social stigma attached to sex work, and a price may be paid in terms of social status, health, harassment, and violence (Ditmore, Levy, & Willman, 2010).

Because what happens online is real—and real in its consequences—flirtatious, romantic, and sexually oriented online behaviors can have just as much meaning and impact as they have in face-to-face settings. And they can be just as highly ambiguous and confusing, if not more so. Online or offline, it is not always clear whether a message is flirtatious, romantic, sexual, or none of these. We live in a time of rapidly changing norms, including romantic and sexual norms. It remains to be seen whether we will develop more flexible societal views and understandings to accompany these changing circumstances or whether we will, as members of groups and societies, continue to penalize and shame those whose behaviors do not fit established norms (see Ben-Ze'ev, 2004; Boon et al., 2014; Whitty, 2005).

trust and social support

It is sometimes seen as surprising that people are as supportive and trusting of one another as they are online. But social support is quite often established in digital spaces, both when people have been in contact over a period of time and even among relative strangers who have just "met" (Ellison et al., 2007, 2011; McCosker & Darcy, 2013; Parks, 2011; Sproull et al., 2005). The online experience lends itself so well to sharing, interacting, and even catharsis that people can find themselves sharing very real needs (information, interpersonal contacts, even money!) and becoming close in a variety of ways.

Some wonder why people spend time, effort, and their own personal funds helping people whom they have never met face-to-face. First, it should be recalled that people met online *really are met*—our brains do not make a distinction between different types of "knowing" others, and we can care about people we meet in any context. Also, it can be gratifying to be seen and known as someone who knows things and helps others. It can raise one's status in a group or community. It can make it more likely that the helper may be helped someday in return. But finally, and most fundamentally, people often assist one another simply because they want to. It is a very human impulse to care about and aid others—to be altruistic—and the internet and digital media provide many opportunities for this impulse to be expressed.

A culture of giving and receiving support and indeed of altruism often develops on sites, blogs, message boards, and electronic mailing lists oriented toward problem solving, especially with regard to medical or other serious issues. Such groups proliferate on the internet. People who need help or answers when in a new or dire situation often turn to the internet for information or resources. A variety of groups have sprung up to address these needs, providing support, companionship, information, and resources. They can truly help people survive, as one of the people I interviewed explained:

> This listserv has been a lifeline to me, especially when I was first diagnosed and could not rely on the few minutes I had with my doctors to help educate me on what my disease was and what I might expect . . . . Until you learn the new language, it is disconcerting to be facing a disease and not know how to communicate effectively. It is like

> being dropped into a new country and told your life will depend on how quickly you learn to communicate in this new language—it is a life altering experience. (Chayko, 2008, p. 53)

In groups with this kind of goal—but really, in all kinds of communities online—people report being especially empowered, supported, and embraced (see McCosker & Darcy, 2013).

Time and space to talk and be listened to, any time of the day or night, can of course be valuable. But an abundance of such sharing can induce feelings of stress. It can be difficult and emotionally overwhelming to hear story upon story of hardship and suffering. It can be a source of stress to be the one in charge of caring for others and to see evidence of such difficulties on digital and social media. It is best to step back from all of this from time to time. But participation in such groups can also help alleviate stress, particularly for women who are tasked with caregiving (see Hampton, Rainie, Lu, Shin, & Purcell, 2015).

In an environment in which much is shared, members of such groups can become tremendously close. They can come to trust one another greatly. This, too, sometimes seems strange, given that they may not have met face-to-face (though it is not uncommon for such groups to begin to host meet-ups and for members to form offline friendships). And certainly, some participants do not become close or trust one another. But in the modern technological world it is rather common to develop trust in people who are not personally known—members of financial, government, medical, and military organizations, or producers of products we use, for example.

Society "would be imperiled were individuals unwilling to trust the legions of physically absent others on whom they are dependent," report Gross and Simmons (2002, p. 533), paraphrasing Giddens (1994, pp. 89–90). We tend to trust institutions like hospitals, schools, and banks as a matter of course. Of course, not everyone should be trusted, online or offline. But trust and social support are commonly and rather freely given and exchanged in modern society, including in online spaces, and personal relationships and friendships can become deepened as a result (see Castells et al., 2004; Chayko, 2008; Geser, 2004; Sproull et al., 2005; Suler, 2004; Turow & Hennessy, 2007).

interpersonal conflicts and harassment

Members of online communities centered on strong mutual interests tend to work quite hard to keep their groups robust and cohesive. Group members who have developed a strong sense of community and identity generally want to protect their communities when conflicts and problems arise. Groups that are not so cohesive can splinter or dissolve much more easily.

There are many ways that online communities, and the relationships that they inspire, can be threatened. Simple disagreements can escalate with ill-chosen words or when expected responses are late or do not arrive. Negative and harsh comments ("flames") can discourage civil, enjoyable, productive interaction. "Trolls," usually outsiders to a group, can derail conversations and upset participants by persistently changing the subject, taking the group off track, and introducing unpleasantness. More serious disruptions can come in the form of harassment, stalking, hacking, spam, viruses, and so on.

Harassment—from trolling and name-calling to stalking and threats—is all too prevalent online and is becoming a major impediment to digital tech use for many, especially women and members of marginalized populations. Roughly four in 10 Americans have experienced online harassment, and 62% have observed it (Duggan, 2017). Additionally, those whose lives are more fully entwined with the internet, have lots of information about them available online, promote themselves online, or work in the digital tech industry experience higher rates of digital harassment than those who are relatively less engaged online.

Nearly one in five Americans has experienced severe forms of harassment online, including physical threats and stalking. Personal or physical features are often targeted, with politics, personal appearance, race or ethnicity, and gender the most common characteristics about which people are harassed. The consequences can be serious and painful, ranging from mental and emotional stress to reputational damage to fear for one's safety or life (Duggan, 2017).

Digital technology—particularly texting and email—is used to harass and intimidate in the overwhelming majority of domestic violence cases (89% by one estimate; Chemaly, 2014). One of my interview subjects found that she and her ex-boyfriend seemed to behave more cruelly to one another online, though she did not characterize this as harassment. Another told me this:

> Writing things online . . . is the new easy way for girls to be mean to each other without having to say things face-to-face. (Chayko, 2008, p. 187)

Contributing factors include lack of face-to-face accountability in digital spaces; the ease with which coarse, cruel comments can be, and so often are, shared online; and disinhibition in online spaces that is so often associated with anonymity. People who troll and bully others online tend to have low self-esteem, conscientiousness, and "agreeability," with internal moral values that have been compromised or with which they are not in touch (Zezulka & Seigfried-Spellar, 2016). Harassment can take place in nearly any online (or offline) environment, but it is increasingly seen on social media, in comments sections on online postings, and in gaming spaces.

Of those who have been harassed online, 45% say that this harassment has been severe, consisting of stalking, sexual harassment, and sustained harassment over a long period of time. Men are more likely to experience name-calling, while young women are more vulnerable to sexual harassment and stalking, which can take a serious emotional and physical toll. It is not uncommon for women who express opinions online to be harassed and threatened—to receive rape and death threats. Young people in general also report higher rates of physical threats and sustained harassment than does the general population.

About half of all people who are harassed online say that they find it only a little or not at all bothersome (of course, this may simply be what they say). But those who experience more serious harassment are quite likely to find it so upsetting as to disrupt their lives. A significant minority (27%), who are more likely to be women, find it extremely or very upsetting to be harassed online. Online gaming sites are seen by internet users as substantially more welcoming to men than to women, while dating sites are seen as much more welcoming to women (Duggan, 2014).

Members of online groups and communities seem to be most supportive of one another when they are strongly connected to one another and motivated to protect their boundaries. These individuals may carefully moderate comments, for example. They may call out those who engage in flaming and trolling and have them blocked from participation. Handling and policing conflict is an important element of digital group organization (Baym, 2010; Chayko, 2008). The flip side of this, however, is that in protecting the group's boundaries, newcomers or outsiders may be trolled or harassed. Negative behaviors can in some cases be counteracted with a strong commitment to positive behavior by existing members of the group (Baym, 2000, 2010; Lee, 2005; Sproull et al., 2005).

Sometimes, though, harassment cannot be counteracted internally with any measure of success. When serious, ongoing threats to safety occur online, there might not be a clear path for reporting such crimes and finding appropriate resolution or prosecution. Laws that might provide protection tend to be unclear and outdated—the Telecommunications Act of 1996 does not hold website administrators responsible for content posted by users, though some evidence suggests that the algorithms and governance of Reddit implicitly rewards misogynism and a "toxic culture" (Massanari, 2017), and Twitter and Facebook have begun investigating and addressing reports of inappropriate behavior on their sites (Duggan, 2014). Many feel that the social media platforms on which harassment occurs should and must do more to hold abusers accountable.

Harassers and abusers tend to operate anonymously or under pseudonyms, while their victims (often women) often appear online under their own names, in the context of their professional and personal lives. Threats may come from a variety of different sources, rather than from a single organization that could be targeted or sued. Policing these behaviors is therefore very difficult and complex. Additionally, the costs are significant—for individuals, law enforcement agencies, and society—and are both financial and emotional (Chemaly, 2014; Duggan, 2014; Hess, 2014).

At the local level, overburdened police forces may not have the resources to investigate online threats and may not see them as local or "real" threats. Amendments to the Violence Against Women Act of 1994 have updated it to apply to new technologies, and 24 states have cyberstalking laws on the books. Still, law enforcement agencies are often ill equipped to handle such cases. County, state, or federal agencies can usually offer more support, but due to their limited resources and the ephemerality of internet postings and anonymity of internet identities, the help they offer is still inconsistent at best. Interacting with other people is a complicated proposition.

Just as people can form close, meaningful, supportive friendships and relationships, they can also experience interpersonal conflicts and harassment that can be personally and collectively destructive. All the risks of human interaction and communality exist online as well, plus a few more that its digital and sometimes anonymous nature inspires. People do not have the same accountability to one another when they are not face-to-face. They can hide online; they can do stupid and dangerous things; they can be moved to frustration and anger; they can seek attention and do harm.

The technology itself need not be blamed for these conflicts, however. As noted earlier, many of the same problems that people face online—like harassment or cruelty—exist in offline spaces as well. But as these problems are discussed publicly, they are sometimes amplified, with technology receiving the blame. This is another example of technological determinism, and it is not the only (nor perhaps the wisest) way to approach the issue of online conflict.

Relationships transacted in digital spaces will necessarily face certain problems, just as any and all relationships do. In addition, special challenges and opportunities exist in the digital realm. Digital relationships lack the full range of information that can be shared and conveyed in face-to-face interaction—body language, subtle gestures and glances, touch, and smell. Diminished accountability and sensory information can exacerbate problems, it is true, but it can also alleviate them (as when a shy person finds himself or herself with more confidence to speak and connect online). Overall, people still do report more positive than negative uses of the internet and digital media (Chayko, 2008). But we have a long way to go to successfully address internet and digital harassment, threats, and harm.

the life span of digital relationships

When relationships have an online component, they are not necessarily bound by some of the limitations inherent in the physical world. Space, as we have seen, can be easily transcended as people gain the means to know of and then become close to people whom they may have never met and may never meet face-to-face. Just as distance no longer prohibits relationships from forming, so too can time be transcended in digital spaces.

Social connections and relationships often outlast and outlive the physical. In hearing stories of people who lived before us (such as ancestors or historical figures), we can feel a connection to them. Photos and videos can help deepen such bonds in some cases. Many of the people I have interviewed told me of connections with long-deceased family members established in exactly this way:

> My grandfather. I didn't know him. And I do feel connected to him. And I wanted to meet him and share with him the grandfather-granddaughter thing. I heard stories. But he died before I was born. (Chayko, 2002, p. 11)

And, this from another interviewee:

> My great-grandmother—there's a giant picture of her in my mom's house. Everyone's always telling me we look alike and that I've got some of her traits. . . . I've heard a lot of stories about her. And yeah, I feel connected to her. (Chayko, 2002, p. 85)

Storytelling on blogs and social media can easily expand and intensify the facilitation of these kinds of spatial *and* temporal connections.

If they are depicted via video, audio, and photos, individuals can remain visually and cognitively present even after they are physically gone. Digital technologies can increase this sense of presence in unique ways. Holograms provide the illusion of movement through space. Through digital editing, musical duets have been sung with people who have passed away. Images can be spliced into an existing photo, video, or movie to make it seem as though people are physically together when they may have been separated by many years. While intellectually it may be understood that someone who has been digitally depicted is no longer alive, the experience can be genuine and resonant and deepen and enhance bonding. The same processes that help us feel connected to people who live many miles away, then, can help us feel connected to the deceased.

The dead also "persist and continue to participate as social actors through the platforms and protocols of social networking sites," as computing and information systems professor Martin Gibbs and his coauthors maintain (Gibbs, Meese, Arnold, Nansen, & Carter, 2015, p. 255; see also Marwick & Ellison, 2012; Stokes, 2012). While individuals were once relegated to funeral parlors and gravesites after their deaths, social media and digital technologies have helped to reposition death as a more visible, even social, event. Internet and social media platforms enable user profiles to be reworked to form ongoing memorials and to gather publics together as mourners around them (Berlant, 2008). Blogs and websites are set up as repositories of photos and testimonials. Funeral homes have created online spaces for memories to be shared.

As the profiles and aspects of the selves of the dead do not remain static, in a sense, the self is not dead but rather continues "to evolve though the participatory construction of memories, bereavement, and remembrance. . . . Memorial pages persist and scale through articulated networks in ways that allow for distributed and collective representations of the dead to be constructed, necessitating curation" (Gibbs et al., 2015; see also Lingel, 2013; Marwick & Ellison, 2012). Those that remain to grieve the dead increasingly view "death, dying, mourning, grieving, and even mortality itself as a hybrid between the physical and the digital" (Moreman & Lewis, 2014, p. 2). Socially and mentally—sociomentally—in many ways the dead have "some life."

Those who have died are not only remembered and spoken *of* but often spoken *to* on social media, demonstrating the desire to keep the memory of the deceased alive and even the desire to remain in some kind of contact with him or her. Social media sometimes seems to have a kind of "airborne" quality that may encourage the feeling that the deceased can be somehow reached across time and space. Though this is obviously a purely emotional response, it can still provide comfort in a very difficult and transitional time. As one of my interviewees related,

> I witnessed and participated in my first electronic memorial service. People gave loving testimonial after testimonial about how this dear woman had helped them in their time of need, how she touched their lives, how much they would miss her and glad they were that her suffering was over . . . in spite of the fact that they had never met her! I will never forget the impact that memorial service had on me. As I read the messages on the screen I literally cried. (Chayko, 2008, pp. 34–35)

As such a testimony indicates, even those who have never met face-to-face can be grieved for, and this grief can be expressed via digital technology.

The deceased can be digitally reimagined as an audience with whom one can "interact." Messages may be directed to those who have passed away, sometimes on memorial sites that persist for many years, even indefinitely. Photos and videos of the deceased may be widely shared and spread. Those who may be unwelcome can intrude on the open online memorial; different audiences or contexts can also come into contact, initiating context collapse even after death (Marwick & Ellison, 2012). Social media, then, can provide a kind of channel by which the dead can remain in physical space and where it can feel as if we are encountering them and experiencing a type of interaction with them.

In all these ways and many more to come, what it means to be present to one another and interacting with each other is changing. Truly, the human life span has in effect become digitally expanded. We can see the flexibility, the malleability, of many aspects of social life as they become digitally enhanced and augmented. In order to understand these changes and their implications for our lives, it is best to remain mentally flexible—open to new ideas and how they enhance current understandings.

At the same time, we must remain *conceptually* flexible as we examine the way that large-scale social institutions, such as the family, the workplace, and the media, are changing in the digital era. In the next chapter, we look at what I call the *techno-social institutions* to see how at the macro level societies are changing—and inspiring changes in their members.

Note

1. Portions excerpted from Chayko (2014).

8

THE TECHNO-SOCIAL INSTITUTIONS

the institutional "heart": the family

We say that something is an *institution* when it is foundational, functional, long-lasting, large in scale, and systemic—when it has been around a long time and it seems like it may always be. *Social institutions* provide a society with structure and order and give its members a framework within which to build their social connections and communities. They are so critical to helping a society (and its members) function that all societies contain some social institutions—mostly, the very same ones that we examine in this chapter.

For eons, some of the most critical social institutions have included the family, business and the workplace, health care, religion, education, politics and governing, the criminal justice system, and the media. Each of these has been strongly influenced by technological developments over time, with the internet and digital media in particular playing a very strong role in this. These newer technologies must be integrated within each institution, while older strategies remain important for the accomplishment of goals (Zickuhr, Purcell, & Rainie, 2014). For this reason, this book refers to these critical institutions as the *techno-social institutions.*

It makes little sense to study social institutions in isolation from one another. To understand how our families operate, for example, we must understand how their members work, are educated, practice their religions and politics, and so on. We must consider the effects of a society's systems of criminal justice, health care, media, and government on its members, and we must consider the effects of the activities in each social institution on one another. The study of all of these systems, all the social institutions, makes the most sense as a concerted whole (Durkheim, 1893/1964).

It is also important to look at how the members of a society construct the social institutions and endow them with meaning and, for our purposes, how technology is employed to do so. For it is in the day-to-day behaviors of individuals making decisions as to how they will act and exercising their agency (individuals are therefore sometimes called *social actors* in this context) that a larger system is gradually built that can then help shape future behaviors of the people within that system. Individuals actually create and build the institutions of society through thousands and millions of everyday acts, large and small. (It is important to note that we cannot grant to institutions the power to act on their own; it is *people* who act.) At the same time, the institutions have a powerful influence on those who exist within them and the decisions those individuals make to act as they do. It's an endless circle—a loop—of structure and agency, representing the way that the macro and micro levels of a society influence and indeed create one another (for a vibrant description of the relationship between structure and agency, see Erdmans, 2004).

I always recommend that when we analyze social institutions, we start with the family because the family is at the center, at the heart, of any strong, functioning society. It is the most intimate of the institutions because it is the first place where most people learn about love and life. It is, in fact, a microcosm of society. As we have seen, the family is a primary group, an agent of socialization that inspires and encourages the development of self and identity over the course of a lifetime. And more than in any other institution, we can see in the family how the micro-level life of the individual and the macro-level life of the social system influence and indeed construct one another.

The internet and digital media are part of the everyday life of families in technologically developed societies. They help keep families connected in much the same way as they help individuals and communities remain connected because a family is really a small (and in some cases, a large!) community. At the same time, technology has changed the dynamics and dimensions of family life. The higher the levels of education and income, the more likely it is that a family will use the internet at home and that it will be central to their lives (Rainie & Wellman, 2012; Wellman, Smith, Wells, & Kennedy, 2008).

In tech-rich societies, many families invest in multiple ICTs that can be found in nearly every room of the house. In addition to computers (desktop and laptop), tablets, and cell phones or smartphones, homes may contain multiple televisions, digital cable boxes, gaming consoles, video recorders, and DVD or Blu-Ray players. Television watching is a very different experience today than it was even in the early 2000s. Individuals can now select from a wide variety of more narrowly conceived programs that they can view in different ways on their own schedules (traditional TV, streamed video via Netflix or YouTube, cable or satellite programs "on demand" via TiVo or DVR), with social media at the ready so that one can interact with other viewers while watching. This is, again, networked individualism in action, as family members use these technologies to remain connected with one another (Rainie & Wellman, 2012, p. 159).

Even in societies in which tech use is common, though, families are not equally "wired." Some families operate under the constraints of limited internet connectivity and mobile data plans. In these families, members may bargain over time spent on the internet. While youths from highly wired families enjoy individualized net time, members of partially wired families divide up household internet time carefully. Families are expected to make sacrifices in order for their children to obtain internet access, as children are increasingly expected to use the internet for homework and for such social capital–building activities as forming social networks and researching and applying to colleges. The presence or absence of the internet in the home can therefore have far-reaching effects on a person's ability to progress in society and remain connected and networked (Robinson & Schulz, 2013).

Members of families also use the internet and digital media to stay in contact with one another and with their extended families. People, usually women, often use social media, usually Facebook, to perform this kin-keeping function. A kind of purposive leisure has developed in which, through chatting, photo sharing, and game playing, members of extended families can enjoy one another's company as they remain in contact (see Boudreau & Consalvo, 2014). While this kind of kin keeping has traditionally been the responsibility of a female caregiver, in about two thirds of American families who use digital technology to accomplish such tasks, the heads of the household (when there are two of them) share the work (though not necessarily equally). They divide up contacts and stay in touch with those contacts by texting or phone calling. Similarly, they generally share the work of staying in touch with children via phone and expect frequent check-ins from children (Rainie & Wellman, 2012).

Social media and texting play important roles in maintaining communication and connectedness among family members near and far, and webcams and email are especially helpful in providing a sense of copresence for spatially separated family members. As children grow older, parents are more likely to use ICTs to communicate with them, and parents are most likely to text with one another when their children are of school age (Rudi, Dworken, Walker, & Doty, 2015). Families also use digital tech together. Just as they may watch TV together, they go on the internet together or spend time talking about digitally generated entertainment or other content (Madianou & Miller, 2011; Rainie & Wellman, 2012; Wellman et al., 2008). And when they vacation together, families use smartphones to document the experience, enhancing the sense of family unity, while also providing opportunities for members to retain their sense of individuality (Yu, Anaya, Miao, Lehto, & Wong, 2017).

Children, using computers and cell phones at ever-younger ages, often teach their parents and caregivers how to use them. This does not necessarily mean that their use of technology is sophisticated or thoughtful (see boyd, 2014). But children who have grown up with digital technology may be particularly comfortable having technology folded into their lives and used in family settings. Older family members who can remember a different way of life may have a harder time with the pervasive, near-constant use and effects of digital technology. Some say that they find the technology "cold" and refuse to use it on that basis; for others, the learning curve to adopt and remain skilled on digital technology is an impediment. In general, those older people who are already strongly connected socially are most likely to adapt and benefit from online digital technology (Luders & Bae Brandtzaeg, 2017; Luders & Gjevjon, 2017).

Children often receive their first phones from caregivers seeking to keep them safe in the event of emergencies. There was a huge spike in cell phones given to children in the United States after the terrorist attacks of September 11, 2001, an event that struck fear in the hearts of many who were (or still are) afraid of another attack or a forced separation from their children. To be better equipped during an emergency is often cited as a reason children are given their first phones (and why many adults purchase theirs as well). In a bit of sad (for children, anyway) irony, while mobile phones may provide the means for children to move about more freely in their parents' absence, they are also the means by which parents check up on them. These obligatory check-ins tend to occur more frequently than they did in the predigital era, so in essence, many children have become more tethered to their parents than ever before (Turkle, 2012).

Many caregivers also do not want their children to be on the wrong side of a perceived digital divide. Owning a cell phone can be an indicator of status, wealth, or power. Children may be concerned with being left out of group texts and activities coordinated and facilitated by phone. They want to be included in games their friends play and content options that their friends are exposed to. Their impulse to be part of the group and to fit in is sometimes misunderstood by parents, who concentrate more on potentially negative impacts of the phone and less on the more positive role it plays in childhood sociality.

Still, many parents help their children go online at relatively early ages. The vast majority of parents assist their children in accessing or signing up for social media sites like Facebook before they are old enough to do so on their own (boyd, Hargittai, Schultz, & Palfrey, 2011). However, many parents spend time on social media sites like Facebook with their children. In 2011, 80% of parents who were social media users and had children who were social media users friended their child on at least one site, and about half of these parents commented on or interacted with their child directly on the site. This can prompt discussion of things seen on the internet and on the site, including behaviors a parent finds problematic, while it furthers the development of social connections inside and outside the extended family.

Many parents worry about keeping their children safe online. They also worry about overuse of and dependency on the technology. They may seek and receive expert advice for controlling the use of technology (such as keeping computers out of the bedroom or using filtering software) and may even implement some of these strategies. Parents often feel more comfortable if their children carry mobile phones with them when out of the house, even as they perceive those phones as being overused.

Of course, smartphones are minicomputers that bring the internet into children's personal spaces wherever they go. While the internet and digital media provide a window through which parents can view what their children do, children also employ strategies for keeping their activities obscured. It is common for children and teens to visit social media sites that their parents do not know about and to communicate with one another there. They may choose apps that are brand new or that their parents do not know about; one of the reasons for the popularity of Snapchat is that evidence of activities disappears from parents' eyes. This is part of kids' efforts to carve out their own identities away from the watchful eye of caregivers, as discussed in Chapter 6. Texting, which often feels private when being used, is also popular among children and teens for much this same reason, as is the ability to stay in touch with groups of friends on an ongoing basis with group chats.

There has been much discussion as to how deeply involved (some say *over*involved) modern "helicopter" parents are in their children's lives. There is strong temptation to use digital technologies to surveil children, track their every move, and contact them with great frequency, even as they grow older and become young (and then older) adults (Hofer & Moore, 2011; Nelson, 2010). But many of the parents interviewed by sociologist Lynn Schofield Clark for her study of parenting in the digital age disclosed that they tried very actively and deliberately to resist these temptations and to provide appropriate space for their children to grow up (Clark, 2013).

At least two distinct patterns seem to have developed as families of different backgrounds and income levels respond to the use of digital technology in their lives (though there is surely overlap between these two, as well as departure from these norms—see Clark, 2013). Among upper-income families there tends to exist what Clark calls an "ethic of expressive empowerment," in which there is a strong ethic and expectation that the internet and digital media be used for education, achievement, and self-development. Among lower-income families, Clark has noticed an "ethic of respectful connectedness," in which children are primarily guided to use digital media to remain compliant and connected to family members. If you look closely at the premises that underlie these two ethics—both admirable but very different—you can see how these different norms and expectations can serve to reinforce the economic and social gaps that currently exist in U.S. society (Clark, 2013).

There are many challenges for families as they attempt to integrate technology into family life (Madden, Cortesi, Gasser, Lenhart, & Duggan, 2012). Parents and caregivers worry that children are online too much, and they worry about what they are doing—including the digital footprint that may remain. Caregivers—especially those of younger teens and preteens, and from upper-income households—also worry about how their children treat one another online and whether they are contacting strangers online or face-to-face. Many attempt to implement strategies aimed at controlling or reducing digital technology use, but these efforts are to some extent limited by the portability of mobile media and the freedoms this gives its users. Providing strategies for appropriate use and using filtering mechanisms or spyware can return some of this power to parents but at the expense of privacy for family members and possibly even the level of trust given by children to their parents and vice versa (Newell, Moore, & Metoyer, 2015). Families should ideally consider how to balance safety and trust as they develop relational strategies for using digital technologies.

All in all, most tech-connected families use digital technology to remain in touch even as they move busily and independently from place to place. Mobile phones in particular help family members "go their separate ways while keeping them more connected" (Rainie & Wellman, 2012, p. 170). Families may have less "face time" than in the past, but they have more "connected time" (p. 170).

health care

The internet and digital media have come to have a profound influence on people's health care and therefore their health, both physical and mental. The storage, management, and transmission of health-related data now increasingly occur digitally. Technology also supports and influences clinical decision-making and facilitates patient care, often from a distance. While it is clear that health care practices are changing in high-tech digital societies, the impact of these *e-health* changes is not yet clear. There is, so far, a dearth of conclusive evidence regarding the quality, safety risks, and cost-effectiveness of implementing health-related digital technologies, especially on a societal scale (Black et al., 2011).

Health care has become biomedicalized in the digital era. Issues and problems once thought outside the realm of medicine (like drug abuse, childbirth, and depression) are now considered medical issues, with an increasing expectation that they be covered in health care plans. Managed care systems, corporatized insurance systems, and computerized patient data banks are supplanting the individualized systems of the independent physician as caregiver. Science and technology are expected to explain and contribute toward best practices and cures, and they have spawned a number of biomedical organizations, infrastructures, and clinical treatments. In addition, information on health and illnesses proliferates via all kinds of media, including the internet, and direct-to-consumer prescriptions, over-the-counter drug advertising, health issues, and ethics are debated in digital media constantly (Clarke, Shim, Mamo, Fosket, & Fishman, 2010). Biomedicine has been considered a fundamental element of mass culture and popular media (Bauer, 1998).

Most people now look for health information online in addition to turning to their physicians, friends, and family (Fox, 2011a; Hesse et al., 2005). What has been called "peer-to-peer" health care is flourishing—reminiscent of the ways that people helped one another in tribal communities that did not have access to modern medicine (or it hadn't been invented yet). In general, both online and offline, the larger one's network, the greater the health benefits. Online, people help one another find information, goods, and services that can improve their health, both physical and mental (Bessiere, Pressman, Kiesler, & Kraut, 2010). Offline, exposure to larger numbers of people provides greater immunity to infectious diseases by exposing people to a wider range of infections, such as common cold viruses (Rainie & Wellman, 2012, p. 132; Song, Son, & Lin, 2011).

Medical information accessed online is not always accurate, however, even when sites look slick and professional. Such sites may help to diagnose certain illnesses, but they generally fall short in providing plans for recovery (Volti, 2014, p. 193). Health care providers must contend with the knowledge that patients have often consulted many other, likely digital, sources. With medical information at their fingertips, individuals have become more intimately involved in decisions related to their health. More and more, they feel an increased responsibility for their own health. Still, most consider their health care providers their most-trusted sources of information (Cotten & Gupta, 2004; Hesse et al., 2005). Most patients are not using the internet to self-medicate; they still look to medical professionals to provide definitive diagnoses that involve the prescribing of drugs (Cotten & Gupta, 2004; Fox, 2011b).

It is becoming more common to take personal charge of one's day-to-day health and fitness. Digital and mobile technology have become valuable tools in this effort. One in three cell phone owners uses a phone to access health information, and one in five smartphone owners has a health app on his or her phone that is usually related to diet, exercise, or both. Younger adults, minorities, and those in particular need of health info are most likely to install and use one of these apps (Fox & Duggan, 2012).

Importantly, the internet has enabled the creation of new pathways for patients to find and help each other (see Bessiere et al., 2010). People find and form groups in which they share health and medical information, fight diseases and addictions, lose weight, and live healthier lifestyles. They share information related to their health and health care and support one another (Hajli, 2014). This is especially critical when one has undergone a significant change in one's health or is faced with a disease of some rarity.

Health-oriented communities can be significant and indeed life changing for their members. Additionally, messages that members exchange are often searchable and can be found later by others with health questions or conditions. This gives people increased control (or a feeling of control) over their health and the means to make decisions and battle problems (Fox, 2011a). Of course, when information is digitized it can be hacked and surveilled; one cannot assume that it is completely secure. In short, digital health platforms, communities, and apps can help people live more productive and healthy lives, but care should be taken as the quality and security of digitized medical information cannot be guaranteed.

religion

For many in technologically developed societies, the practice of religion has been transformed by the ubiquity of the internet and social media in their lives. At one time, religious ceremonies took place only or primarily in sacred places, built and consecrated by the faithful. To go to a special physical space—perhaps a church, synagogue, or mosque—and practice one's religion was a ritual. Now, many religious services take place online and can be attended from a distance. *Cyberchurches* have evolved from web forums to fully interactive sites in which members can view and engage in a service online or even take part in one as an avatar in the virtual reality "world" of Second Life (www.secondlife.com; Campbell, 2012).

Information about sects, places of worship, and religions themselves are spread widely through electronic and social media channels. Religious leaders write blogs and record podcasts; sermons and music can be accessed via a cyberchurch website. Apps have been developed that allow people to more easily interact with fellow worshippers and with faith leaders—there is even a confession app that allows Catholics to digitally approximate the ritual of confession (although it is not recognized by the church as an actual confession; see Cheong & Ess, 2012). Religious texts can be accessed online and prayer requests can even be placed (Campbell, 2012). One in five people who practices religion talks about it online, and about half have seen others do so. One in five has also followed his or her faith using a mass media platform, such as a religious talk radio program, TV show, or music (Pew Research Center, 2014).

Media use not only increases people's access to religion but can also supplement their understanding of it. Websites, forums, and social media permit people to share, discuss, and debate religious issues. More obscure religions and religious views can be discovered and their tenets brought to light; new ones can be developed and find an audience. Spirituality in general has received a boost from the number of sites devoted to spiritual issues and from the use of the internet to find places in which to explore it. "Faith brands" can be successfully developed through publicizing the mission of a church or religion and encouraging loyalty and membership (Cheong & Ess, 2012).

Using social media to follow and discuss religious issues does not necessarily lead to engagement in brick-and-mortar places of worship, however. For many, the engagement stops with the click of a like button or a follow. Those who join Facebook groups for religious organizations usually limit their religious participation to the online group, communication scholar Mark D. Johns has found. They do not necessarily consider the next step to be physical attendance at a place of worship. Rather, the act has symbolic meaning or serves as an indicator of identity rather than a commitment to take a more physically active role in one's faith (Johns, 2012).

Open discussion of and participation in religion can challenge what has previously been considered sacred. In sociologist Emile Durkheim's analysis of the sacred and the profane (1912/1965), the sacred carries special meaning because it is somewhat hidden and must be appreciated in a private space. Religious practice is now a more public activity. A religious service might seem to some to be less special and sacred when it is broadcast or streamed to an internet audience. On the other hand, this can publicize the religion and permit access to those who might otherwise be unable to attend.

For people who wish to keep such activities private, though, this can be a problem. In some societies, people are free to practice a religion (or not to do so) without fear of reprisal or penalty. But in many places, people can be profiled and persecuted for their religious views and targeted, harmed, even killed. Digital technology can assist in the detection of people who hold certain views and can therefore help those who hold opposite views organize against them (see Kjuka, 2013). But, as we have seen, it can also help people who share the same views find one another, form communities, and give and receive social support.

The practice of religion is changing in the modern world. Whether or not these developments represent a "commercialization" that is not in keeping with the mission of religion is increasingly debated. Worldwide, *religiosity*—the belief in or practice of religion—is on the decline, especially among those under age 40, while atheism is on the rise. Many who consider themselves not to be religious have not left their faiths, though; they continue to practice them in their own way but have opted not to define or identify themselves as a "religious person." In general, women and people with lower incomes are more likely to consider themselves religious than their counterparts, a finding that holds across global cultures. And about 60% of the global population still considers itself to be religious (WIN-Gallup, 2012). It will be interesting to see how the incorporation of ICTs into religion, worship, and spirituality affect these trends.

work and commerce

Work has undergone a massive transformation in the digital age, as the internet and digital media have become a critical part of organizing and transacting all kinds of business. Computers and mobile media are used in countless organizational settings in a number of ways, from gathering data to organizing it to providing shared spaces for work. In many companies and organizations, work is done and business is transacted in a number of spatially distributed settings, all coordinated via computer. Over 60% of American workers use the internet on the job (Madden & Jones, 2008).

E-commerce—buying and selling products, services, and information online—is a big part of internet work. In most cases, it is much less expensive to set up an online "storefront" (usually in the form of a website with the ability to take in money) than to rent store space. Information transmission costs are also relatively inexpensive over the internet. Even companies that have a physical location often now do a good portion of their business over the internet, and those that do business primarily over the internet may still have one or more physical locations.

Many people appreciate the convenience and value of online commerce. The online shopping industry grows every year, a trend that is projected to continue. The largest share of online revenue in the United States is generated in retail shopping, with Amazon the top vendor, and travel booking websites generate one third of e-commerce revenue (Statista, 2014). Some businesses have not translated to e-commerce as well as others, but due to the large profits possible, innovations to them are being explored. For example, grocery shopping, which as of 2014 had not found major success online, seems to have a brighter future in e-commerce. Amazon is fronting the cost of an expensive delivery infrastructure, without which the business could not take off, and customers are getting used to the idea of buying fresh food online. It takes both a technological and a psychological shift for some businesses to succeed.

Forty percent of worldwide internet users have bought products or goods online via desktop or mobile devices. This amounts to 1 billion online buyers, a number that is projected to continuously grow. They are not evenly distributed around the globe, however. More than four times as many people in the United States, Great Britain, Norway, Japan, Korea, and Denmark have shopped online compared to Hungary, Italy, Greece, Mexico, and Turkey (Curran, 2012). Internet access is likely one of the biggest reasons for this difference; also, e-retail confers an economic advantage only when warehousing and distributions costs are low.

Online commerce also has a deliberately communal dimension. In rating, commenting on, or sharing opinions and information regarding sales transactions, social connections can be formed that have real impact on the business. On online auction sites, for example, people tend to be willing to pay more for an item if others express an interest in it (Kauffman & Wood, 2006). The dynamics of online sharing and connecting, then, can be critical to the success of the online organizations that engage in such activities. At the same time, data mining and surveillance should be kept in mind. Consumers and companies alike should be aware of the implications of widespread sharing on people's privacy and safety and of the (in)security of data in online spaces.

Internet usage on the job tends to vary by field of work. Nearly three out of four professionals, managers, or executives use the internet at work, either constantly or several times a day. About half of clerical, office, and sales workers also use the internet on the job several times a day at least. Service workers and those in the skilled trades are far less likely to report internet use at work (Madden & Jones, 2008). Use of the internet and digital media at work generally leads to more time spent working and more productivity overall—although, for sure, such behaviors as checking email and Facebook can pull one's focus from more productive activities (this has been called *cyberloafing*; see Andreassen, Torsheim, & Pallesen, 2014). Research indicates, however, that when colleagues get to know one another via Facebook and social media, they are more satisfied with their jobs (Hanna, Kee, & Robertson, 2017).

Virtual organizations—sometimes called *distributed work groups*, *virtual teams*, or *knowledge networks*—are now prevalent. These online work groups and their mobile equivalents can be quite successful in helping spatially separated people accomplish tasks together. People can work on multiple projects with multiple teams online. Digital technologies like Skype and social media enable people to work and network together efficiently and effectively. The introduction of such technologies has provided sizable gains in productivity for many businesses (Volti, 2014, p. 194).

Some jobs are in danger of becoming obsolete in modern digital economies, though. Automated software and machines have replaced workers in clerical tasks and on the factory floor (Brynjolfsson & McAfee, 2014). ATM machines have displaced some bank tellers, bloggers have pushed out some journalists, online travel sites have supplanted some travel agents, and robots, already being used in manufacturing, may someday replace some kinds of personal assistants and even caregivers. Because some jobs can be done anywhere once digitized, they can be outsourced to other areas, including other countries, where they may be done for lower wages.

This trend depresses wages and the economy overall, as more people compete for fewer lower skilled jobs, and increases overall income inequality (Brynjolfsson & McAfee, 2014). It also shifts economic risk away from companies and organizations to the individual, who is now expected to adapt and to constantly adjust to new economic realities. While companies gain flexibility, employees lose job security (see Neff, 2012). This can be truly disruptive of people's lives, for there is dignity and purpose, not only wages and labor, involved in work.

However, while demand for less skilled labor may diminish in some contexts, demand for highly skilled digital labor is generally on the increase. People with digital design experience, analytic and engineering skills, and creativity in envisioning and implementing innovative technologies are sought in many fields. College degrees and even graduate education are required for many of these kinds of high-tech jobs (Brynjolfsson & McAfee, 2014). Education, reskilling, and the creation of new jobs are critically important in the modern technological age.

While some small companies have found great success doing business via the internet, overall, large corporations continue to dominate all major market sectors—from automobile manufacturing to supermarkets. This is partly due to the difficulties that smaller firms have in penetrating foreign markets due to language and infrastructure problems, and partly because of the inherent advantages conferred by size and power: bigger budgets, greater access to capital, lower costs of production, and the expertise and resources to continually innovate and grow. While small internet companies can leverage social media and the power of networks to grow and scale in ways that would not have been possible pre-internet, and some (like Facebook and Twitter) can become wildly successful, most are squashed or sometimes bought out by large corporations and conglomerates. Competition is unequal in the internet age (Curran, 2012; Curran, Fenton, & Freedman, 2012). Many companies find they must adapt to or integrate new technology, or die (Brynjolfsson & McAfee, 2014).

It is interesting to note that when younger people enter modern workplaces, their digital skills are often different than those of some veterans of their occupation. They tend to excel at gathering information quickly (though not necessarily at assessing the credibility of this information), at completing discrete tasks, and at adapting to new, emerging technologies and reskilling (Rainie, 2006). At the same time, it should not be assumed that all young adults entering the job market are technologically skilled or, if they are, that those skills are what will serve an organization best. Sophisticated analyses and judgments often require experience.

Contacts developed online can help people find new jobs and new areas in which to become skilled, but it requires a certain level of access and digital literacy to know how and where to look for them. The exchange of information regarding work, including the most effective ways to work, is a primary use of social networks online. But we must keep in mind that this information is not equivalently available to all, so this is not a level playing field. And there are still many kinds of jobs, particularly those involving manual labor, which must be obtained in a more "analog" (i.e., traditional) fashion. The internet is by no means the only way to find and procure a job (see Fountain, 2005).

There is significant work/home spillover in the digital age, most often by those who use the internet or email on the job (Berkowsky, 2013; Madden & Jones, 2008). Fifty-six percent of those whose work requires them to be digitally connected report doing some work at home, and 20% say they do so every day or almost every day (Madden & Jones, 2008). Sometimes, this work is done after hours. One in five internet users says that internet use has increased the amount of work he or she does from home, and one in 10 says that he or she does more work because of the internet (Rainie & Wellman, 2012). Workers who use ICTs are "more productive, flexible, collaborative, and better connected," Rainie and Wellman conclude. "However, they also work longer hours and are more distracted and stressed" (2012, p. 177). This kind of stress can come from the extra work that those who use the internet for their jobs may feel that they need to accomplish, or it can be the result of the pressures of combining one's work and home lives satisfactorily.

At any rate, the work/home boundary has become redefined (see Nippert-Eng, 1996). Many workers are accessible by employers, family, and friends at all times (or most of the time). Aspects of one role can impact or impede upon another; for example, a parent may become torn as to whether to tend to a child's needs or meet a work deadline. Frequency of checking email and using Facebook and other ICTs on the job has been found to be associated with negative spillover in both directions. In other words, the more a worker uses the internet and digital technology on the job, the more difficult it may be to disengage from them when need be and attend to issues at home (Berkowsky, 2013).

However, ICT use in connection with work means that it is much easier to remain in contact with coworkers, clients, and people in one's field or discipline than might otherwise be the case. Colleagues near and far can be contacted conveniently and fairly easily by email or social media, which can even lead to coworkers getting to know one another better and perhaps even becoming friends. Work in which digital social networks are developed has the potential to become warm, creative, relaxing, and highly companionable, filled with people available to give advice or support at a moment's notice. This can help to stave off some of the more tedious aspects of work (Rainie & Wellman, 2012).

New modes of digitally enabled work, and the ongoing development of new norms and values surrounding them, are a challenge to workplaces and workers alike. We are living through a time of change and uncertainty. Increasing numbers of people can work anywhere and conduct business at any time. Without a given space in which to work, these individuals may have an especially difficult time "logging off" when they get home. They may feel that they should always be working, or they may come to view life as a continuous blend of home and work, without a firm boundary between the two. One might then do personal tasks at work and work tasks at home and find that there is not a big difference in these types of time. It may provide a competitive advantage *not* to compartmentalize work and leisure. While bringing work home can intrude on family or personal time, it can also allow individuals to get needed work done and advance their careers or make more money, which can benefit their families. The flexibility to work in different spaces and at different times can potentially have great value for people who are able to and who want to work somewhat nontraditionally.

education and libraries

Knowledge is growing at an exponentially accelerating rate. According to futurist-inventor Buckminster Fuller's knowledge-doubling curve, prior to 1900, knowledge doubled approximately every century. By the end of World War II, knowledge was doubling every 25 years. Today, different types of knowledge have different rates of growth, but, on average, human knowledge is doubling every 13 months and at some point may double as often as every 12 hours (Schilling, 2013).

To sort through all this knowledge and data, much of it specialized, requires higher-level understanding and skills that can be obtained in the course of becoming formally educated. To obtain jobs in modern technological societies, higher-education credentials are helpful. Workers with a high school education or less have seen a reduction in wages in the digital age, as mechanization has eliminated many jobs that once paid decent wages but required few technological skills (Volti, 2014, p. 194).

Education has been transformed in many ways by the internet and digital media. Computers and digital technology are found in classrooms at all levels. Informational materials, lessons, and whole curricula can be delivered in online *e-learning* (or *distance learning*) environments, and this has become a popular option for the delivery of educational materials. Additionally, "hybrid" or "blended" educational settings, which are partly online and partly face-to-face, are becoming more prevalent. Information about educational opportunities and offerings is plentiful online.

Colleges and universities are considered the primary hub for knowledge production and gathering in modern societies (Anderson, Boyles, & Rainie, 2012). Distance learning via digital technology is also critical to the long-term strategies of educational institutions, including approximately 70% of higher education institutions in the United States. About one third of college students have taken a class that is primarily delivered online, and three quarters of academic leaders and officers rate the learning outcomes as the same as or superior to those achieved in face-to-face classes. Online learning does not come easily to all students, though; it requires facility and skill with digital technology and a preponderance of discipline and self-motivation (Allen & Seaman, 2013; Ellis, Goodyear, Prosser, & O'Hara, 2006).

With digital and mobile media, learners can search for, find, create, and consume content on the go (Alexander, 2004). The culture of sharing and spreading information lends itself to prosumption in education, as members of learning communities consider themselves simultaneously producers and consumers of knowledge. This is a much more active and engaged model for education than one in which learners are passive recipients. With numerous resources at their fingertips, learners can develop a deeper, more focused approach to learning. On the other hand, individuals can become distracted by tech options and social media and lose focus on tasks.

Many who use technology in teaching or who teach online report this to be beneficial, especially when instructors become actively involved in the experience and establish trusting relationships with students. Well-designed digital classroom environments have proved to be structured yet flexible (see Cuthbert, Clark, & Linn, 2002; Haythornthwaite, 2002; Renninger & Shumar, 2002; Young, 2006). Discussion boards, online journals, and classroom social media use can provide opportunities for interaction and networking among students, instructors, and even course authors. In one study, students who used Twitter in the classroom to share information and interact in a planned and structured way achieved markedly higher grades than those in a class that covered the same material without engaging with Twitter (Junco, Heiberger, & Loken, 2011). Overall, the use of participatory technological tools such as social media and blogs has been found to enrich student learning and engagement (Allen & Seaman, 2013; Ellis et al., 2006).

Classes can also now be "flipped," allowing instructors to provide some of the content ordinarily provided face-to-face in the classroom in a digital space (such as via video lecture) for the student to view during homework time. This frees up class time for interactive lab work and other creative applications of that time. It also allows students to watch or listen to the digitized information as many times as needed at home. Digitally enabled educational activities, then, can be adapted to instructors' and students' needs and have been linked to higher grades and greater student satisfaction and motivation in both children and adults (Bennett & Fessenden, 2006; Cramer, Collins, Snider, & Fawcett, 2006; Guldberg & Pilkington, 2006; MacKinnon & Williams, 2006; van't Hooft & Kelly, 2004). There is still much to be learned about online educational practices and how to reap their greatest benefits, though.

The very notion of what a school *is*, is changing and expanding in the digital age. Brick-and-mortar institutions now face digital competitors, some of which throw into question what schools should be and do (and whether they should financially profit for providing education). Public education has had a long tradition in America, even though inequalities in resources and delivery have seen outcomes vary widely. In recent years, however, challengers, such as for-profit universities and charter schools, commercial providers of lectures and online educational content, online services like iTunes U, and nonprofit learning organizations like the Khan Academy, have shaken up the institution of education. A number of specialized training centers provide instruction and credentialing for trades and professions (Anderson et al., 2012). Massive open online courses (MOOCs) developed by universities and by other organizations are fascinating and controversial experiments in scaling the delivery of instruction and information exponentially. MOOCs seem to draw interest primarily among the already highly educated or high-income earners, even when the courses are free (Ferenstein, 2015). In short, schools, schooling, and institutions of higher education no longer resemble their counterparts of the early 2000s—or even 2010. That's how fast some of these digitally influenced changes are coming about.

Libraries, too, have been transformed in the technological age. Libraries are systems in which information in both disaggregated and cumulative forms is organized and managed. They represent the knowledge of a society and the ability of people to access and contribute to that knowledge. The library is, therefore, a key institution for the preservation and advancement of democracy. About half of all Americans age 16 or older used a public library in some form in 2014 (Zickuhr et al., 2014).

Libraries and other systems of knowledge management face many challenges in the modern technological world since information has become digitized and plentiful and flows so widely and often freely. A library must respond to people's needs for materials, skills, and the management of knowledge and must have a strategy to stay ahead of the technological curve regarding these issues. Libraries are also important public access sites for internet connectivity. However, public access users in one study saw the library as a rather undesirable place to use the internet. Women tended to associate the library with nostalgia for books and family. Male interviewees associated libraries with technology (Dixon et al., 2014).

Many libraries face serious fiscal challenges. Their funding is often decreased at the same time as they are expected to maintain services critical to the acquisition and sharing of knowledge. Providing internet access and digital services are expected. These offerings can range from online "Ask a Librarian" services and personalized reading recommendations to media kiosks and mobile apps. Librarians need to periodically update their skills in data management and digital information literacy and support ever-changing electronic educational practices. They also need to understand how customers access and use digital content, including the library's own resources, on a number of mobile devices in a variety of formats. And digitized collections that can be accessed on numerous platforms must be constantly updated (Clegg, 2015; Zickuhr et al., 2014).

While digital technology has to some extent infiltrated and helped to transform teaching, libraries, and reading, print books remain central to these experiences. While more Americans than ever are reading e-books (28% of American adults aged 18 and older, as of January 2014), few have stopped reading print books entirely. Just 4% of American readers read e-books exclusively. But reading books and other online material via e-books and on the internet has become a primary way to access information, especially up-to-date information (Zickuhr et al., 2014). Interestingly, material consumed electronically rather than from print may be more difficult to absorb and remember. Studies have found that the placement of text on a printed page and the tactile experience of reading printed content helps people better comprehend what they have read (Flood, 2014; Mangen, Walgermo, & Brønnick, 2013).

Educational and learning groups can function as full-fledged communities when members gain a feeling of belonging and purpose, share knowledge, and develop an image of themselves as a unit. These communities then operate as social networks in which members work collaboratively, exchanging information, advice, and social support (see Cuthbert et al., 2002; Guldberg & Pilkington, 2006; Renninger & Shumar, 2002). But there are still many challenges ahead for schools, libraries, and learning communities, as access to a quality education is far from universal throughout the world, and digital access—along with a full understanding of the ways that digital technology can be used in education—is, so far, inconsistently realized.

politics and governing

It has long been hoped that the internet and digital technology would assist governments in serving their constituents. A government is tasked with maintaining and improving opportunities for its citizens in a centralized, organized way. Properly implemented, digital technologies could assist in the coordination of government agencies, increase efficiency, and help boost economic growth. In a time of fiscal pressures and burdens and, often, political unrest, this is greatly needed. Unfortunately, governments still often operate in inefficient ways and do not make the best use of the digital tools and strategies available to them. Thus, few governments have been able to benefit fully from digitization.

Government agencies (treasury, defense, education, social services) generally have distinct communication systems and infrastructures. They may use ICTs, but their systems are frequently separate from one another and uncoordinated, in part because the various bureaus do not want a loss of autonomy. The result can be "excessive government investment, often spread across or duplicated within a large number of diverse capabilities in different areas, and a support system that fluctuates in response to changing political pressure and policies," technology experts David Hovenden and Chris Bartlett report. "As with companies whose strategies are poorly aligned with the capabilities needed for success, this leads to a lack of focus on the true mission of the government or agency, and an inability to carry it out successfully" (2013).

The thoughtful integration and use of digital technologies can help governments meet these kinds of challenges. A strong digital infrastructure can enable governments to marshal their capabilities, bring agencies together, and develop cost-effective solutions to problems. The government can be a kind of broker for its constituent parts, bringing agencies together and into conversation with each other by using shared digital technology. Greater flexibility and lower costs would likely result, although security issues would remain. But so far these opportunities are largely ignored due to political constraints and the difficulties of making (and funding) changes to the status quo.

Smaller, poorer countries with limited resources face even greater challenges in implementing digital infrastructure initiatives. While they must operate in a global economy and society, their technology is often not up to the task. For example, countries in sub-Saharan Africa currently attempting to coordinate agencies and services digitally are experiencing overwhelming problems. Technological obsolescence, a concern for all organizations with a digital component and presence, is even more of a worry when resources are very limited. And the problems of capturing, maintaining, and preserving electronic records in a secure and sustained fashion are felt by all governments, industries, and organizations (Ngulube, 2012).

An even more comprehensive rethinking and redesign of governmental communication and information infrastructures—an *e-government*—is increasingly possible. The digital infrastructure of a nation can be rebuilt from the ground up, coordinating critical systems like citizen identification, record keeping, taxing, social services, and health care. With an entire system designed for digital interconnection, individuals can be afforded a measure of privacy and control over their data. The tiny country of Estonia has undergone just such a comprehensive rebuilding of its ICT infrastructure, proving that it can be done—albeit on a much smaller scale than would be possible in many nations (Tamkivi, 2014). And, as always, it should be noted that the security of so much interconnected digitized information cannot be assured.

Election cycles also favor short-term, not long-term, solutions to problems. Those who govern must often consider reelection strategies relatively early in their terms of office and may prioritize the consideration of issues that have simpler and more straightforward solutions. Tech issues are not always visible and rarely have quick fixes. Additionally, some citizens are literally and figuratively cut off from these conversations due to their own lack of technology access.

Some governments use digital technology to keep tabs on other governments, political groups, and even their own citizens. Tasked with providing security for the citizenry, governments, including that of the United States, have viewed and listened to what people are doing by accessing and monitoring their internet activity, text messages, and/or phone calls. In the United States, this raises constitutional issues of whether such surveillance is legal when no specific threats have been made. The government generally counters with the argument that some monitoring is necessary in order to prevent and subvert danger, as was the justification for the mass collection of data of U.S. citizens authorized by the 2001 PATRIOT Act, legislation passed swiftly following the September 11, 2001, terror attacks. It is important for people to make their views on this type of surveillance known, for the larger issue—the appropriate scope of government involvement in the lives of its citizens—affects us all.

Technology also influences the ways that leaders are chosen to govern our societies. In the 1800s, when railroads were the primary means of long-distance travel, politicians would embark on "whistle-stop" railway tours of the countryside to meet the electorate. When television became prominent, it followed that the most telegenic candidates (beginning with John F. Kennedy) had a distinct advantage. Now that the internet and digital media have become such prominent parts of everyday life, candidates with the superior grasp of how to connect with voters online and on social media have a better chance of being elected. Social media specialists are now a key component of political campaign staffs.

President Barack Obama's candidacy for U.S. president in 2008 was the first large-scale example of this to date. He entered the race a relative unknown in 2007, but his campaign's shrewd use of social media introduced him in a lively, modern way to a large number of potential voters, many of whom became interested in politics for the first time. Perhaps even more significantly, social media was used to break down financial barriers and leverage interest in Obama in innovative ways—using YouTube, for example, rather than more expensive television ads, to present him to the electorate and providing ways for people to donate small amounts of money to the campaign (Discovery, 2012; Katz, Barris, & Jain, 2013).

The use of social media (particularly Twitter) by President Donald Trump during his U.S. presidential campaign of 2015 and 2016 and upon assuming the presidency in 2017 is perhaps an even more dramatic example of the power of social media in politics. Trump used social media, usually Twitter, as a platform to speak directly to the American voters and populace, sidestepping traditional media outlets and disrupting traditional practices of dealing with the press. This change is rather in line with his charge to disrupt long-standing practices and patterns in general. Trump even communicates directly with world and national leaders, and members of his own administration and cabinet, publicly via Twitter, rather than privately, which can also have major implications for his relationships with them (and for U.S. global relations). The impact of such major changes will likely be felt for years to come, as candidates for elected office, including those with little prior political and governing experience, leverage social media platforms and audiences to meet new aims in new ways, establishing new norms along the way. It would not be a stretch to predict that our methods of choosing and electing candidates, their relations with the press, their methods of governing, and even democracy itself, may be in a period of transition and overhaul, with highly uncertain results.

In America and worldwide, social media use can open the door to less-experienced candidates and can jump-start fund-raising and political social movements in new ways. Social media is frequently used to express political views and to find like-minded others with whom to engage politically (see Chapter 5 for more on the role of social media in social movements). While surely some people change their political views after considering online political information, research indicates that most people's existing political views are merely reinforced after spending time online. People generally talk politics with those who share their views. The tendency *not* to speak up about political or policy issues when it is perceived that one's audience might disagree with those views is called the "spiral of silence," and it can spill over from online to offline contexts, making it less likely for people to discuss things that might prove controversial or divisive (Hampton, Rainie, Lu, Dwyer, Shin, & Purcell, 2015). This is also an example of *confirmation bias*: the tendency for individuals to be protective of their initial positions on a topic, even in the presence of contradictory evidence (Leeper, 2014; Maximino, 2014).

Information related to politics and governing is often highly charged and politically skewed; never more so that in the current environment (see Campbell, 2016; Himelboim et al., 2016). This is all the more reason to educate oneself on various issues and points of view. About 20% of social media users *do* modify or change their social or political views when exposed to new and different ones in the course of social media use (Anderson, 2016). The internet and digital media have the potential to remake political systems and governments in important and consequential ways. And one of the roles of their citizens is to call for these changes.

the media

The mass media, which include print media like newspapers, magazines, and books and electronic media like television, radio, and movies, are increasingly thought of, collectively, as constituting a social institution. In recent years, the internet and digital media have begun to be included in the mass media when the role of the media as a social institution is invoked. Together, these means of communication have had an impact on the world that is nothing less than revolutionary.

While the government exerts substantial control over the mass and digital media in many countries worldwide, in democratic societies the media is considered separate from the institution of governing. It is organized as a market, not a state, system and is expected to be controlled and staffed by professionals who seek to be accurate, impartial, and informative. Although political power and the media intersect in different ways in different societies, American media and news reporting are often looked to globally as an example of the free and independent press. This independence has been compromised, though, by the media's domination by a small number of conglomerates.

A conglomerate exists when a set of companies that may not necessarily be similar to one another are owned by the same larger company. This has happened with mass and digital media companies across the globe, as most of them have become owned by certain parent companies. In 1996, the Telecommunications Reform Act was passed by the Federal Communications Commission (FCC), allowing radio and television stations in different regions to be owned by the same company and paving the way for continued deregulation in which a relatively small number of corporations could own more and more media organizations.

At this writing, six corporations in the United States—Disney, Viacom, News Corp/20th Century Fox, Time Warner, Comcast, and CBS—act as conglomerates, controlling 90% of what is read, watched, or listened to via the media. As recently as 1983, 50 countries owned the same percentage of television and radio stations, magazines, newspapers, movies studios, and the like. Today's media conglomerates even own some sports teams and theme parks. It has been estimated that 232 media executives control the information diet of 277 million Americans—that's one media executive to every 850,000 subscribers (Lutz, 2012). In other countries, the media is similarly concentrated in a handful of corporations or, in some cases, political parties.

This concentrated consolidation of media ownership is often critiqued as detrimental to the free and open exchange of information so important to a democracy. The potential exists for fewer points of view to be expressed as a predominant corporation sets standards of tone and content. It is also important to keep in mind that many media organizations are for-profit ones, with their main objective to make money rather than to educate or to serve the public interest. Dominant points of view may not be contested, and censorship can result as these corporations favor special interests and profits over newsworthiness. The quality and diversity of the information that is shared can become sacrificed for standardization, a charge often made in a globalized culture.

Journalism and news dissemination have changed dramatically with the advent of the internet and digital technology, especially social media. Journalists and news organizations today work within a 24/7 news cycle—that is, they are expected to provide newsworthy information to the public around the clock, throughout the week. Twenty-four-hour cable news networks and online news sites are examples of this. While all-news radio stations have existed for decades, this relatively recent innovation in television (the first all-news cable network was CNN in 1980) has transformed the process of news gathering and dissemination because much more product is required to fill the time. It is also important for media outlets to entice viewers and readers to their product, as many of the outlets are profit-making organizations that need audiences to survive.

Some claim that the 24/7 news cycle and its voracious need for content played a key role in the election of Donald Trump. Cable news networks such as CNN, MSNBC, and Fox News have a lot of airtime to fill, and Trump's 2015–2016 campaign for president was an incredibly juicy story. This resulted in near-constant coverage of the campaign and its unconventional candidate's every move. The ethical and possibly legal troubles of his opponent Hillary Clinton, who had used a private email server in her home to conduct government business while Secretary of State under President Obama, was another story to which the networks devoted much time. It will be interesting to see how the highly dramatic presidential election of 2016—and the journey of a president (Trump) who had never held political office—will impact media narratives and content with respect to elections and governing in the near and distant future.

The structure of online internet-based journalism and news is also changing (Pavlik, 1997). While content can be reproduced on the internet in much the same way as it exists in print form, it can also contain hyperlinks that enable readers to access additional information. Online news stories can also contain original content designed specifically for the internet, include multimedia content, and permit readers to contribute by posting their own opinions, commentary, or even links to related information sources (Bruns, 2005; Chung, Nam, & Stefanone, 2012). In the early 2000s, these innovations culminated in the emergence of news blogs, which have faster production cycles, integrated hyperlinks, and user-generated content that creates alliances with other blogs and user-generated content sites (Weber, 2012). Digital journalism has not only evolved considerably from print and earlier online efforts but has also become a more communal enterprise.

Many news organizations now use social media and incorporate it into their work. Symbiotic relationships are formed that improve the strength and long-term success of the organization (Weber, 2012). Journalists must be engaged with the public, and people reading and following what reporters are doing on social media is a prime way for this to occur. Journalists, celebrities, politicians, and many other professionals also use social media like Twitter to promote news stories and to interact with the public directly. Video, photos, and posts and tweets contributed by audience members have also become sources of news and appear in news stories (Kim, Kim, Lee, Oh, & Lee, 2015). In addition, the dissemination of news, once solely the task of journalistic entities, now increasingly takes place via internet and social media content creators, resulting in the proliferation of media aggregation sites and even less formal information-oriented blogs (see Chapter 5). It can be quite difficult to ascertain the source and credibility of the information found in these varied digital spaces.

The number of adults who get their news from social media has risen sharply over the last decade—62% of American adults look to social media for their news, and 18% do so often (Gottfried & Shearer, 2016). In fact, because they are on social media so often and follow news sources, many people trust that the news that they need to know will come to their attention, that it is "out there" widely and generally (this is called *ambient news*), and that they need not actively seek it out. This passive approach to accessing and following news has been called the "news-finds-me perception," and while it explains modern patterns of news consumption, it is linked to lower levels of political knowledgeability (Gil de Zuniga, Weeks, & Ardevol-Abreu, 2017).

While many consumers of aggregated news appreciate the ease and convenience of obtaining a variety of sources of information in one place, the practice can be seen as exploitation—even theft—of the original work of others. It has also weakened traditional journalistic organizations and the industry as a whole. In 2011, hundreds of U.S. newspapers ceased publication even as news aggregators were on the rise. Media diversity has been reduced, and misinformation can be easily amplified. Widespread reuse of information can create a "spiral of sameness" (Boczkowski, 2010, p. 174; Martin, 2014, p. 88).

As journalism faces reinvention and redefinition, digital and mass media have begun to assume some of the functions that other institutions have traditionally performed. Via the electronic media, people become educated, practice their religions, amass health and fitness information, elect candidates, follow and influence (and become influenced by) the practices of politicians and governments, and come together as families. These media are, therefore, a primary way that people learn about and come to understand how other social institutions operate (see Silverblatt, 2004). Their practitioners, though, have been under some siege and have been called biased, failing, fake, and worse in the era of the Trump candidacy and presidency.

But because the internet is not currently centralized (and this does not mean that it could not *become* centralized at some point) and because ordinary people and citizen journalists can share information widely along its channels and networks, many alternative sources for news and information exist. These channels do not have the power that media conglomerates have, and they may or may not hold their content creators to high standards of accuracy, but they do represent potential and actual avenues for the free exchange of information. As we saw in Chapter 5, some nations endeavor to censor and shut down the internet, especially during times of internal turmoil, and there are no guarantees that even in the United States free access could be threatened. The net is not "neutral"; in many cases, powerful interests influence what is available and accessible, though the *net neutrality* principle argues that information on the internet must be made available to all, regardless of ability to pay. Social media and a variety of other decentralized internet forums for discussion and sharing provide an important alternative information flow to the media conglomerates.

The internet and digital media have made possible what can be called a *convergence culture* (Jenkins, 2006). Information and media flow across—or *converge* on—multiple platforms on the same time: television, books, social media, and online forums. As multiple media industries present different versions or aspects of stories, audiences can migrate from place to place as they follow or participate in a media offering. A single cultural franchise, such as Batman, *Star Wars*, the *Matrix* movies, or Harry Potter, can now be distributed through a range of media delivery methods. Audiences can actively search the form of entertainment experience they want. More stories can now be told over more platforms, reaching more people (Jenkins, 2006).

Because of media convergence, pop culture products attract and inspire a much greater degree of audience participation than has ever before been possible. It may be, sociologist Howard Becker has argued (albeit in a predigital era), more sensible to see cultural products as the joint creation of the artist, the audience, the industries involved, and even the distributors. Together, these are the elements of an "art world," he says, and all of them are an integral part of the process of making and enjoying art in any of its forms (Becker, 1984).

In varied but important ways, all the techno-social institutions are experiencing convergence. Lines between home and work, government and business, media and commerce, and politics and religion are becoming so blended and blurred that it is difficult to see them as separate. This can either lead to a sense of powerlessness in the face of change and convergence or to a desire to effect change in these areas and make a difference, perhaps using the internet and digital media to do so.

Clearly, we are seeing pronounced shifts in our social institutions. Though influenced by technology, these changes are less about the technologies involved and more about the cultures of which they are a part. Many aspects of modern life are shifting and converging, and individuals and societies are attempting to cope with and understand these changes. In the next chapter, we look at more of the pros and cons—the benefits and hazards—of living in a technology-saturated environment of continuous superconnectedness.

9

MORE BENEFITS AND HAZARDS OF 24/7 SUPERCONNECTEDNESS

constant availability

Prior to industrialization, people used to be in fairly frequent contact with small groups of others. They could not and therefore did not venture as far from their homes and from one another as modern individuals can now do. Instead, people spent their time in the company of the same groups of others—their friends, families, and neighbors. In the last century and a half or so, advancements in transportation (railroads, cars, air travel) have allowed people to travel great distances and to commute to work, thus separating their work lives from their home lives. At the same time, advancements in communication technology have allowed people to stay in better contact with others both far and near.

Because of these and other technological advancements, people's availability to one another has increased over time. The internet and digital media, which represent some of the most recent of these advancements, have brought people who may have become separated in the industrial age back together—mentally and emotionally, if not always physically. As anthropologist Kate Fox has noted,

> much has been written about the loneliness, isolation and alienation of modern urban life, but few commentators have noted the important role of the mobile as an antidote to these evils. You may be surrounded by uncaring strangers in a busy city street, or working in a competitive, unfriendly office, but your mobile gives you a lifeline connection to your own social world, your village green, your garden fence. Carrying your social support network in your pocket, you'll never walk alone. (Fox, 2001, para. 44)

In this sense, "tribes" that might once have met over a fire pit or in a village green can once again gather frequently. Their gathering place, though, is now the internet or a social media site.

Digital and mobile technologies provide the means for social networks to be constructed and available to members nearly all of the time. They pervade people's online *and* offline spaces and lives. Though an individual might not be able to contact a particular other person in a given community at will, if one's social networks are large and diverse enough, usually *someone* in at least one of those communities can be contacted most any time of the day or night (Chayko, 2008). This can be both comforting and empowering. As one woman whom I interviewed told me,

> I feel empowered to be able to connect with whoever I need instantly. (Chayko, 2008, p. 118)

Another explained it as follows:

> My connections are more important than whatever I'm doing that might force me to shut my cell phone off. (Chayko, 2008, back cover)

Many cell phone users even sleep with their phone under their pillow or on their bedside table, providing the feeling that they are constantly connected to the world and therefore less alone (Clayton et al., 2015; Srivastava, 2005). Keeping a phone close by at all times can provide a feeling of constant companionship. Individuals are afforded access to information, resources, and other people when and where they need them. But they can also become so used to the ease and convenience of connecting digitally that they feel anxious, lost, and unmoored when disconnected.

Constant availability and continuous connectedness provides digital tech users with an ambient awareness of one another that is remarkably persistent. As we go through our lives, we feel the nearness, the connection with others, and this is important and generally satisfying. It helps relationships and communities persist and thrive (Hampton, 2016) and allows us to gather information and get help when needed conveniently and swiftly. But it is also implicated in many of the troubling by-products of techno-social life that we have discussed in this book: vertical and horizontal surveillance, lack of privacy, data mining, cybercrime, and cyberterrorism. Data and information in digital spaces are vulnerable to destructive hacking, to information being "outed" or made public at any time, and continuous connectedness helps make this so. But for better or worse, an always-on, always-connected, 24/7 culture has arrived and is in full swing and has become a hallmark of modern techno-social life.

convenience and microcoordination

Because the internet and digital media permit individuals to contact one another at a moment's notice, people often expect to be able to reach one another and to make plans at any time. These rational expectations can be heightened when people want or need extra attention. They may have a condition that requires it (like an illness), they may have moved away from family or friends, or they may just feel a greater need for connection. In these cases, while they might wish to be in frequent contact with their loved ones anyway, the desire can become heightened.

People who live in tech-intensive societies can come to truly depend not just on digital technologies but on the convenience they afford. The internet and digital media allow their users to accomplish tasks that once involved much more time and trouble. People can now communicate with others much faster, more frequently, and with greater ease (Chayko, 2008; Sakkopoulos, Lytras, & Tsakalidis, 2006). Asynchronous communication can provide an additional layer of convenience, as people can send and receive messages when it makes sense for them, without fear of interrupting the important activities of others. They can work or be entertained or relax nearly anywhere, anytime. This can all be both a convenience and an inconvenience. One of my interviewees told me this:

> The pro side is I'm available, and that is the down side, also. (Chayko, 2008, p. 114)

Digital technologies, especially mobile phones, have become critical to the coordination of day-to-day activities. They have even changed the ways that we plan and enjoy activities. Individuals now frequently make or reconfigure plans last minute or while in transit; they do not plan ahead in the way that was required before cell phones. Sociologist Rich Ling calls this last-minute, in-progress coordination of activities *microcoordination* (2004; for more examples, see Castells et al., 2004; Eldridge & Grinter, 2001). And once the activity is underway, it is more likely to be altered midstream, or take on a new quality, because with phones and apps at the ready it is so easy and convenient to implement a change.

There are upsides and downsides to microcoordination. Gatherings that might otherwise not have taken place can come together at the last minute; events can be reconfigured even as they are happening; people can be added to a guest list at any time. But it can also help contribute to a climate in which plans and schedules are generally seen as vague, indefinite, and perpetually incomplete. The "implicit contracts around time" become relaxed (Ling, 2004, p. 74). This may discourage people from making needed plans in advance or from taking plans seriously. Events are scheduled more loosely, with time allotted for changes and an expectation that changes, even major ones, may occur. Responding to invitations may seem an unnecessary formality, but the failure to do so can spoil plans and gatherings and impact relationships.

It can sometimes seem, Rich Ling has observed, that the use of digital and mobile technologies in these ways has resulted in time itself being "softened" (2004). Time can be perceived as more porous, less fixed. The expectations people have of one another relative to time are often softened as well, with norms frequently seen as uncertain and malleable. Perhaps ironically, given the ubiquity of tech that provides the correct time, lateness has become increasingly common.

In an example of what has been called *the irrationality of rationality*, the convenience that these technologies can bring to our lives can actually result in tremendous *in*convenience. The tools that help make life more convenient and productive may do their job so well that rational or sensible behavior, such as planning or paying strict attention to details, can decrease. If we count on the technology to rescue us if we make mistakes, we can be prone to making more mistakes. This can actually limit the effectiveness and convenience of using the technology.

Sociologist George Ritzer theorizes that whole societies are following this path (2009). He claims that many societies have become "McDonaldized," adopting certain characteristics of fast-food restaurants, such as their efficiency, predictability, calculability (desire to quantify things to the extent possible), and control. Control, he explains, is achieved by the use of nonhuman technologies, including digital technologies, that help bring about standardization. It can be argued that many aspects of a society, including social systems such as education, health care, and the government, have become McDonaldized—so concerned with moving people through their systems in predictable, calculable ways that individuals are becoming more controlled, less empowered, and somewhat dehumanized in the process.

It is wise to consider the role of information and communication technologies (ICTs) on schedules, time, and rationalization. But we should keep in mind that people use the internet and digital media to a great extent to relax and unwind as well. People head to digital spaces when they want to have fun, play games, and be entertained. As such, their impact on everyday life may end up being humanizing far more than they are dehumanizing.

fun, play, and entertainment

It can be tempting for those who are digitally connected to fill moments that might otherwise be quiet or dull with a constant stream of interaction or entertainment. With great frequency, people go online to enjoy themselves, play games, engage in cultural activities, or otherwise be entertained or have fun. There is always some kind of entertainment that can be sought, found, or even created online. Consequently, time spent on the internet or with digital media often has a light, playful, escapist dynamic. To have the ability to leave behind a busy or stressful physical environment even while in the midst of it and relax and enjoy oneself is a popular affordance of internet and digital media use (Fallows, 2006; Glasser, 1982, 2000; Rainie, 2011; Stephenson, 1964a, 1964b; Wasko & Faraj, 2000). Of course, this can certainly lead to procrastination and what might be perceived as the "wasting" of time.

Play is important, though; it is not necessarily frivolous. It meets critical needs and thus is a consistent part of the lives of people across cultures. Play is activity that is "bounded from everyday life, separated from pressures and obligations . . . freely chosen, noninstrumental, often absorbing and escapist" (Chayko, 2008, p. 63; see also Danet, 2001; Glasser, 1982, 2000; Huizinga, 1938/1950; Sandvig, 2006). Play is also relational—it is an important way that people make social connections.

It turns out that quite a bit can be accomplished in relaxed, playful environments. Skills can be honed, information can be obtained, friendships can be made and solidified. Skills and information matter not only for their own sake but because in this context they build common ground—a common stock of knowledge and norms and values that can become part of the culture of a group or a subculture. Playful activity can be a respite from everyday work and worry as well. I interviewed an L.A. Lakers fan who told me of his affection for the people with whom he plays and talks about basketball online:

> We're all interested in the same thing . . . and we've all got something in common, and we're all there to enjoy it. (Chayko, 2002, p. 105)

This individual made it clear to me that enjoyment was only part of the reason to follow a team or sport. He was very aware that the relationships that arose along the way were central to the experience.

In the course of prosuming entertainment and games and talking about them, either digitally or face-to-face, interpersonal connections and bonds are established. As people share their cultural interests with one another, they explore their like-mindedness—they may come to feel that those with whom they interact in these spaces are similar to themselves. Talk about celebrities, movies, books, or media preferences can pave the way for deeper understandings and provide an entry point for friendships to develop.

As discussed in Chapter 8, audiences of all forms of entertainment (television, movies, music, books) now often enjoy them on multiple platforms at once—electronic, print, and digital. This kind of *transmedia entertainment* can provide an extremely engaging experience for fans of these different kinds of genres and texts, allowing people to read or enjoy a given text in multiple ways, in various formats, deepening their involvement and commitment to the content (Jenkins, 2006). Some texts are highly serialized, continuing in some fashion from day to day and perhaps over many years, which substantially enhances the involvement and enjoyment of their audiences.

Technologically connected and networked fans are also able to participate in their favorite media offerings via the internet and digital media, especially social media. These platforms supplement the original texts by providing additional information and a means to connect with other audience members. Fans can readily discuss and critique programs; contribute to social media threads, blogs, and hashtags; and engage in communal discussions. Social media, particularly Twitter, has become a sort of second screen for people choosing to connect with other television viewers while a program or event is happening, especially a live one, creating a kind of electronic lounge where an audience can digitally commune and simultaneously share the experience (Harrington, 2014). As we have seen, digital hangouts are important in a society; they provide spaces for people to get together and feel one another's presence without the obligation of productivity or even direct interaction. And they can be lots of fun, which is important in and of itself, providing a welcome respite from more burdensome, taxing obligations.

Those who share cultural interests can go on to build groups and communities together. Such social circles abound in digital spaces and can provide a place for fans of any particular interest to come together. As with any community, these communities can become full-fledged cultures, with rules, rituals, symbolic boundaries, and initiation practices by which fans gain access to an inner circle. There is no guarantee that such a group will be egalitarian; it is as likely to contain hierarchies, cliques, and conflict as is any social organization, which can be seen in the phenomenon of the uber-fan or BNF (big name fan; Jenkins, Ford, & Green, 2013; Pearson, 2010).

Fans also have the opportunity to play new roles in digitally mediated systems. In addition to discussing and critiquing media products, fans can contribute to mediated stories by composing and sharing fan fiction, which is becoming a very popular way for fervent (or "cult") fans of a story to enjoy it together and even appropriate the story for their own pleasure (see Šesek & Pušnik, 2014). As these are essentially remixed works that do not necessarily have the imprimatur of the maker, they can be seen as piracy—as a copyright violation. Of course, another way of viewing such works is that they are a flattering means by which the original can be honored, expanded, and further promoted. It depends completely on one's perspective.

Such creations can spread widely, especially via blogs and social media, and the creators can become amateur experts (Baym & Burnett, 2009). Amateur experts often don't ask for any kind of economic compensation because there are other, perhaps more satisfying, rewards. They may receive attention (sometimes measured in social media likes and follows), interpersonal connections and relationships, status within the community, and/or other kinds of rewards. Media industries in general seem unsure whether and how to deal with this phenomenon, but some media producers value and learn from these audiences and may direct some messages or content (or advertising) directly to them, helping entertainment in the digital age be multidirectional and interactive across the board (Jenkins et al., 2013).

Gaming is another very popular online activity. Whether they are individualized, small group, or involve massive numbers of people, games can be intensely involving and can stretch over long periods of time, even years. They create environments that players insert themselves into, inhabit, and can become deeply immersed in. Highly social, video games are populated on and "behind" the screen with others that a player gets to know (see Juul, 2005; Klastrup & Tosca, 2004). Some games are even enabled with the technology of *virtual reality*, an immersive, computer-generated, multimedia environment that replicates physical experience in a highly realistic way. Virtual reality experiences and immersive games can be preparations for and simulations of embodied experiences, such as military combat or medical interventions (Gee, 2011; also see Chayko, 1993).

Digital and online gaming is also a culture. This culture may seem to be a youth-oriented and male-dominated one, but it would be a mistake to assume that all game players are teenage males. In fact, 67% of people aged 18 to 29 play online games, while 40% of those aged 50 to 64 do, and a full quarter of those 65 and over. Men and women are almost equally likely to play—50% of men and 48% of women report that they play games online (Corneliussen & Rettberg, 2008;

Duggan, 2017). Some games are more intense, featuring intricate environments that may require external headgear or other means to take part in immersive *virtual reality* or *augmented reality* environments. In massive multiplayer online role-playing games (MMORPGS) like World of Warcraft, the average player has been estimated at about 26 years old, with 36% of its players married and 22% having children (Yee in Corneliussen & Rettberg, 2008, p. 6).

In general, the gaming culture has seen more than its share of harassment, specifically of women. Representations of women in video games and game advertisements are frequently sexualized, and games featuring violence are a major source of revenue and profit. Women report disproportionately high levels of harassment in competitive games involving strangers, as do other nondominant groups, such as gays and racial minorities. Some women (and others) play games anonymously, while others play in safer communities or "clans" where egalitarian behavior is the norm (O'Leary, 2012). The "Gamergate" controversy (and hashtag) of 2014 erupted after female game developers experienced brutally misogynistic harassment and threats online. A flood of attacks and counterattacks ensued, many of them serious and frightening (for more on harassment, see Chapter 7).

Online games can be challenging, competitive, and highly strategic. Tasks are mastered, strategies are crafted, and social environments are quite often created. Skills are gained that can prove useful outside of a game and are highly transferable to different situations. Proper game play can teach decision-making, problem solving, discipline, delayed gratification, and even the scientific method, for in successful game playing, the gamer must often establish a hypothesis about some aspect of the game, test it, and then evaluate the results (Chayko, 2008, p. 68; Suellentrop, 2007, p. 62). Logical thinking and behavior is rewarded in many video and online games. These skills can serve people well in the digital workplace and in education, and a number of games are now being used to prepare members of the military and the police for dangerous situations (Volti, 2014, p. 273).

Some worry that people who live tech-saturated lives (especially the young) have come to expect and even to require instant stimulation, fun, entertainment, and/or digital connection at all times—that they expect never to be bored. To be sure, the generation of younger people that has grown up with these technologies at their disposal is so accustomed to them that they may be less tolerant than older people of things that do not entertain them, that are slower-paced, perhaps, or that seem to be "boring" (Chayko, 2008). They may seek to fill practically every moment with something to do and look for this gratification online. In the process, they may find themselves trying to multitask in many aspects of their lives.

multitasking and the attention span

Because people can use the internet and digital media to move fluidly from place to place and from screen to screen, they can find that directing their attention to any one topic and having it remain there is a challenge. They may feel easily distracted, their minds jumping from thing to thing. It may be becoming difficult for individuals to focus on one specific thing for an extended time, challenging the modern attention span and social institutions (which rely on focused individuals) alike (Kurtzberg & Gibbs, 2017; McHale, 2005; Ophir, Nass, & Wagner, 2009).

Attention is the act of giving mental concentration to a given task or unit of information. It is very difficult for most people to give full concentration to a task for a long period of time. While the length of the average attention span has not been accurately estimated, attention lapses—in which one's attention is at least momentarily diverted—occur very frequently, as often as every few minutes (Bunce, Flens, & Neiles, 2010). The ability to pay attention differs, of course, by individual and by task. One can pay significantly longer attention to a task if they feel engaged and immersed in it. This can happen when people take on a challenge at just the right level of complexity—not too easy but not too hard—generating a state of absorbed, energetic, long-term concentration called *flow* (Csikszentmihalyi, 1990). When one is involved in this way in a task, experience, or hobby (like a game), it is not difficult to pay attention to it for sustained periods. But most of the time, for most of us, it is a struggle to sustain unbroken engagement in a lengthy task or experience.

There is much concern that attention spans are diminishing in the digital era, though this, too, is difficult to quantify with precision. Many have become accustomed to posting digital updates frequently or checking in with friends or simply looking at or scrolling through digitized screens. It seems likely that these activities serve as a distraction to sustaining engagement in longer-term tasks. And to be sure, detrimental effects have been found; when students check Facebook, text, or instant message for personal use while they are studying, for example, grade point averages and overall study time suffer (Junco & Cotten, 2011; Kirschner & Karpinski, 2010). In other contexts, though, cognitive immersion in digital activities relevant to a specific task have been found to promote concentration and can improve academic outcomes (Prensky, 2001; see also Grimley, Allan, & Solomon, 2010). And when elementary school students with communicative disorders, specifically nonverbal autism, were given mobile digital devices to complete educational tasks, they demonstrated increased attention spans and levels of social interaction (McEwan, 2014).

How and whether people multitask, especially where ICTs are concerned, is a rich topic of study. *Multitasking* is a somewhat misleading term. It is not really possible to do several complex cognitive tasks simultaneously. More often, people move back and forth from task to task, switching as rapidly as they can or need to. Some people are better than others at doing this and can maintain focus on different tasks fairly well without their concentration suffering substantially, while others are not able to do so. Relatively fewer extreme multitaskers may even be able to split their attention among several tasks very effectively. The overall cognitive and attentional costs to individuals who switch frequently among tasks and attempt to multitask on a regular basis are still being debated (Alzahabi & Becker, 2011; Grimley et al., 2010; Ophir et al., 2009).

In general, people who attempt to multitask regularly and chronically suffer cognitive and behavioral deficits. They have difficulty recalling information and are slower at processing information. It is cognitively (and sometimes physically) demanding to try to do several things at once, and the result can be frustration and a sense of being overwhelmed (Ophir et al., 2009). I got very strong responses along these lines when I asked people how they managed their information flow, both online and offline. "It can be overwhelming at times—sometimes WAY too much information thus causing me to shut down," as one person whom I interviewed put it (2008, p. 128).

To persist in trying to multitask—which, again, is not only difficult but impossible for some people—can result in an individual giving *continuous partial attention* to many things at once. This phenomenon—scattering bits of one's attention among a number of things at any given time—is common in the modern media age (Stone, 2005). It happens chiefly because people frequently scan the media (or physical) landscape for new and different alternative opportunities even as they are supposed to be concentrating on a single one. They are, in a sense, optimizing for the best connections, activities, and contacts at any given time. To give continuous partial attention has become a norm in tech-rich cultures, technologist Linda Stone (who invented the term) says, because in these societies seeming to be busy and connected is to be alive, to be recognized—to matter (Stone, 2005).

A mobile device at one's fingertips provides easy access to a number of "places" to wander through and people to "visit." To pay attention to a single topic with this breadth of diverse stimuli so readily available is indeed a challenge. But managing these options properly can enhance people's capability to learn about and take part in a number of things. It is possible that losses of depth may be offset by gains in breadth, in learning more, in doing a greater number of different activities. "If we've lost something by not reading ten books on one subject," says novelist Naomi Alderman, "we've probably gained as much by being able to link together ideas easily from ten different disciplines" (as quoted in Naughton, 2010).

It is important to look at both the gains and the losses of taking on tasks in a media-saturated environment. Concerns about the ability of the human being to do a number of things at once are valid. There are limits to how much one can effectively do in a short time. But the brain is malleable and develops and changes over time as it is used in different ways. According to media studies researcher Ulla Foehr (2006), modern brains may be undergoing an evolutionary adaptation to the technology-rich media environment. "In this media-heavy world, it is likely that brains that are more adept at media multitasking will be passed along and these changes will be naturally selected," she says. "After all, information is power, and if one can process more information all at once, perhaps one can be more powerful" (2006, p. 24). In this theory, the ability to multitask can be developed via natural selection over time—a provocative prospect (see also Jenkins, 2009; Rose, 2010). Of course, whether that would represent a positive or negative development for the human race is up for debate.

stress, information overload, and FOMO

There are many tasks and expectations associated with the frequent use of digital technology. Keeping up with a flood of stimuli and information can be challenging and burdensome. Tasks may start to snowball; people can feel that they need to work and/or be digitally connected day and night, lest they fall behind the curve. Social connections and friendships need to be tended to, and superconnected people make and maintain many of them. But as we have noted so often in this book, these stresses are not caused by technology use. In fact, some of these stresses are simply the "cost of caring" (Hampton, Rainie, Lu, Shin, & Purcell, 2015).

While modern people certainly experience their share of stress, digital technology and social media users do not generally have higher levels of stress than those who are less digitally connected. In fact, for women the opposite is often true. Women who use Twitter and email and share photos by mobile phone report lower levels of stress than do those who do not because these technologies help them ascertain how their friends and family members are doing. It is often the responsibility of women to keep track of and check in on family, friends, and loved ones. By giving women an easy, convenient way to do this, social media can reduce their stress levels (Hampton et al., 2015).

Of course, in the course of using social media people sometimes hear about stressful or difficult events happening in the lives of others. They may learn that people they care about have been fired, lost loved ones, or are undergoing other hardships. This *awareness* of stress in the lives of others can and does cause stress—especially, again, for women, who are more likely to be attending personally to these kinds of issues. Stress—like the flu—is contagious. When your loved ones are experiencing stress, you may feel it as well because you care about them and "feel their pain." But these feelings and stresses are not due to spending time on social media. They are, again, simply the cost of caring about others (Hampton et al., 2015).

There is much talk about FOMO on social media (see Turkle, 2012). FOMO is the "fear of missing out" on the many interesting things that always seem to be happening online. Research indicates, however, that most social media users do not find FOMO particularly stressful and that, again, social media is not necessarily to blame if and when people feel overwhelmed. Indeed, fear of information overload predates the web. There is much to do in busy, fast-paced societies. Social media can ease or mitigate such pressures and requirements. Again, it's *how one uses the technology* that causes the outcome. Active social media users, then, need not feel more stress than those who do not use it regularly (Hampton et al., 2015).

Since people are exposed via social media to so much that is happening, there will always be something—many things—that are missed. As one woman told me,

> I feel like I need to check [my favorite sites] regularly or I'll be left out. (Chayko 2008, p. 125)

This concern was echoed by many whom I interviewed. It can seem overwhelming to keep up with news, information, entertainment and leisure pursuits, and all of one's social connections. It is impossible to remain completely "in the know." Many people pull back when presented with too much information in a short period of time. Research suggests that people are increasingly likely to unfollow people or organizations on Twitter when they provide what seems like too much information in a compressed period of time, as by sending a disproportionately high number of tweets in a time period (Liang & Fu, 2017). A kind of retreat may feel necessary.

The problem isn't having "too much information at our fingertips," says futurologist Jamais Cascio, "but that our tools for managing it are still in their infancy" (as quoted in Naughton, 2010). Some worries about information overload can be alleviated by the strategic use of digital tools to help us filter, sort, and organize information. Still, there is a limit as to how much information can be processed by the human brain in a given period of time. Information overload can lead to feelings of low self-esteem, when it seems that others have a better life than you have, and anxiety, when it seems impossible to keep up with it all.

Anxiety can be experienced even when people are simply unable to answer their ringing cell phones. In a study by journalism professors Russell Clayton, Glenn Leshner, and Anthony Almond (2015), iPhone users who were unable to answer their ringing phones while completing a puzzle reported feelings of anxiety and unpleasantness. Their heart rates and blood pressure increased. Their cognitive functioning was impaired, and they had a hard time paying attention to the task at hand.

In life, too many choices, like too much stimulation, can be overwhelming. This is an issue commonly experienced and is not unique to internet and digital tech users. As writer Martin Gronborg has described psychology professor Barry Schwartz's identification of *the paradox of choice*, "[Schwartz's] point is that choices also make us unhappy. There is no proportionality between our range of choices and our degree of happiness. Actually, quite the contrary. Only an adequate number of choices is good" (Gronborg, 2012, para. 2). According to Schwartz, after a certain point, the more choices one has, the harder and harder it becomes to feel happy.

In digital and social media use, individuals can become highly aware of how others depict themselves and seem to live their lives. Carefully edited depictions of lives and selves, as we discussed in Chapter 6, abound in digital spaces. In comparison, one's own life may sometimes seem less interesting, exciting, or happy than those of others. Social occasions to which one has not been invited may be documented in all their entertaining glory. Relationships between others can develop and be publicly documented, which may be uncomfortable to witness. Jealousy and insecurity are understandable reactions in a heavily mediated environment. There is so much going on, and only a small portion of it is happening to you!

It is important to keep in mind that others likely feel the same as you do with regard to stresses and possible feelings of inadequacy. No one's life is a perfectly crafted video or a well-framed, well-filtered photo. Social media, and media in general, offer us a window on the world, but what we see through that window need not necessarily be exactly as it seems, and probably isn't. As we learned in Chapter 6, identities and lives are being carefully shaped and presented online, and they undergo constant change. It is generally a mistake to assume that what you think is true *is* true, that everyone else has got it together, or that you're the only one who feels overwhelmed and inadequate sometimes. These are the by-products of a superconnected life.

Modern life also brings frequent decision dilemmas. Individuals must decide exactly how available they want to be at any given time, and to whom, and in what context. They must determine which bits of information should be shared in each of the environments in which they find themselves, for as we have seen, multiple, diverse audiences constantly converge online and contexts easily collapse. It takes skill and effort to navigate all these contexts (Castells, 2011; Chayko, 2008; Fortunati, 2002; Katz & Aakhus, 2002; Marwick & boyd, 2011).

Norms and values are frequently in flux in tech-rich societies. Sometimes they are even disrupted—changed so substantially and rapidly that they can seem to eclipse what came before. In such situations, it is easy to feel (or to actually *be*) displaced, confused, left behind. Jobs and entire industries may disappear or be replaced by those with entirely new practices. It can be challenging to understand and keep up with change. On the other hand, there is still much societal continuity. Change—even tech-influenced change—is far more frequently incremental than fully disruptive (see Marvin, 1988; Shapin, 2007).

It is useful to keep in mind that many of these dilemmas are understandable responses to living in modern societies in which much is going on, much is expected, and much is changing. The internet and digital media are not responsible for the stresses and pressures of modern life; in fact, they often help people manage these stresses. These difficulties are present wherever and whenever people come together, learn about one another, and care about one another.

emergencies

With mobile phones at the ready, people can now take care of one another and reach out to one another more easily in emergencies. Many people report needing or wanting to have a cell phone nearby at all times because they feel safer and more comfortable in the event that an emergency might occur. This is, again, a prime reason that phones are purchased in the first place, especially for one's children. It gives many people comfort to know that their children can contact them at any time and that they, in turn, can reach out to their children as needed and to always know (or to believe that they know) where their children are.

Many schools have relaxed prior strict requirements against cell phones because parents expect to be able to contact their children in the event of an emergency. Some schools allow students to use their devices at lunchtime or on breaks. What would once have been unusual (parents and children contacting one another during the school day) may be becoming normative. This further encourages regular and continuous family communication, even when children go to college or become adults and leave the house.

One of the central images of mobile phones is that of a "lifeline"—a direct connection to safety (Castells et al., 2004, p. 66). It provides both symbolic and real protection. Sometimes people—particularly women—pretend to talk on their phones to act as a kind of shield against unwanted attention; doing so sends the message that they are not alone. It is common for people to turn to their phones to text or talk when on their own, just to feel like they are in touch with someone. The cell phone can provide what Rich Ling calls "vicarious protection," which signals to the world that we are safely connected and not alone (2004; see also Geser, 2004).

In the case of true emergencies, rescue efforts are generally coordinated via computerized technology. Public safety and security networks are coordinated and mobilized by digital means. Citizens can hear of an emergency via mass and digital technology and may either aid in the rescue or avoid danger. Unfortunately, crimes and attacks are often coordinated this way as well. The same tech that can be used to help others can also harm them, depending, as always, on the technology's use.

Technologies that can be helpful and critical in times of emergency can also contribute to an environment in which more and more events come to take on the quality of an emergency. In addition, the pace of life in modern technological societies is often very fast. People expect one another to be available at all times. Thoughts and feelings become expressed quickly and immediately, sometimes without reflection. While digital technology can provide comfort and safety in the sense of emergency, it can also contribute to an environment in which people are more prone to doing things quickly and recklessly.

As we have seen, in tech-intensive environments the very prospect of disconnection can produce anxiety. Carrying a cell phone in the event of an emergency can prevent certain worries and create others, as one of my interviewees told me:

> I always have my cell phone on me. It's reassuring to know it's unlikely that I'll be stuck somewhere with no way to contact anyone, but when I find myself without it it's like I panic. I think, "Oh no I forgot my phone at home, what if something happens? What if someone needs to get ahold of me in the next few hours?" It takes a few minutes for me to realize how unlikely it is that someone will not be able to wait for me for a couple of hours. (Chayko, 2008, p. 123)

Technology anchors people in spaces and relationships. If a person is accustomed to constant connectedness and availability, it can be uncomfortable to be out of touch, even temporarily. Accordingly, individuals can become dependent on—some would say addicted to—digitally mediated experiences.

dependency and addiction

There is real concern over whether too-frequent use of the internet, digital media, and mobile devices like cell phones can create a dependency on or addiction to these technologies. Models of internet addiction posit that the criteria for such an addiction would include an individual's loss of control over internet use; ensuing psychological, social, or professional problems; and preoccupation and cravings when not using the internet. Though there is debate as to whether technology use can be considered an actual addiction or more of a dependency, there is little doubt that when these devices are used, people often feel a desire to use them more and more (Kurtzberg & Gibbs, 2017; Van Rooij & Prause, 2014).

The dopamine loop of information seeking and reward in digital tech use described in Chapter 7 comes into play here. Once we use technology and it feels good, there is incentive to use it again and again. Activities that stimulate the production of dopamine entreat the individual to want to do them over and over so that the positive feelings that flood the brain and body can be repeated. Online video gaming, social media socializing, and sexual uses of technology are said to be among the most compulsive or addictive internet-based activities. Offline, behaviors such as drug and alcohol use, exercising, eating, shopping, game playing, gambling, pornography use, and even sex are known to entice excessive continuation and be difficult to stop doing. These behaviors are sometimes considered addictions.

Some scholars, however, claim that the addiction model is not quite appropriate when chemical or physiological disease is absent. They maintain that there is not sufficient evidence to consider excessive use of the internet and digital media an actual addiction (Van Rooij & Prause, 2014). As psychologist and professor of gambling studies Mark Griffiths notes, use of the internet might more properly be considered a nonchemical dependency (2001). Experts explain that dependencies become problematic when the individual becomes enmeshed in a downward behavioral spiral characterized by mounting life problems, the failure of coping skills, and intensified cravings (LaRose et al., 2001; LaRose, Lin, & Eastin, 2003).

Those who are enmeshed in superconnected social networks and spend a lot of time online can certainly develop such symptoms. The attainment of social status and feelings of being involved and valued online can be heady; they can provide a sense of belonging and purpose. In online gaming, a person who plays games in order to avoid or escape other problems rather than simply for entertainment or socialization purposes may be more likely to become excessively involved in the experience (Khazan, 2006). Forty-five percent of the gamers that communication and game researcher Nick Yee studied in his large-scale study of people who played massive online games seemed to display such symptoms, while 42.7% of the internet gamblers gaming researchers Robert Wood and Robert Williams studied could be classified as "problem gamblers" (Khazan, 2006; Wood & Williams, 2007). It may be less important to determine whether to classify the condition as an addiction than to understand and help those who become afflicted.

It is interesting to question why the term *addiction* is invoked when certain kinds of activities are undertaken and not others. "If a person was reading novels excessively, we'd be less likely to call that 'addiction' because we value reading as culture," says communication scholar Dmitri Williams (as quoted in Khazan, 2006). He continues, saying that "we see game play as frivolous due to our Protestant work ethic" (as quoted in Chayko, 2008, p. 78). The same could be true of internet and digital media use, which is also sometimes dismissed as frivolous but is obviously used for a wide range of purposes with a vast range of effects.

To be sure, people can become deeply and troublingly immersed in behaviors like gambling, pornography use, compulsive online shopping and consumerism, the pursuit of unhealthy relationships, and so on. These problems all exist outside of internet and digital media use as well, however; they were problems before the advent of the internet and would be considered problems in any context. As we have seen repeatedly throughout this book, technological determinism, or looking to technology as the sole root cause of a problem, can impede a full understanding of the multifaceted ways that these technologies impact people's lives. It also does not suggest potential solutions to problems. As we seek to better understand the forces and desires that underlie technological use, we can try to minimize these very real problems while maximizing the positive potential of these technologies.

health and moods

Sometimes, what seems to be an addiction or a dependency may be a symptom of something else. Slapping a quick label on something without seeking deeper understanding is unhelpful and can indeed be harmful. A seeming addiction to or dependence on the internet and digital media may more accurately be indicative of a health problem (see LaRose et al., 2001; Morahan-Martin, 2005; Sanders, Field, Diego, & Kaplan, 2000).

Research indicates that too much time spent in front of computer and mobile screens is associated with low energy and fatigue. An increase in hours spent shopping, playing games, and doing research on the internet is associated with increased depressive symptoms (Morgan & Cotten, 2003). But using the internet to remain in close contact with friends and family is associated with declines in depression over time (Bessiere et al., 2010), and using it primarily to email, chat, or instant message others is also associated with decreased depressive symptoms (Morgan & Cotten, 2003). So the internet and digital media cannot be said to cause fatigue or depression per se, and they can also help people find ways to alleviate these states.

Physical inactivity is associated with higher levels of internet use and is also associated with depression (Fortunati, 2002; LaRose et al., 2001). By definition, if one is taking part in a sedentary activity, one is not getting exercise or doing much moving. Physical pain can also accompany too much time spent in front of a computer or looking at a screen. One's back can begin to hurt, and eyesight can become strained. In fact, numerous physical ailments have been correlated with time spent in front of computers, including headaches, hip pain, and even deep vein thrombosis, which is a very dangerous condition in which too much time spent physically inactive can incite the development of potentially fatal blood clots in the legs (Chayko, 2008). Physical movement is critical for the properly functioning body and for stress and anxiety reduction. It has been recommended that people who engage in stationary computer use for long periods take frequent breaks to stretch and walk around to keep the body and brain alert.

One does not have to be immobile while using digital devices, however. Cell phones, tablets, and other portable devices can be propped up in front of treadmills, stationary bikes, and other exercise equipment. Additionally, health-oriented apps and devices can be used to keep track of steps that are taken, calories consumed, and countless other bits of useful information. Digital technology can be used to promote and achieve good health. And as we have seen, medical information and advice are widely sought online and are enabled by the social networks that are formed there, and larger social networks are positively associated with good health and social support (Rainie & Wellman, 2012).

Using social media can also help delay the effects of aging and improve the physical and mental well-being of elderly people. In a University of Exeter study, elderly participants considered at serious risk of mental and physical decline were trained in using social media. When compared to a control group who did not use social media, study participants showed improvements in cognition and confidence, a strengthened sense of identity, and lessened feelings of loneliness. The risk of depression was also lowered. Playing games online has also been found to help fight the effects of aging in the areas of reaction time, attention span, and visual recognition (see Sass, 2014). Virtual reality experiences can even introduce a simulated therapist that can lower anxiety, and robots are beginning to be used as caretakers (Aronson, 2014; Kellerman, 2012; Turkle, 2012).

Moods can also be enhanced as a consequence of using the internet and digital media. When people spend time in positive, meaningful conversation and in communities online, their moods and well-being tend to improve (see Chayko, 2008; Green et al., 2005; Lindsay, Smith, Bell, & Bellaby, 2007). And, of course, giving and receiving social support, establishing friendships, and hearing from faraway friends and family can feel good and be an enormous boost to one's mood and health.

The physical and mental impact of spending lots of time online is a critical one of which to be cognizant and is an area in which much research is still needed. A reluctance to disconnect—and difficulty in disconnecting—would be quite concerning. Even when internet and digital media use does not occur in the extreme, it can still be a challenge for people to know how and when it is appropriate and necessary to turn off their devices and screens.

A balanced, blended approach to gathering life experiences and experiencing social interaction can help to create the healthiest life possible. Interacting in diverse environments and settings is important as well. Many of these settings can be sought and found online. But, of course, it is healthy and valuable to pursue activities that are offline also.

Solitude and disconnection are important in providing the brain and body with rest and restoration. It can be enriching to be bored sometimes—to allow the emotionality and intensity that so often accompanies digital technology use to cool. In order to be truly reflective, peace and stillness are generally required. When we carve out peaceful spaces for reflection, clarity and depth can be brought to our thinking and our bodies can feel refreshed as well. Children and teens, in particular, who have only known a world of continuous digital connectedness, may need to be guided in these respects.

It can be enlightening to induce a temporary separation from those with whom one is most consistently connected—to be temporarily out of touch. As I have written, "If we never leave one another, we can never miss one another, or experience the joy of being reunited" (Chayko, 2008, p. 136). Or as Hans Geser puts it, "Human existence is enriched by feelings of longing or homesickness . . . by sadness when a loved one leaves and joy when he/she finally comes back" (2004). Temporary disconnection, then, not only from technology but also from one's regular experiences, can be enriching and enlightening in a number of ways, both obvious and subtle.

On the other hand, social media theorist Nathan Jurgenson warns that "fetishizing" the offline—the time we spend away from technology in general—can be problematic (2012b). To overly praise (and even brag about) offline experiences simply *because* they are offline is to miss the point of going offline, he opines. It grants the experience (and the offline) a disproportionately exalted status. People go offline all the time, he points out, gathering the experiences that they may (or may not) choose to post about later. As we learned in Chapter 3, the online and the offline are enmeshed and are generally experienced as an integrated whole. They are not separate spaces or separate realities. When we brag or obsess about going offline, do we reinforce the "digital dualism" that claims that these spheres are separate?

A somewhat controversial set of ideas, Jurgenson's theory addresses the relative significance of the online and the offline worlds and speaks to the importance of considering all experience to be gratifying. All forms of lived experience can and *do* have value. We might remain more objective and open-minded when exploring them if we use research and theory to guide us, as opposed to giving way to emotional, sometimes fear-influenced reactions (sometimes called *moral panics*) to the newness of living life amid always-emerging technologies.

being plugged in . . . to society

Human beings need to feel at home in the world. We need to feel that the world will not change too dramatically, too suddenly, too unexpectedly. Even the most solitary among us need to feel "plugged in" to the world around us—plugged in to *society*. For humans are social animals and cannot develop mentally, emotionally, or physically if they do not have regular sources of interaction and a sense of connection to and understanding of the world around them.

Just as surely as cords and chargers plug our devices into electric outlets, technology plugs us into society. It connects us, again and again, to pathways, networks, and communities. At least some subset of one's network of friends, family, and acquaintances is nearly always reachable and can provide us with information, continuity, and community. Literally *and* figuratively, members of tech-rich societies are more plugged in than ever before.

This can be a satisfying, rewarding feeling. It can also be an ongoing challenge, as contexts collapse, multiple audiences must be attended to, and selves are constructed in these complex visible spaces. But most importantly, being plugged in can provide us on a very deep level with the comforting feeling that we are not alone. Some people assume that internet and digital media use makes us feel more alone. But the research does not bear this out. The research conducted on this topic and reviewed in Chapter 7 (and more comprehensively in Chayko, 2014) overwhelmingly indicates that internet and digital media use help people feel and be more connected with others.

But even in a more general and diffused sense, people feel that they are part of a larger whole when they go online. When spending time in online hangouts, playing games or visiting social media sites, or simply emailing a friend or colleague, we are reminded of the huge *net* of people that surrounds us all. "Just as the individual's deprivation of relationship with his significant others will plunge him into anomie," sociologists Peter Berger and Hansfried Kellner explain, "so their *continued presence* will sustain for him that *nomos* by which he can feel at home in the world" (1964, p. 7, emphasis added). To sense, even vaguely, the continued presence of others in the world and one's connectedness with them helps people feel more securely rooted in the world and provides a deep and real feeling of societal continuity.

All of us desire what Anthony Giddens calls *ontological security*—"the confidence or trust that the natural and social worlds are as they appear to be" (1984, p. 375). A world that was to reflect constant disruption, its sands always shifting beneath our feet, would be too difficult to bear. We require some kind of continuity and sameness from day to day. Taking part in techno-social life online can provide this kind of constancy, for it (and at least some others with whom we are connected) is always, dependably, there. It is a kind of gift that a tightly connected society gives to its members—the means to feel plugged in, superconnected, part of a whole (Chayko, 2002, 2008).

This sense of continuity and security persists even when we are offline. We do not need to check our phones constantly to know that friends and family are out there and that our connections and networks and communities, for the most part, persist. To be sure, it is highly satisfying to check in with friends and family—to feel their presence and the sense of security that, ideally, they confer. This is something people want to experience and verify regularly. But in a very real way, we carry these others with us wherever we go, making ontological security in the modern technological age truly a portable, mobile phenomenon. As Kate Fox was quoted on the first page of this chapter, "Carrying your social support network in your pocket, you'll never walk alone" (2001).

"Carrying others with us" mentally—when we are not physically together—predates online connectedness. The ability to think about and retain memories of other people in our minds predates the internet era, of course. We do not need to be literally plugged in, connected by technology, to feel connected to others. But technology—and remember, technology can be understood broadly to indicate a wide range of tools, techniques, and means of connecting people—can be a great boon in allowing us to feel, facilitate, and reinforce these feelings at any time. Some of the most interesting conversations I had with my interview subjects were on this topic:

> When I am online, I am always checking up on friends, making plans, or keeping in touch with distant friends and relatives. More often than not, I am in interaction with at least one other person. . . . Knowing I can email with friends makes me feel less "trapped" at work—I have access to everyone I know, so I don't need to feel trapped or isolated and therefore can better focus on my work. (Chayko, 2008, pp. 90, 106)

> I feel like I have all my friends with me. I feel like I've got this support group that I carry around in my head. (Chayko, 2002, p. 97)

The internet and digital media and technology connect us to one another and to the networks and communities of which we are a part, persistently and pervasively. They allow us to become superconnected., with all the accompanying benefits and hazards. And they raise a number of interesting questions about the techno-social future.

10 OUR SUPERCONNECTED FUTURE

new and emerging technologies

As we look toward the future, it is clear that digital technological innovation will continue at a high rate and that superconnectedness will only increase. Soon, half of the world's population will be online. The speed with which broadband technology can be used to access the internet will reach 10 megabits per second, which will be 200 times faster than dial-up service took only a couple of decades ago (and for roughly the same price). New and emerging technologies and applications of technology are being developed at unprecedented rates. Digitally enabled devices are used in almost all aspects of everyday life. The result, as we have seen, will be a combination of change and continuity, as some technologies have transformative effects on the ways that we live, while others have a more modest impact (Broadband Commission, 2014; Marvin, 1988; McKinsey & Company, 2014).

Some of the most important developments encompass digital structure itself. The computing capacity of computer hardware, for example, has been doubling every 18 to 24 months, and this is projected to continue in the future. Known as *Moore's law*, this means that in 15 years, computing capacity will have increased 1,000 times. Meanwhile, as computing becomes smaller and more powerful, the internet and mobile media can be increasingly accessed on smaller and more powerful devices, and graphical displays are becoming increasingly interactive, detailed, and graphically dense. A number of devices used to access digital content can now be worn, such as Google Glass and the Apple watch. The use of cell phones and smartphones continues to spread through the developed and undeveloped worlds, as larger and more expensive computing systems are no longer necessary to obtain or sustain internet or mobile access.

The miniaturization of computer technology has resulted in the development of computer chips that are now so tiny that they are called nanochips. As we saw in Chapter 4, these chips can now be implanted in the body, raising serious questions about external access to the most private personal information, as well as human dignity and individuality. Although most chips are not permanent, they require surgery to remove that causes scarring. At least one state has felt the need to pass a law prohibiting the forced implantations of chips under the skin by employers. While some argue that "chipping" is not so different from the implantation of pacemakers, artificial limbs, and the like into the body, others say that it is vertical surveillance at its most intrusive and troubling. It also begs the question as to how machinelike, how cyborg-like, humans are willing to allow themselves to become (Chayko, 2008).

Of course, humanlike machines, called robots, have existed for decades. They already perform tasks that humans might not want to do or be able to do or that are tedious, repetitive, or dangerous, such as working on space stations or assembly lines. But the tasks they perform are becoming more complex and lifelike. At one Silicon Valley hotel, a bellhop robot delivers items to people's rooms. Software algorithms can write news articles (Miller, 2014).

Caring for the elderly, young, or those who are sick or in distress can be challenging, and in some places, robots are taking on tasks associated with such care. In one Seattle hospital, robots administer sedatives to patients. In Japan, where they are considered *iyashi*, or "healing," robots help provide care to the elderly. In Europe, human-looking "social companion" robots are being developed to offer people reminders about appointments and medications and to encourage social activity, healthy eating, and exercise. Researchers in the United States have developed robots to assist in surgery, deliver medications and other supplies in hospitals, and assist with rehabilitation efforts. Advanced robots can seem quite empathetic, friendly, and even warm and can provide a real sense of companionship. Social companion robots that are even more humanlike are in the works, but development of these has elicited a strong reaction from the American populace, much of it negative (Aronson, 2014; Miller, 2014; Turkle, 2012).

People's use of mass and digital media is changing as well. New innovations render digital and social media more interactive and place based, and the physical location of users are frequently revealed. They have also changed how the more traditional mass media, both electronic (radio, TV, film) and print (newspapers, magazines, books), are used. Mass media users are increasingly able to access content over the internet and digital media and to share and discuss and even shape that content (see Harrington, 2014). People can now stream and view media content on all kinds of digital and mobile devices, on various platforms (such as Netflix), and on their own schedule, which restores some control to the viewer (who may choose, for example, to binge watch a television show rather than to watch it on a network's schedule).

New social media platforms, apps, and blogs that continue to be developed represent additional opportunities for audience members to customize their mediated experiences and to have more choices. This can lead to audience members developing a more enhanced media influence and voice. Entrepreneurial opportunities are available in this media environment as well. As we have seen, though, large media conglomerates have distinct advantages and power over smaller companies and individuals.

All these changes present new ways for people to work, relax, study, practice religion and politics, be entertained, and attend to their health. The techno-social institutions, like society itself, are living, changing, breathing entities. They consist of and are created by the accumulated actions of people living their lives, responding to change, and building the future.

the techno-social path ahead

Here is where you, the reader, are on a nearly level playing field with the experts cited throughout this book. This high-tech revolution has happened so quickly that no one can be absolutely sure where the path forward leads. Theories abound, many of which have been presented in this book. I want you to understand these theories, of course, but also to develop your own and debate them. I'll mention here some of the most prominent predictions of our techno-social future being offered as of the writing of this book, but if you are thinking as a scholar and you've absorbed most (some?) of what this book has covered, you should be equipped to make some predictions of your own. As no one can say for sure exactly what might or might not happen in the future, you have every chance of being right.

Perhaps the most likely predictions that could be made regarding tech societies of the future involve ever-increasing surveillance. More kinds of information are likely to be unearthed by more companies in an attempt to profile individuals and groups more and more specifically. It will become even harder to keep aspects of one's life private. People may become incentivized to share and sell their personal information directly, even bypassing some forms of data mining. Data mining and gathering will become more stealthy and pervasive. Environments may become laden with sensors that collect information as we move through them. In some areas, these sensors already exist. Implantable chips are being used. Drones are deployed in public. Such practices could result in a world in which it would become difficult if not impossible to escape being monitored. And to log off or disconnect might not be a realistic option, as digital technology is becoming a requirement for participation in more and more aspects of everyday life and work.

Most of us are not in control of the digital data that describes and is associated with us and do not have digital rights over much of our own data. Governments can restore some digital rights to citizens with comprehensive digital infrastructure design, such as that undertaken by Estonia and described in Chapter 8. But whether other nations move in such a bold direction—and whether citizens demand it—remains to be seen. Laws can be passed to permit and uphold the legality of invisible, invasive data searches. How aware is the citizenry of the implications of such policies?

Computing devices can become embedded in almost anything. In what has been called the *internet of things*, items that surround us daily are becoming digitally enabled and connected. Such items as TVs, kitchen and home appliances, toys, and cars can now be connected to the internet and to one another in large systems. These systems can generate information, collect data, and provide feedback as to how they are being used. Information on the human beings in their surroundings can also be gathered, making everyday objects tools for surveillance. While the internet of things can enhance lifestyles and safety, it can also have environmental and ethical impacts that are in many cases unregulated. Whether more regulation of digitized items and environments is to come or whether efforts to minimize regulatory oversight (such as Creative Commons) will predominate also remains to be seen.

Entire cities now can become technologized (or "smart"). Technologies that sense people's behaviors and even atmospheric conditions like the weather can be combined with data-mining and surveillance tools integrated with the city's infrastructure such that much of what is happening in the city can be observed and recorded. We already see some of this with cameras (often hidden) placed at traffic intersections to inform you (and law enforcement) when a breach has occurred and allow police to implement the associated penalty. Data such as traffic and crime patterns and energy and utility use can be tracked, and citizens' everyday activities can be observed. Many large cities in Europe are slated to become "smart cities." How will our natural environment and surroundings be affected? Will we use our technological knowledge to preserve nature or destroy it?

While all this information can certainly be used to keep people safer and to enhance the efficiency of a city, it brings up important questions of large-scale systematic monitoring. How might freedom, agency, and human rights be compromised and changed in such an environment? Does what tech scholar Jathan Sadowski calls *cyborg urbanization* diminish inhabitants' ability to have a say in the policies of the cities they live in (see Eschrich, 2014)? As we considered throughout Chapter 4, who has the power here, and how might it be used for and against the individual, the community, the society?

As appliances, computers, and entire workplaces become "smart" and equipped with artificial intelligence, the question as to the extent to which human workers might be replaced remains. While automation and robots are already displacing some workers (see Chapter 8), it should be noted that much of this work is underpaid, undervalued, and often unhealthy and dangerous, in addition to being tedious. It is unclear exactly how the economy would adapt to a workforce with a substantial nonhuman segment. Whether machines like robots should be used in military combat, be designed to more closely resemble humans, and even have rights are among the controversies surrounding their future development and incorporation into everyday life. How much "intelligence" and power can robots amass? How will humans and robots decide to share the planet?

Virtual and augmented reality applications in work, play, and leisure have expanded our abilities to create true immersive environments. Except in extreme cases, people do not seem to want or allow these environments to substitute for the face-to-face experience. But what is the long-term impact of spending large amounts of time in them? And how will we, and our traditional institutions, change in response to them?

People who live in communities and societies rich in digital technology have access to an unprecedented level of communication resources and a wealth of information. They also have multiple platforms through which to contribute and collect knowledge. They may share or gain insights via social media or blogs, in online courses, and in open source spaces. The potential of all this "recombinant innovation" to boost human progress is significant. With artificial intelligence and human brains potentially working together, the world can be better understood and, ideally, radically improved. As Erik Brynjolfsson and Andrew McAfee predict, such collaborations could be so impactful that they "make a mockery of all that came before" (2014, p. 96).

Social norms and values in groups, industries, institutions, and societies are changing in the digital era. Some of these changes involve the appropriate use of digital devices in certain spaces; the acceptability of sharing information widely; how, where, and when work should be done; and what is most appropriately considered public or private. Still, it should be kept in mind that humans experience most of this in terms of continuity rather than change. Except in rare cases of sweeping revolution, a society generally does not remake itself overnight. On an everyday basis, change is more often modest and incremental rather than disruptive and reconfigured.

The internet and digital media have resulted in the mainstreaming of certain behaviors once considered to be more deviant or profane. This is a change at the cultural level. For example, gambling is increasingly tolerated and promoted as a positive social activity for adults and even children. As consumerism continues to rise, it sometimes seems that nearly everything around us carries advertisements or is for sale. Pornography and sexual images are more widely available and contribute to a more highly sexualized culture. Norms and values, the material products of culture, and the culture as a whole are always dependent on the practices and agency of group members—although those members must work within a power structure that often limits their choices.

New and emerging technologies are changing the ways that our households, classrooms, cities, and governments look and operate. As technologies develop, change, and spread, physical spaces change as well. Decisions will need to be made about how technology is allowed to intrude into the physical world, such as whether unmanned drones can be used in warfare or whether self-driving cars will become accepted in everyday life. These decisions are critical because norms will develop in response to them. These norms and behaviors are a signal to what societies value and can guide us through changes.

We need to think carefully, therefore, about the norms, policies, and laws we establish because they help shape the society that we live in and that generations that follow us will inherit. We need to think about what is gained and lost as technologies continue to be invented that allow us to connect almost constantly. When possible, thinking about these things with an open mind will be more optimal than allowing fixed ideas to guide our way. Empowered by collective organization, which is often coordinated and enhanced by digital technologies like social media, individuals have the opportunity to influence these changes.

As we examined in Chapter 5, societies across the globe are changing in response to the incorporation of the internet and digital media into social life at the micro, meso, and macro levels. It is not uncommon to see cell phones in some of the world's poorer areas, although internet access, literacy, and widespread usability are far still from universal. Mobile technologies are contributing to social transformation in these less developed areas, allowing people greater access to information, services, and jobs, but this transformation is nowhere near total. Those who own and control the technology and the media have more power than those who do not, and those power centers are located in the developed world. For a country or region to fully participate in a technological world, it must have the ability to develop its own technological culture, which requires a substantial commitment of capital, education, and infrastructure. Much more is required to lift people out of poverty and provide the basic necessities of life.

Governments are often slower to respond to these issues than are their constituents. Many who use the internet and digital technology wish to better their worlds and the lives of themselves and others. The organization of citizens to advocate for social change is a powerful collective use of the internet and digital media. Those who have political power will often try to hold onto it, however. They will use the technology to do so—to try to ensure that their ideas and ways of life predominate. It is incumbent on citizens who wish to challenge the status quo to do the same. Though individuals and groups are becoming adept in using digital technologies to speak out against those in power and in some cases to make substantial changes, it is, again, difficult to do this in some of the areas of the world where people's lives are in greatest need of transformation. There, people may not have access to digital technology at all and must rely on the awareness and assistance of those with more social capital and tech readiness. At the very least, this book implores you to be aware of and knowledgeable about these serious global divides and impacts.

Power dynamics can shift, and shift radically, in this technological age. Those who have digital technology access and skills have the means to stir things up, to make and remix products (as well as the culture), and to effect change. Internet users under the age of 30 are increasingly likely to contribute to politically oriented discourse online (Smith, Schlozman, Verba, & Brady, 2009) and to host or contribute to blogs about political or civic issues. It remains to be seen whether younger users will continue these patterns or will be less inclined to remain politically active as they age. Perhaps civic and political engagement will in the future be correlated less with income and education and more with high levels of internet use.

the human–machine connection

As you can see, there are far more questions than answers here. Still, it is important to make some educated guesses and predictions as to how a superconnected future may unfold and what it may look like, including the new kinds of connections that are made between humans and machines. We all want to be as prepared as possible to move confidently and successfully through a world in which an ever-more sophisticated "internet of things" ensures that machines and people will relate to one another in new kinds of ways.

On some level, it is easy to perceive digitally enabled "others" as interactants with whom we have a relationship (Chayko, 2002; Reeves & Nass, 1996). Voices (like the iPhone's Siri), images (like an avatar), and even actors who appear on our media screens are cognitively and affectively encountered and can sometimes even be communicated with. These encounters can in certain ways resemble those of human-to-human interaction and relationships.

Robots and *bots*—humanlike machines and web-based software applications that run automated tasks—are becoming in some cases more interactive and seemingly personable. Such machines and applications can be comforting and help people cope with challenges and even provide some forms of social support (see Kellerman, 2012), although there are limits to the types of communication that the artificial intelligence of computers can perceive (Siri, for example, cannot detect sarcasm; see Zawacki, 2015). Despite the rich, seemingly human interactions enjoyed by the fictional protagonist Theodore and his computer's automated intelligence system Samantha in the movie *Her* or the relationship between Caleb and the robot Ava in the movie *Ex Machina*, computers and software as currently configured lack the experiences and understanding of emotional subtext necessary for communication to be deep, nuanced, and truly human.

Still, people can engage in meaningful ways with digital technology and especially those machines that are most realistic. Robot dogs, dolls, and toys have been known to comfort those who spend time with them—particularly those in greatest need of comfort, such as the elderly (see Turkle, 2012). Parents have reported that their children with special challenges and needs have been helped through mediated interaction. Parent Ron Suskind, for example, has described how his autistic son came out of his shell through engagement with Disney characters, while Judith Newman has written of how her autistic son Gus's conversations with Siri improved his communication skills and provided him with companionship (Newman, 2014). Newman reports that Gus's practice conversations with Siri have resulted in increased facility in interacting with human beings. So many people now indulge in conversations (whether playful or serious) with these kinds of digital tech "assistants" that SRI International, the research and development company behind the voice of Siri (now owned by Apple), is focusing research efforts on enhancing the ability of the assistant to engage in even more complex and realistic conversations (Newman, 2014).

For the most part, those who use such technologies understand the difference between physical and mediated realities. Judith Newman makes it clear that her son Gus is well aware that Siri is mechanized and not an actual human. Fictional characters and disembodied tech voices are generally encountered as created constructions that retain a strong element of reality. One can be well aware of but still "play with" the difference between fiction and nonfiction. In enjoying fictional or mediated experiences, it is common to play freely and flexibly with the concepts of reality and fantasy. In other work, I have theorized that mentally approaching fictional characters as real heightens the pleasure of the fictional experience and can even provide a practice space for making and maintaining digital relationships with real people (Chayko, 2002; see also Chayko, 1993; Harrington & Bielby, 1995; Jenkins, 1992).

While nobody can know exactly what form future human–technology relationships may take, consultation with tech experts and scholars can help us wrap out brains around, and better prepare for, this new wave of human–machine superconnectedness. In 2017, the highly regarded Pew Research Center gathered information from 1,201 experts in industry, government, and academia on this very issue. The experts rendered opinions on how deeply and intensively people and technology-enabled "smart" objects would be connected in the future, and then the researchers identified predictive patterns in the responses (Rainie & Anderson, 2017). Eighty-five percent of the experts who shared their thoughts on this topic with Pew (of which, full disclosure, I was one) indicated that they believe that technological connectivity will continue to increase in the future (and after reading this book, it should not surprise you that I fall into this camp!). The other 15% indicated their belief that a tendency to disconnect and withdraw from technology in the future is more likely, given the inherent vulnerabilities of mechanized technology (hacking, surveillance, etc.).

Most of the experts felt that because humans crave connectivity, they will always and inevitably seek more of it "due to its convenience and out of necessity because it will simply be embedded in more and more things," Rainie and Anderson reported (2017). As one expert said, "The stickiness and value of a connected life will be far too strong for a significant number of people to have the will or means to disconnect." Many of the experts, even those who thought that human–machine connectivity would increase in the future, also acknowledged the downside—that it can be dangerous, scary, and frustrating to rely on digitized systems that have inherent frailties and can at any point be hacked or attacked. Still, "people can get used to anything," a professor of history and information claimed. "Just as with terrorism, the inevitable occasional damage from deliberate or inadvertent failures in highly networked systems will become routine" (2017).

Some of the trends toward greater connectedness predicted in the Pew report:

- The always-on younger generation can't imagine being anything but connected. "The individuals who will be using this technology (in the future) are the teens of today. It will be second-nature for them to use and interact daily across many devices and modalities."

- Unplugging isn't easy now, and by 2026, it will be even tougher. "It will be increasingly difficult to unplug, as more and more aspects of ordinary daily life are plugged in. Unplugging will require a religious level of commitment."

- Resistance is futile: Businesses will penalize those who disconnect; social processes will reward those who connect. "Even if individuals are concerned about the risks, they'll find it difficult or impossible to opt out of these connections if they want to continue with the products or services they want and/or need."

On the other hand, 15% of the experts consulted by Pew felt that greater disconnection was likely, arguing that lack of trust, safety and privacy issues, and more may move those with fears to withdraw: "More, and more serious, data breaches are likely to push people away from the Internet of Things."

In the end, the report concludes that whether or not connection "trumps" disconnection, the dangers are real. Security and civil liberties issues will be magnified. "Most people are totally oblivious to the fragile and easily pierced nature of the Net and the total lack of protection of their medical/financial information," offered a programmer/data analyst. "They will continue to not care or understand the issues."

It is one of the goals of this book that its readers will indeed come to care about and understand issues relevant to living in a techno-social society in a deeper, richer way. With tech change happening so quickly, especially in the digital realm, there is truly no way for anyone—expert or student—to chart a road ahead or predict the future with perfect accuracy. That is why it is so important to be knowledgeable and vigilant regarding the impact of our (and our society's) technology use—and to actively and thoughtfully forge our personal paths forward.

our personal paths

There are many more questions than answers surrounding the future of the internet, digital media, and technology in our rapidly changing society. As we have seen, uncertainty as to how technology can affect norms, practices, the world around us, and our very *selves* can lead some to blame the tools themselves, calling on technological determinism to explain the changes they see around them. Change is constantly underway in tech-rich societies, and it is not always easy to handle.

Living in modern technologized times can be a shock to the system, claims media theorist Douglas Rushkoff (2013). The technologies that we have created are of indispensable assistance in helping us compile knowledge, gather news, and connect with one another, he notes. But great challenges accompany each of these developments. And the more we become aware of these challenges—economic troubles, climate change, wars, any of a host of social problems—the more we can become overwhelmed with the prospect of actually solving them.

It is easiest, Rushkoff (2013) says, to think of these problems as so complex as to be unsolvable. To try to fix them seems so daunting that many turn away. This is perhaps an understandable response. But it cedes control of our lives and our societies—which, we have already learned, *are* us—to others. Technology and society are human creations. All of us have a stake in determining their future course.

Fears tend to worsen when people feel that they cannot participate in decisions that impact their lives. Individuals need to feel that they have a voice in the shaping, development, and use of the technologies that surround them and that they may be able to affect the course of technological change. To feel disempowered regarding one's future can produce "a mixture of naïve hope and paranoid reaction" (Volti, 2014, p. 17). There is no need for either naïveté or paranoia when one lives in a society where the tools and skills to influence that society can be learned and employed.

The challenges of being faced with so much information and so many avenues for tech exploration are very real. However, technology can aid in the development of solutions. People can use social media to raise money for and awareness of social problems. They can check in with family members and friends frequently and maintain stronger, deeper social ties. They can develop the weak ties in social networks that allow them to exchange information, opportunities, resources, and social support. They can collaborate to solve problems and do research and present their findings widely. Health-oriented apps and products can be used in ways that will improve the quality of their lives and of the lives of friends and family.

Research into robotics is pushing the frontiers of exactly how, and how far, humans and machines will mesh. As chips, artificial hearts, and prosthetic limbs are being incorporated into the human body, and as robots are becoming more humanlike, we are seeing a human–machine symbiosis (Kelly, 2010). Whether robots might be able to become truly empathic or creative—or so "smart" that their intelligence could eclipse that of humans—are questions currently being researched (see Carstensen, 2015). But we can always keep in mind that human life, even in the era of the robot, bot, and algorithm, is qualitatively different from any kind of intelligence that can be developed by a machine.

Researchers are currently creating computer models of the brain and consciousness that could theoretically be uploaded into a machine for posterity. According to bioengineer Kwabena Boahen, "We envision building fully autonomous robots that interact with their environments in a meaningful way, and operate in real time while their brains consume as much electricity as a cell phone" (as quoted in Sadowski, 2013). The goal of this research is for human and computer intelligence to be melded in ways that will allow human beings to live forever—in digital form. Do you have a stake in the results of such research? How might it impact your personal path forward?

Debates over the ethics and implications of this kind of progress—truly, whether it represents "progress" at all or something more threatening, even sinister—are raging and will continue to do so as this research continues. For futurist Ray Kurzweil and a number of scientists, human beings are just one stage in the evolution of matter toward higher levels of complexity. By 2029, Kurzweil predicts, artificial intelligences will routinely fool us into thinking that they are flesh-and-blood people, and bots that have been implanted in one's brain will be able to shut down the signals coming from the physical senses and replace them with those that have been digitally generated (in Rushkoff, 2013, pp. 254–255).

The counterargument to this, of course, is that the human self is unique, special. It is irreplaceable by machines. It is worth standing up for. As Rushkoff puts it, the human being contains an "unquantifiable essence . . . something too quirky, too paradoxical, or too interpersonal to be imitated or re-created by machine life" (2013, p. 258). Many agree, while some are unconvinced. Where do you stand on this? What does it mean, really, to be human?

Individuals will continue to express their humanity and to think in new, different ways as they explore uses and implications of the internet and digital media. Highly abstract, categorical, and logical thinking can be developed through reading and writing in digital spaces. Hyperlinking encourages less linear, more expansive, more connective modes of thinking. As interpersonal similarities and like-mindedness are increasingly identified and pursued, collaboration becomes more prevalent and sophisticated. Minds, as we have seen, can even become synchronized and work together more effectively, leading to greater and deeper interpersonal and intercultural understandings (Chayko, 2008; Thompson, 2013).

The rise and proliferation of the internet, digital media, and ICTs represent the potential for individuals to live richer lives but also lives that are more closely scrutinized and surveilled. The harnessing of collective knowledge and superconnectedness yields infinite possibilities, but the outcomes are unclear, uncertain. The future holds infinite possibilities, which can be daunting and overpowering or exciting and freeing. As science writer James Gleick looks at it, "We can be overwhelmed or we can be emboldened" (2011, p. 419).

Upcoming generations of digital connectors will likely find digitality in and of itself to be neither daunting nor confusing. Children and young adults growing up in a technology-intensive environment have several advantages, such as comfort with and practice in interacting and building social worlds online, agility in moving between online and offline spheres, and a default consideration of that which occurs in digital spaces to be very much "real." They tend not to have a problem seeing the online and offline as enmeshed. Soon, children in tech-rich communities and societies will never have known a world without these digital advancements. When that time arrives, what will be lost? What will be gained?

Individuals will always be challenged to create cohesive identities and communities and to understand the workings of both. In the modern technological world, people are, and will remain, superconnected. Thoughtful, strategic, shrewd use of the internet and digital technology can help people better manage their techno-social lives and create a future filled with rich, diverse experiences. To do this, they—we—must become and remain educated and literate about techno-social life.

The internet and digital media provide countless opportunities for making, shaping, critiquing, and improving technology, the world around us, and our own lives. Passive consumption of technology and of changes that have been decreed by others inevitably leads to feelings of weakness and hopelessness. Individuals need to feel some control over their lives, and democracies require that people have a voice. If we outsource technological expertise and decision-making to others, we give them control over all the aspects of techno-social life discussed in this book.

So I invite you again, as I did when we began our exploration of techno-social life in Chapter 1, to take this book's lessons and explore more deeply those issues most relevant to you, that you care most about. Network. Create. Remix. Act. Use the technologies at your disposal and those to come—including those that you build—to shape the kind of world you want to live in. Connect with others who believe as you do. Use a combination of the internet, digital media, and face-to-face gatherings to build and sustain those connections. With curiosity, creativity, and a critical mind—all of which I hope this book has helped you to develop—there are almost no limits to the journey you can take, and the difference you can make, as you chart your own path into the wild, superconnected, techno-social future.

ACKNOWLEDGMENTS

When my good friend, the sociologist, author, and community organizer Corey Dolgon, suggested I write this book, my initial impulse was to ignore him *and* the suggestion. I had a bunch of reasons and excuses for not writing it, some of which were actually legitimate, but the truth was that I wondered whether I was up to the task. The project I envisioned would be broader in its scope than anything I had yet done and would take substantial research, energy, and time.

But once I started envisioning the project and imagining how I would approach it, I realized I was already "in." I found myself scribbling down ideas and then whole sections in between other projects. An outline of the topics and chapters that I wanted the book to include began to take shape. SAGE expressed interest in publishing it. Suddenly, there was no turning back.

Preparing both editions of this book has provided me with unforgettable experiences: days spent learning interesting things and writing about what I learned, fascinating conversations with friends new and old, the joys of accomplishing tasks and meeting goals. I'm glad to have undertaken the work, but I'm even happier for the relationships and networks that have come about and become strengthened along the way.

I must, therefore, thank Corey Dolgon first and foremost for proposing this book to me and providing constant, steadfast encouragement. His influence on my life as colleague, confidant, coauthor, and singing partner has been paramount, and our decade-plus friendship is one of the great pleasures of my life.

I can't mention Corey without thanking in the next breath the third member of our little social justice–oriented folk group, the superb sociologist and singer–songwriter Jim Pennell. Jim and his wife, education professor and sociologist-by-marriage Greta Pennell, have been family to me since our graduate school days at Rutgers. There's something very special about remaining close with your grad school buddies, supporting one another and making music together as the years roll on. Thanks, you three, for always having my back.

I also thank the following:

Eviatar Zerubavel, for teaching me how to think.

Karen Cerulo, for her peerless mentorship, role-modeling, and all-around brilliance.

Ira Cohen, for his boundless generosity and care.

Jeff Lasser and the editors and staff at SAGE, especially Adeline Wilson, Laureen Gleason, Amy Hanquist Harris, Victoria Reed-Castro, May Hasso, Gail Buschman, Kara Kindstrom, and the team at Hurix, for their expert steering of this project to publication.

Dave Repetto, for his early interest in and acquisition of this book when with SAGE.

Jim McGlew, for being my first phone call whenever life turns upside down.

Shravan Kumar Sathyanarayana Iyer, my extraordinary research assistant, and Lorena Cunningham, my extraordinary teaching assistant, whose excellent work helped make this second edition possible.

My students—past, present, and future—for influencing and inspiring all my professional activities. I write to, and for, them, always.

The School of Communication and Information (SC&I) at Rutgers University, my professional home, and especially my colleagues and buddies "in the trenches": Steve Miller, Brian Householder, and Sharon Stoerger. My friend Denise Kreiger helped me design and realize all my most ambitious projects, even though I became a completely useless collaborator about an hour into every work session. I will always thank and appreciate Keith Hampton, my forever friend and colleague, even though he left SC&I for green pastures (literally!) and now encourages and inspires me from a distance. Finally—actually this probably should have been first—I thank Rutgers deans Mark Aakhus, Paul Gilmore, Dafna Lemish, Matt Matsuda, Claire McInerney, Harty Mokros, Karen Novick, and especially Jonathan Potter for their strong support of me and this project.

My many other colleagues and friends at Rutgers, SC&I, The College of Saint Elizabeth, and numerous colleges and universities across the globe: There are too many of you to name, but I thank you for your contributions to my life and this work from the bottom of my heart. Having said that, I'd be remiss not to express my deep love and appreciation to my dear friends Kim Grant, John Marlin, Lisa Mastrangelo, and Margaret Roman. They somehow got tasked with keeping me sane and happy, and they are brilliant at it.

And those who matter most:

Glenn Crooks, for loving me without conditions or expectations—and for taking me camping.

Ryan Lizotte, my wonderful son, for helping me think through the complexities of digital technology (along with politics, music, and life itself) and for creating with me the special, unique bond that is the joy of my life.

Morgan Crooks, for our own irreplaceable, unique, joyful bond of mother–daughter friendship, our silly laughter, and her remarkable self-sufficiency, or this book would never have gotten done.

Terri Chayko, for making me eggs (sometimes) and being my mom.

Bob Chayko, whose love and life lessons still resonate daily, if not hourly.

Aunt Pat, just for being Aunt Pat.

Rob Pincelli, the "big bro" I otherwise would never have had.

Marco Masucci, for all the laughter and all the love.

My siblings and best-buds-for-life Cathy Chayko and John Chayko, their children Anna and Joe Wassmer and Alex and Josh Chayko, their spouses Scott Petry and my girl Claudia Scotti, the whole Scotti clan (especially Goog), Lainie Aldrich and the Wassmers, and last but in no way least, Crazy Aunt Jan and her gang: Norm, Melanie, Devin, Jeff, Amanda, Addy, and Samantha.

Heartfelt thanks to all of you. I'll take my village over any other.

publisher's acknowledgments

SAGE wishes to acknowledge the following peer reviewers for their editorial insight and guidance:

Nicole A. Cooke
Graduate School of Library and Information Science,
University of Illinois

Steve Jones
University of Illinois at Chicago

Julia Nevarez
Kean University

Joong-Hwan Oh
Hunter College–CUNY

Julie B. Wiest
West Chester University of Pennsylvania

REFERENCES

Abidin, C. (2014). #In$tagLam: Instagram as a repository of taste, a brimming marketplace, a war of eyeballs. In M. Berry & M. Schleser (Eds.), *Mobile media making in the age of smartphones* (pp. 119–128). New York, NY: Palgrave Pivot.

Adams, R. G., & Allan, G. A. (1998). *Placing friendship in context.* Cambridge, UK: Cambridge University Press.

Akamatsu, C. T., Mayer, C., & Farrelly, S. (2006). An investigation of two-way text messaging use with deaf students at the secondary level. *Journal of Deaf Studies and Deaf Education, 11*(1), 120–131.

Albright, J. M. (2008). Sex in America online: An exploration of sex, marital status, and sexual identity in internet sex seeking and its impacts. *Journal of Sex Research, 45*(2), 175–186.

Alexander, B. (2004). Going nomadic: Mobile learning in higher education. *Educause Review, 39*(5), 28–35.

Alkalimat, A., & Williams, K. (2001). Social capital and cyberpower in the African-American community. In L. Keeble & B. G. Loader (Eds.), *Community informatics: Shaping computer mediated social relations* (pp. 174–204). London, UK: Routledge.

Allen, E., & Seaman, J. (2013). Changing course: Ten years of tracking online education in the United States. *Sloan Series of National and Regional Surveys of Online Education.* Retrieved from http://www.onlinelearningsurvey.com/reports/changingcourse.pdf

Alzahabi, R., & Becker, M. W. (2011). In defense of media multitasking: No increase in task-switch or dual-task costs. *Journal of Vision, 11*(11), 102.

Amichai-Hamburger, Y., & Ben-Artzi, E. (2003). Loneliness and internet use. *Computers in Human Behavior, 19*(1), 71–80.

Amit, V. (2002). Reconceptualizing community. In V. Amit (Ed.), *Realizing community: Concepts, relationships, and sentiments* (pp. 1–20). London, UK: Routledge.

Anderson, B. (1983). *Imagined communities.* London, UK: Thetford Press.

Anderson, J., Boyles, J. L., & Rainie, L. (2012). The future impact of the internet on higher education. *Pew Research Center.* Retrieved from http://www.pewinternet.org/files/old-media/Files/Reports/2012/PIP_Future_of_Higher_Ed.pdf

Anderson, M. (2016, November 7). Social media causes some users to rethink their views on an issue. *Pew Research Center.* Retrieved from http://www.pewresearch.org/fact-tank/2016/11/07/social-media-causes-some-users-to-rethink-their-views-on-an-issue/

Andreassen, C. S., Torsheim, T., & Pallesen, S. (2014). Predictors of use of social network sites at work: A specific type of cyberloafing. *Journal of Computer-Mediated Communication, 19*(4), 906–921.

Andrejevic, M. (2012). Estranged free labor. In T. Scholz (Ed.), *Digital labor: The internet as playground and factory* (pp. 149–164). New York, NY: Routledge.

Annafari, M. T., Axelsson, A., & Bohlin, E. (2013). A socio-economic exploration of mobile phone service have-nots in Sweden. *New Media and Society, 16*(3), 415–433. doi:1461444813487954

Aronson, L. (2014, July 19). The future of robot caregivers. *The New York Times.*

Retrieved from http://www.nytimes.com/2014/07/20/opinion/sunday/the-future-of-robot-caregivers.html

Associated Press. (2013, January 12). Reddit co-founder Aaron Swartz dies at 26. *CBC News.* Retrieved from http://www.cbc.ca/news/technology/reddit-co-founder-aaron-swartz-dies-at-26-1.1364575

Associated Press. (2016). *Associated Press stylebook.* New York, NY: Basic Books.

Astor, M. A. (2017, July 25). Your Roomba may be mapping your home, collecting data that could be shared. *The New York Times.* Retrieved from https://www.nytimes.com/2017/07/25/technology/roomba-irobot-data-privacy.html?module=WatchingPortal®ion=c-column-middle-span-region&pgType=Homepage&action=click&mediaId=thumb_square&state=standard&contentPlacement=1&version=internal&contentCollection=www.nytimes.com&contentId=https%3A%2F%2Fwww.nytimes.com%2F2017%2F07%2F25%2Ftechnology%2Froomba-irobot-data-privacy.html&eventName=Watching-article-click&_r=1

Aviram, I., & Amichai-Hamburger, Y. (2005). Online infidelity: Aspects of dyadic satisfaction, self-disclosure, and narcissism. *Journal of Computer-Mediated Communication, 10*(3).

Baker, A. J. (2005). Double click: Romance and commitment among online couples. Creskill, NJ: Hampton Press.

Bakshy, E., Rosenn, I., Marlow, C., & Adamic, L. (2012). The role of social networks in information diffusion. In *WWW'12—Proceedings of the 21st Annual Conference on World Wide Web* (pp. 519–528). New York, NY: ACM. doi:10.1145/2187836.2187907

Baller, S., Dutta, S., & Lanvin, B. (2016). The Global Information Technology Report 2016: Innovating in the Digital Economy. *World Economic Forum and INSEAD.* Retrieved from http://www3.weforum.org/docs/GITR2016/WEF_GITR_Full_Report.pdf

Bargh, J. A. (2002). Beyond simple truths: The human-internet interaction. *Journal of Social Issues, 58*(1), 1–8.

Bargh, J. A., McKenna, K. Y. A., & Fitzsimons, G. M. (2002). Can you see the real me? Activation and expression of the "true self" on the internet. *Journal of Social Issues, 58*(1), 33–48.

Bastani, S. (2000). Muslim women on-line. *The Arab World Geographer, 3*(1), 40–59.

Bauer, M. (1998). The medicalization of science news—from the "rocket-scalpel" to the "gene-meteorite" complex. *Social Science Information, 37*(4), 731–751.

Baym, N. (2000). *Tune in, log on. Soaps, fandom, and online community.* Thousand Oaks, CA: SAGE.

Baym, N., Zhang, Y. B., & Lin, M. (2004). Social interactions across media: Interpersonal communication on the internet, telephone and face-to-face. *New Media and Society, 6*(3), 299–318. doi:10.1177/1461444804041438

Baym, N. K. (1995). The emergence of community in computer-mediated communication. In S. G. Jones (Ed.), *Cybersociety* (pp. 138–163). Thousand Oaks, CA: SAGE.

Baym, N. K. (2010). *Personal connections in the digital age.* Cambridge, UK: Polity.

Baym, N. K., & Burnett, R. (2009). Amateur experts: International fan labour in Swedish independent music. *International Journal of Cultural Studies, 12*(5), 433–449.

Becker, H. (1984). *Art worlds.* Berkeley: University of California Press.

Beer, D. (2008). Social network(ing) sites . . . revisiting the story so far: A response to danah boyd and Nicole Ellison. *Journal of Computer-Mediated Communication, 13*(2), 516–529.

Belk, R. W. (1998). Possessions and the extended self. *Journal of Consumer Research, 15*(2), 139–168.

Bell, C., & Newby, H. (1974). *The sociology of community: A selection of readings.* London, UK: Frank Cass and Company.

Bell, G., & Gemmell, J. (2009). *Total recall.* New York, NY: Dutton.

Bellah, R. N., Madsen, R., Swidler, A., Sullivan, W. M., & Tipton, S. M. (1985). *Habits of the heart: Individualism and commitment in American life.* Berkeley: University of California Press.

Bellur, S., & Sundar, S. S. (2010). *Psychophysiological responses to media interfaces.* Paper presented at the proceedings of the ACM, Atlanta, Georgia. Retrieved from http://www.eecs.tufts.edu/~agirou01/workshop/papers/Bellur-CHI2010-BrainBodyBytes2010.pdf

Beniger, J. R. (1987). Personalization of mass media and the growth of pseudo-community. *Communication Research, 14*(3), 352–371.

Benkler, Y. (2014). Distributed innovation and creativity, peer production, and commons in networked economy. In Turner Publishing (Ed.), *Change: 19 key essays on how internet is changing our lives* (pp. 290–306). Nashville, TN: Turner.

Bennett, L., & Fessenden, J. (2006). Citizenship through online communication. *Social Education, 70*(3), 144–146.

Ben-Ze'ev, A. (2004). *Love online: Emotions on the internet.* Cambridge, UK: Cambridge University Press.

Berger, P., & Kellner, H. (1964). Marriage and the construction of reality: An exercise in the microsociology of knowledge. *Diogenes, 12*(46), 1–24.

Berger, P. L., & Luckmann, T. (1967). *The social construction of reality: A treatise in the sociology of knowledge.* Garden City, NY: Doubleday.

Berkowsky, R. W. (2013). When you just cannot get away: Exploring the use of information and communication technologies in facilitating negative work/home spillover. *Information, Communication and Society, 16*(4), 519–541.

Berlant, L. (2008). *The female complaint: The unfinished business of sentimentality in American culture.* Durham, NC: Duke University Press.

Bernstein, E. (2007). *Temporarily yours: Intimacy, authenticity, and the commerce of sex.* Chicago, IL: University of Chicago Press.

Berridge, K. C., & Robinson, T. E. (1998). What is the role of dopamine in reward: Hedonic impact, reward learning, or incentive salience? *Brain Research Reviews, 28*(3), 309–369.

Bessiere, K., Pressman, S., Kiesler, S., & Kraut, R. (2010). Effects of internet use on health and depression: A longitudinal study. *Journal of Medical Internet Research, 12*(1). doi:10.2196/jmir.1149

Bilton, N. (2013, June 30). Disruptions: Social media images form a new language online. *The New York Times.* Retrieved from http://bits.blogs.nytimes.com/2013/06/30/disruptions-social-media-images-form-a-new-language-online/?_r=0

Biocca, F., & Levy, M. R. (1995). *Communication in the age of virtual reality.* London, UK: Routledge.

Birch, B. A. (2011, November 9). Studies show internet plagiarism on the rise. *Education News.* Retrieved from http://www.educationnews.org/k-12-schools/studies-show-internet-plagiarism-on-the-rise/

Black, A. D., Car, J., Pagliari, C., Anandan, C., Cresswell, K., Bokun, T., . . . Sheikh, A. (2011). The impact of eHealth on the quality and safety of health care: A systematic overview. *PLoS Medicine, 8*(1). doi:10.1371/journal.pmed.1000387

Blank, G. (2013). Who creates content? Stratification and content creation on the internet. *Information, Communication & Society, 16*(4), 590–612.

Blood, R. (2002). Weblogs: A history and perspective. In J. Rodzvilla (Ed.), *We've got blog* (pp. 7–16). Cambridge, MA: Perseus.

Blum, A. (2013). *Tubes: A journey to the center of the internet.* New York, NY: HarperCollins.

Blum-Ross, A., & Livingstone, S. (2016). Families and screen time: Current advice and emerging research. *Media Policy Brief 17.* London: Media Policy Project, London School of Economics and Political Science.

Boase, J., Horrigan, J. B., Wellman, B., & Rainie, L. (2006, January 5). The strength of internet ties. *Pew Research Center.* Retrieved from http://pewinternet.org/Reports/2006/The-Strength-of-Internet-Ties.aspx

Boase, J., & Wellman, B. (2006). Personal relationships: On and off the internet. In A. Vangelisti & D. Perlman (Eds.), *The Cambridge handbook of personal relationships* (pp. 709–723). Cambridge, UK: Cambridge University Press.

Boczkowski, P. J. (2010). *News at work: Imitation in an age of information abundance.* Chicago, IL: University of Chicago Press.

Boesel, W. E. (2012, December 18). Social media and the devolution of friendship: Full essay (pts I & II). Retrieved from http://thesocietypages.org/cyborgology/2012/12/18/the-devolution-of-friendship-full-essay-pts-i-ii/

Boon, S. D., Watkins, S. J., & Sciban, R. A. (2014). Pluralistic ignorance and misperception of social norms concerning cheating in dating relationships. *Personal Relationships, 21*(3), 482–496.

Boudreau, K., & Consalvo, M. (2014). Families and social network games. *Information, Communication and Society, 17*(9), 1–13. doi:10.1080/1369118x.2014.882964

Bourdieu, P. (1985). The social space and the genesis of groups. *Theory & Society, 14*(6), 723–744.

boyd, d. (2006). Friends, friendsters, and top 8: Writing community into being on social network sites. *First Monday, 11*(12). doi:http://dx.doi.org/10.5210/fm.v11i12.1418

boyd, d. (2007). Identity production in a networked culture: Why youth heart MySpace. *Médiamorphoses*, (21), 69–80.

boyd, d. (2014). *It's complicated: The social lives of networked teens.* New Haven, CT: Yale University Press.

boyd, d., & Ellison, N. B. (2007). Social network sites: Definition, history, and scholarship. *Journal of Computer-Mediated Communication, 13*(1), 210–230.

boyd, d., Hargittai, E., Schultz, J., & Palfrey, J. (2011). Why parents help their children lie to Facebook about age: Unintended consequences of the "Children's Online Privacy Protection Act." *First Monday, 16*(11). doi:http://dx.doi.org/10.5210/fm.v16i11.3850

boyd, d., & Heer, J. (2006). Profiles as conversation: Networked identity performance on Friendster. *Proceedings of the 39th Annual Hawaii International Conference on System Sciences (HICSS'06). IEEE Computer Society*. Retrieved from http://www.danah.org/papers/HICSS2006.pdf

Brenner, J. (2013, September). Social networking fact sheet. Pew Research Center. Retrieved from http://www.pewinternet.org/fact-sheets/social-networking-factsheet/

Broadband Commission. (2014). The state of broadband 2014: Broadband for all. *Broadband Commission for Digital Development, International Telecommunication Union (ITU)*. Retrieved from http://www.broadbandcommission.org/Documents/reports/bb-annualreport2014.pdf

Brown, S. (2006). The criminology of hybrids: Rethinking crime and law in technosocial networks. *Theoretical Criminology, 10*(2), 223–244.

Bruns, A. (2005). *Gatewatching: Collaborative online news production*. New York, NY: Peter Lang.

Bruns, A. (2008). *Blogs, Wikipedia, Second Life, and beyond: From production to produsage*. New York, NY: Peter Lang.

Bruns, A., & Burgess, J. (2011). *The use of Twitter hashtags in the formation of adhoc publics*. Paper presented at the Sixth European Consortium for Political Research General Conference, Reykjavik, Iceland. Retrieved from http://eprints.qut.edu.au/46515/

Brynjolfsson, E., & McAfee, A. (2014). *The second machine age: Work, progress, and prosperity in a time of brilliant technologies*. New York, NY: W. W. Norton.

Bunce, D. M., Flens, E. A., & Neiles, K. Y. (2010). How long can students pay attention in class? A study of student attention decline using clickers. *Journal of Chemical Education, 87*(12), 1438–1443.

Bush, V. (1945). As we may think. *Atlantic Monthly, 176*(1), 101–108. Retrieved from http://www.theatlantic.com/magazine/archive/1945/07/as-we-may-think/303881/

Calhoun, C. J. (1986). Computer technology, large-scale social integration, and the local community. *Urban Affairs Quarterly, 22*(2), 329–349.

Campbell, H. A. (2012). Introduction: The rise of the study of digital religion. In H. Campbell (Ed.), *Digital religion: Understanding religious practice in new media worlds* (pp. 1–22). New York, NY: Routledge.

Campbell, J. E. (2016). *Polarized: Making sense of a divided America*. Princeton, NJ: Princeton University Press.

Career Builder. (2017, June 15). Number of employers using social media to screen candidates at all-time high, finds latest Career Builder study. Retrieved from http://press.careerbuilder.com/2017-06-15-Number-of-Employers-Using-Social-Media-to-Screen-Candidates-at-All-Time-High-Finds-Latest-CareerBuilder-Study

Carmichael, P. (2003). The internet, information architecture and community memory. *Journal of Computer-Mediated Communication, 8*(2). doi:10.1111/j.1083-6101.2003.tb00208.x

Carr, N. (2011). *The shallows: What the internet is doing to our brains*. New York, NY: W. W. Norton.

Carstensen, J. (2015, January 22). Robots can't dance. *Nautilus*. Retrieved from http://nautil.us/issue/20/creativity/robots-cant-dance

Cassell, J., & Cramer, M. (2007). Moral panics about girls online. In T. McPherson (Ed.), *Digital youth, innovation and the unexpected* (pp. 53–75). Cambridge, MA: MIT Press.

Cassidy, J. (2006, May 15). Me media. *The New Yorker*. Retrieved from http://www.newyorker.com/magazine/2006/05/15/me-media

Castells, M. (2000). *The rise of the network society* (2nd ed.). Oxford, UK: Oxford University Press.

Castells, M. (2001). *The internet galaxy*. Oxford, UK: Oxford University Press.

Castells, M. (2011). *The rise of the network society: The information age: Economy, society, and culture*. New York, NY: John Wiley & Sons.

Castells, M., Fernandez-Ardevol, M., Qiu, J. L., & Sey, A. (2004, October 8–9). *The mobile communication society: A cross-cultural analysis of available evidence on the social uses of wireless communication technology*. Paper presented at the International Workshop on Wireless Communication Policies and Prospects: A Global Perspective, University of Southern California, Los Angeles.

Caughey, J. L. (1984). *Imaginary social worlds: A cultural approach*. Lincoln: University of Nebraska Press.

Cavanagh, A. (2009). From culture to connection: Internet community studies. *Sociology Compass, 3*(1), 1–15.

Cerf, V., Dalal, Y., & Sunshine, C. (1974). Specification of internet transmission control program. Network Working Group Document. Retrieved from https://tools.ietf.org/html/rfc675

Cerulo, K. A. (1995). *Identity designs: The sights and sounds of a nation*. New Brunswick, NJ: Rutgers University Press.

Cerulo, K. A., & Ruane, J. M. (1998). Coming together: New taxonomies for the analysis of social relations. *Sociological Inquiry, 68*(3), 398–425.

Cerulo, K. A., Ruane, J. M., & Chayko, M. (1992). Technological ties that bind. *Communication Research, 19*(1), 109–129.

Chayko, M. (1993). What is real in the age of virtual reality? "Reframing" frame analysis for a technological world. *Symbolic Interaction, 16*(2), 171–181. doi:10.1525/si.1993.16.2.171

Chayko, M. (2002). *Connecting: How we form social bonds and communities in the internet age*. Albany: State University of New York Press.

Chayko, M. (2008). *Portable communities: The social dynamics of online and mobile connectedness*. Albany: State University of New York Press.

Chayko, M. (2014). Techno-social life: The internet, digital technology, and social connectedness. *Sociology Compass, 8*(7), 976–991.

Chayko, M. (2015). The first web theorist? The legacy of Georg Simmel and "the web of group-affiliations." *Information, Communication & Society*. doi:10.1080/1369118X.2015.1042394

Chemaly, S. (2014, September 9). There's no comparing male and female harassment online. *Time*. Retrieved from http://time.com/3305466/male-female-harassment-online/

Chen, Y., Pavlov, D., Berkhin, P., Seetharaman, A., & Meltzer, A. (2009). Practical lessons of data mining at Yahoo! *Proceeding of the 18th ACM Conference on Information and Knowledge Management*, 1047–1056. doi:10.1145/1645953.1646087

Cheong, P. H., & Ess, C. (2012). Introduction: Religion 2.0? Relational and hybridizing pathways in religion, social media, and culture. In P. H. Cheong, P. Fischer-Nielson, S. Gelfgren, & C. Ess (Eds.), *Digital religion, social media, and culture: Perspectives, practices, and futures* (pp. 1–25). New York, NY: Peter Lang.

Chmiel, A., Sienkiewicz, J., Thelwall, M., Paltoglou, G., Buckley, K., Kappas, A., & Holyst, J. A. (2011). Collective emotions online and their influence on community life. *PLoS One, 6*(7). doi:10.1371/journal.pone.0022207

Choi, S. M., Kim, Y., Sung, Y., & Sohn, D. (2011). Bridging or bonding? A cross-cultural study of social relationships in social networking sites. *Information, Communication and Society, 14*(1), 107–129.

Chung, C. J., Nam, Y., & Stefanone, M. A. (2012). Exploring online news credibility: The relative influence of traditional and technological factors. *Journal of Computer-Mediated Communication, 17*(2), 171–186.

Citron, D. K. (2014). *Hate crimes in cyberspace*. Cambridge, MA: Harvard University Press.

Claburn, T. (2009, March 4). Court asked to disallow warrantless GPS tracking. *Information Week*. Retrieved from http://www.informationweek.com/architecture/court-asked-to-disallow-warrantless-gps-tracking/d/d-id/1077257?

Clark, H. H., & Brennan, S. E. (1993). Grounding in communication. In R. M. Baecker (Ed.), *Readings in groupware and computer-supported cooperative work* (pp. 222–233). San Mateo, CA: Morgan Kaufmann.

Clark, L. S. (2013). *The parent app: Understanding families in the digital age*. Oxford, UK: Oxford University Press.

Clarke, A. E., Shim, J. K., Mamo, L., Fosket, J. R., & Fishman, J. R. (2010). Biomedicalization: Technoscientific transformations of health, illness, and US biomedicine. *Biomedicalization: Technoscience, Health, and Illness in the US, 68*(2), 47–87.

Clayton, R. B., Leshner, G., & Almond, A. (2015). The extended iSelf: The impact of iPhone separation on cognition, emotion, and physiology. *Journal of Computer-Mediated Communication, 20*(2), 119–135. doi:10.1111/jcc4.12109

Clegg, H. (2015). Review of "Web metrics for library and information professionals." *Library Management, 36*(1/2), 183–185.

Cobb, S. (2012, March 20). Google's data mining bonanza and your privacy: An infographic. *ESET Threat Blog*. Retrieved from http://blog.eset.com/2012/03/14/google-data-mining-bonanza-and-your-privacy-infographic

Computer Hope. (2014, June 3). Computer history. Retrieved from http://www.computer hope.com/history/

Cooley, C. H. (1964). *Human nature and the social order*. New York, NY: Schocken. (Original work published 1922)

Cooper, A., McLoughlin, I. P., & Campbell, K. M. (2000). Sexuality in cyberspace: Update for the 21st century. *CyberPsychology and Behavior, 3*(4), 521–536.

Corneliussen, H., & Rettberg, J. W. (2008). *Digital culture, play, and identity: A World of Warcraft reader*. Cambridge, MA: MIT Press.

Cotten, S. R., & Gupta, S. S. (2004). Characteristics of online and offline health information seekers and factors that discriminate between them. *Social Science and Medicine, 59*(9), 1795–1806.

Cramer, K. M., Collins, K. R., Snider, D., & Fawcett, G. (2006). Virtual lecture hall for in-class and online sections: A comparison of utilization, perceptions, and benefits. *Journal of Research on Technology in Education, 38*(4), 371–381.

Csikszentmihalyi, M. (1990). *Flow: The psychology of optimal experience*. New York, NY: Harper and Row.

Curran, J. (2012). Reinterpreting the internet. In J. Curran, N. Fenton, &

D. Freedman (Eds.), *Misunderstanding the internet.* London, UK: Routledge.

Curran, J., Fenton, N., & Freedman, D. (2012). *Misunderstanding the internet.* London, UK: Routledge.

Curtis, A. (2011). The brief history of social media. Retrieved from http://www.uncp.edu/home/acurtis/NewMedia/SocialMedia/SocialMediaHistory.html

Cuthbert, A. J., Clark, D. B., & Linn, M. C. (2002). WISE learning communities: Design considerations. In K. A. Renninger & W. Shumar (Eds.), *Building virtual communities: Learning and change in cyberspace* (pp. 215–246). Cambridge, UK: Cambridge University Press.

Cyber Telecom. (2014, January 14). Internet history: NSFNet. *Cybertelecom: Federal Internet Law and Policy.* Retrieved from http://www.cybertelecom.org/notes/nsfnet.htm#aup

Daer, A. R., Hoffman, R., & Goodman, S. (2014). *Rhetorical functions of hashtag forms across social media applications.* Paper presented at Proceedings of the 32nd ACM International Conference on the Design of Communication, New York, NY.

Danet, B. (2001). *Cyberplay: Communicating online.* Oxford, UK: Berg.

Davenport, T. H., & Beck, J. C. (2002). *The attention economy: Understanding the new currency of business.* Boston, MA: Harvard Business Review Press.

Davis, M. S. (1983). *Smut: Erotic reality/obscene ideology.* Chicago, IL: University of Chicago Press.

Davis, O. (2015, February 16). Hackers steal $1 billion in biggest bank heist in history: Could they take down the whole system next time? *International Business Times.* Retrieved from http://www.ibtimes.com/hackers-steal-1-billion-biggest-bank-heist-history-could-they-take-down-whole-system-1818010

Dead Media Archive. (2011). Car phone. *Dead Media Archive.* Retrieved from http://cultureandcommunication.org/deadmedia/index.php/Car_Phone

DePaulo, B. M. (2004). The many faces of lies. In A. G. Miller (Ed.), *The social psychology of good and evil* (pp. 303–326). New York, NY: Guilford Press.

Diefenbach, S., & Christoforakos, L. (2017). The selfie paradox: Nobody seems to like them yet everyone has reasons to take them. An exploration of psychological functions of selfies in self-presentation. *Frontiers in Psychology, 8.* Retrieved from https://www.ncbi.nlm.nih.gov/pmc/articles/PMC5239793/

DiMaggio, P. (2014). The internet's influence on the production and consumption of culture: Creative destruction and new opportunities. In Turner Publishing (Ed.), *Change: 19 key essays on how internet is changing our lives* (pp. 362–391). Nashville, TN: Turner.

Discovery. (2012, December 12). Topic: Big question—how has the internet changed politics? Retrieved from http://dsc.discovery.com/tv-shows/curiosity/topics/big-question-how-has-internet-changed-politics.htm

Ditmore, M. H., Levy, A., & Willman, A. (2010). *Sex work matters: Exploring money, power, and intimacy in the sex industry.* London, UK: Zed Books.

Dixon, L. J., Correa, T., Straubhaar, J., Covarrubias, L., Graber, D., Spence, J., & Rojas, V. (2014). Gendered space: The digital divide between male and female users in internet public access sites. *Journal of Computer-Mediated Communication, 19*(4), 991–1009.

Duggan, M. (2014, October 22). Online harassment. *Pew Research Center.* Retrieved from http://www.pewinternet.org/2014/10/22/online-harassment/

Duggan, M. (2017, July 11). Online harassment, 2017. Retrieved from http://www.pewinternet.org/2017/07/11/online-harassment-2017/

Dunbar-Hester, C. (2014). *Low power to the people: Pirates, protest, and politics in FM radio activism*. Cambridge, MA: MIT Press.

Durkheim, E. (1964). *The division of labor in society*. New York, NY: Free Press. (Original work published 1893)

Durkheim, E. (1965). *The elementary forms of religious life*. New York, NY: Free Press. (Original work published 1912)

Durkheim, E. (1966). *Suicide: A study in sociology*. New York, NY: Free Press. (Original work published 1897)

Dutta, S., Geiger, T., & Lanvin, B. (2015). The Global Information Technology Report 2015: ICTs for inclusive growth. *World Economic Forum and INSEAD*. Retrieved from http://www3.weforum.org/docs/WEF_Global_IT_Report_2015.pdf

Dyson, E., Gilder, G., Keyworth, G., & Toffler, A. (1994). Cyberspace and the American dream: A magna carta for the knowledge age. *Future Insight*, *1*(2). Retrieved from http://www.pff.org/issues-pubs/futureinsights/fi1.2magnacarta.html

Eddy, M., & Scott, M. (2017, June 30). Delete hate speech or pay up, Germany tells social media companies. *The New York Times*. Retrieved from https://www.nytimes.com/2017/06/30/business/germany-facebook-google-twitter.html

Egan, M. (2017, June 19). What is the dark web and deep web? *Tech Adviser*. Retrieved from http://www.techadvisor.co.uk/how-to/internet/what-is-dark-web-deep-web-3593569/

Eldridge, M., & Grinter, R. (2001). *Studying text messaging in teenagers*. Presented at the CHI 2001 Workshop on Mobile Communications: Understanding Users, Adoption and Design, Seattle, WA.

Ellis, R. A., Goodyear, P., Prosser, M., & O'Hara, A. (2006). How and what university students learn through online and face-to-face discussion: Conceptions, intentions and approaches. *Journal of Computer Assisted Learning*, *22*(4), 244–256.

Ellison, N., Heino, R., & Gibbs, J. (2006). Managing impressions online: Self-presentation processes in the online dating environment. *Journal of Computer-Mediated Communication*, *11*(2), 415–441.

Ellison, N. B., Lampe, C., & Steinfield, C. (2009). Social network sites and society: Current trends and future possibilities. *Interactions*, *16*(1), 6–9. doi:10.1145/1456202.1456204

Ellison, N. B., Steinfield, C., & Lampe, C. (2007). The benefits of Facebook "friends": Social capital and college students' use of online social network sites. *Journal of Computer-Mediated Communication*, *12*(4), 1143–1168. doi:10.1111/j.1083-6101.2007.00367.x

Ellison, N. B., Steinfield, C., & Lampe, C. (2011). Connection strategies: Social capital implications of Facebook-enabled communication practices. *New Media and Society*, *13*(6), 873–892. doi:10.1177/1461444810385389

Erdmans, M. P. (2004). *The Grasinski girls: The choices they had and the choices they made*. Athens: Ohio University Press.

Erikson, K. T. (1966). *Wayward puritans: A study in the sociology of deviance*. New York, NY: Wiley.

Eschrich, J. (2014, October 14). Interview: Jathan Sadowski on the future of cities. *Hieroglyph*. Retrieved from http://

hieroglyph.asu.edu/2014/10/interview-jathan-sadowski-on-the-future-of-cities/

Ess, C. (2011). Self, community and ethics in digital mediatized worlds. In C. Ess & M. Thorself (Eds.), *Trust and virtual worlds: Contemporary perspectives* (pp. 3–30). New York, NY: Peter Lang.

Etgar, S., & Amichai-Hamburger, Y. (2017). Not all selfies took alike: Distinct selfie motivations are related to different personality characteristics. *Frontiers in Psychology, 8*. Retrieved from https://www.ncbi.nlm.nih.gov/pmc/articles/PMC5445188/

Fallows, D. (2006, February 15). Surfing for fun. *Pew Research Center.* Retrieved from http://www.pewinternet.org/2006/02/15/surfing-for-fun/

Feldman, R. S., Forrest, J. A., & Happ, B. R. (2002). Self-presentation and verbal deception: Do self-presenters lie more? *Basic and Applied Social Psychology, 24*(2), 163–170.

Ferdman, R. A. (2014, October 2). 4.4 billion people around the world still don't have internet. Here's where they live. *Washington Post.* Retrieved from http://www.washingtonpost.com/blogs/wonkblog/wp/2014/10/02/4-4-billion-people-around-the-world-still-dont-have-internet-heres-where-they-live/

Ferenstein, G. (2015, January 16). Netflix binges and the new tech utopia. *The Atlantic.* Retrieved from http://www.theatlantic.com/technology/archive/2015/01/netflix-binges-and-the-new-tech-utopia/384471/

Fernback, J. (2007). Beyond the diluted community concept: A symbolic interactionist perspective on online social relations. *New Media and Society, 9*(1), 49–69. doi:10.1177/1461444807072417

Fischer, C. S. (1982). *To dwell among friends: Personal networks in town and city.* Chicago, IL: University of Chicago Press.

Flanagin, A. J., Hocevar, K. P., & Samahito, S. N. (2014). Connecting with the user-generated web: How group identification impacts online information sharing and evaluation. *Information, Communication and Society, 17*(6), 683–694.

Flood, A. (2014, August 19). Readers absorb less on Kindles than on paper, study finds. *The Guardian.* Retrieved from http://www.theguardian.com/books/2014/aug/19/readers-absorb-less-kindles-paper-study-plot-ereader-digitisation

Floridi, L. (2007). A look into the future impact of ICT on our lives. *Information Society, 23*(1), 59–64. doi:10.1080/01972240601059094

Foehr, U. G. (2006). *Media multitasking among American youth: Prevalence, predictors and pairings.* Menlo Park, CA: Henry J. Kaiser Family Foundation.

Fortunati, L. (2002). The mobile phone: Towards new categories and social relations. *Information, Communication & Society, 5*(4), 513–528.

Fountain, C. (2005). Finding a job in the internet age. *Social Forces, 83*(3), 1235–1262.

Fox, K. (2001). Evolution, alienation and gossip: The role of mobile communications in the 21st century. *Social Issues Research Centre.* Retrieved from http://www.sirc.org/publik/gossip.shtml

Fox, S. (2011a, February 28). Peer-to-peer health care. *Pew Research Center.* Retrieved from http://www.pewinternet.org/2011/02/28/peer-to-peer-health-care-2/

Fox, S. (2011b, May 12). The social life of health information, 2011. *Pew Research Center.* Retrieved from http://www.pewinternet.org/2011/05/12/the-social-life-of-health-information-2011/

Fox, S., & Duggan, M. (2012, November 8). Mobile health 2012. *Pew Research*

Center. Retrieved from http://www.pewinternet.org/2012/11/08/mobile-health-2012/

Gabrial, B. (2008). History of writing technologies. In C. Bazerman (Ed.), *Handbook of research on writing: History, society, school, individual, text* (pp. 27–40). New York, NY: Routledge.

Gabriels, K., Poels, K., & Braeckman, J. (2013). Morality and involvement in social virtual worlds: The intensity of moral emotions in response to virtual life versus real life cheating. *New Media and Society, 16*(3), 451–469. doi:10.1177/1461444813487957

Gajjala, R. (2004). *Cyber selves: Feminist ethnographies of South Asian women*. Walnut Creek, CA: Rowman Altamira.

Gee, J. (2011). Learning theory, video games and popular culture. In M. Bauerlein (Ed.), *The digital divide* (pp. 38–43). New York, NY: Tarcher Penguin.

Gergen, K. (1991). *The saturated self: Dilemmas of identity in contemporary life*. New York, NY: Basic Books.

Gergen, K. J., Gergen, M. M., & Barton, W. H. (1973). Deviance in the dark. *Psychology Today, 7*(5), 129–130.

Gerrig, R. J. (1993). *Experiencing narrative worlds: On the psychological activities of reading*. New Haven, CT: Yale University Press.

Geser, H. (2004). Towards a sociological theory of the mobile phone. *Sociology in Switzerland: Sociology of the Mobile Phone*. Retrieved from http://socio.ch/mobile/t_geser1.htm/

Gibbs, J. L., Rozaidi, N. A., & Eisenberg, J. (2013). Overcoming the "ideology of openness": Probing the affordances of social media for organizational knowledge sharing. *Journal of Computer-Mediated Communication, 19*(1), 102–120.

Gibbs, M., Meese, J., Arnold, M., Nansen, B., & Carter, M. (2015). #Funeral and Instagram: Death, social media, and platform vernacular. *Information, Communication & Society, 18*(3), 255–268.

Gibson, W. (1984). *Neuromancer*. New York, NY: Ace.

Gibson, W. (2010, August 31). Google's earth. *The New York Times*. Retrieved from http://www.nytimes.com/2010/09/01/opinion/01gibson.html?_r=0

Giddens, A. (1984). *The constitution of society: Outline of the theory of structuration*. Berkeley: University of California Press.

Giddens, A. (1991). *Modernity and self-identity*. Stanford, CA: Stanford University Press.

Giddens, A. (1992). *The transformation of intimacy: Sexuality, love, and eroticism in modern societies*. Palo Alto, CA: Stanford University Press.

Giddens, A. (with Beck, U., & Lash, S.). (1994). *Reflexive modernization: Politics, tradition, and aesthetics in the modern social order*. Cambridge, UK: Polity Press.

Gil de Zúñiga, H., Jung, N., & Valenzuela, S. (2012). Social media use for news and individuals' social capital, civic engagement and political participation. *Journal of Computer-Mediated Communication, 17*(3), 319–336.

Gil de Zúñiga, H., Weeks, B., & Ardèvol-Abreu, A. (2017). Effects of the news-finds-me perception in communication: Social media use implications for news seeking and learning about politics. *Journal of Computer-Mediated Communication, 22*, 105–123. doi:10.1111/jcc4.12185

Giles, D. C. (2002). Parasocial interaction: A review of the literature and a model for future research. *Media Psychology, 4*(3), 279–305.

Glaser, J., Dixit, J., & Green, D. P. (2002). Studying hate crime with the internet: What makes racists advocate racial violence? *Journal of Social Issues, 58*(1), 177–193.

Glasser, T. L. (1982). Play, pleasure and the value of newsreading. *Communication Quarterly, 30*(2), 101–107.

Glasser, T. L. (2000). Play and the power of news. *Journalism, 1*(1), 23–29.

Gleick, J. (2011). *The information: A history, a theory, a flood.* New York, NY: Vintage.

Goffman, E. (1959). *The presentation of self in everyday life.* New York, NY: Anchor.

Goldsmith, J. L., & Wu, T. (2006). *Who controls the internet? Illusions of a borderless world.* New York, NY: Oxford University Press.

Goleman, D. (2006). *Social intelligence: The new science of human relationships.* New York, NY: Bantam Books.

Google Arts and Culture. (2013). The origin of the internet in Europe. *Google Arts and Culture.* Retrieved from https://www.google.com/culturalinstitute/beta/exhibit/the-origins-of-the-internet-in-europe/QQ-RRh0A

Gottfried, J., & Shearer, E. (2016). News use across social media platforms 2016. *Pew Research Center.* Retrieved from http://www.journalism.org/2016/05/26/news-use-across-social-media-platforms-2016/

Gottschalk, S. S. (1975). *Communities and alternatives.* Cambridge, MA: Schenkman.

Granovetter, M. (1973). The strength of weak ties. *American Journal of Sociology, 78*(6), 1360–1380.

Gray, T., Liscano, R., Wellman, B., Quan-Haase, A., Radhakrishnan, T., & Choi, Y. (2003). Context and intent in call processing. *Feature Interactions in Telecommunications and Software Systems VII*, 177–184. Retrieved from http://groups.chass.utoronto.ca/netlab/wp-content/uploads/2012/05/Context-and-Intent-in-Call-Processing.pdf

Green, M., Hilken, J., Friedman, H., Grossman, K., Gasiewski, J., Adler, R., & Sabini, J. (2005). Communication via instant messenger: Short- and long-term effects. *Journal of Applied Social Psychology, 35*(3), 445–462.

Griffin, S. (2000). Internet pioneers. *Ibiblio.Org.* Retrieved from http://www.ibiblio.org/pioneers/

Griffiths, M. (2001). Sex on the internet: Observations and implications for internet sex addiction. *Journal of Sex Research, 38*(4), 333–342.

Grimley, M., Allan, M., & Solomon, C. (2010). Exploring the association between leisure time digital immersion, attention and reasoning ability in pre-teens. *International Journal of Web-Based Learning and Teaching Technologies, 5*(4), 56–69.

Gronborg, M. (2012). FOMO. *Scenario.* Retrieved from http://www.scenariomagazine.com/fomo/

Gronewold, N. (2009, November 24). One-quarter of world's population lacks electricity. *Scientific American.* Retrieved from http://www.scientificamerican.com/article/electricity-gap-developing-countries-energy-wood-charcoal

Gross, N., & Simmons, S. (2002). Intimacy as a double-edged phenomenon? An empirical test of Giddens. *Social Forces, 81*(2), 531–555.

Guillén, M. F., & Suárez, S. L. (2005). Explaining the global digital divide: Economic, political and sociological drivers of cross-national internet use. *Social Forces, 84*(2), 681–708.

Guldberg, K., & Pilkington, R. (2006). A community of practice approach to the development of non-traditional learners through networked learning. *Journal of Computer Assisted Learning, 22*(3), 159–171.

Guo, B., Bricout, J. C., & Huang, J. (2005). A common open space or a digital divide? A social model perspective on the online disability community in China. *Disability and Society, 20*(1), 49–66.

Haberman, C. (2014, December 7). Grappling with the "culture of free" in Napster's aftermath. *The New York Times.* Retrieved from http://www.nytimes.com/2014/12/08/technology/grappling-with-the-culture-of-free-in-napsters-aftermath.html?_r=0

Hafner, K. (1998). *Where wizards stay up late: The origins of the internet*. New York, NY: Simon & Schuster.

Hafner, K. (2004). The epic saga of the WELL. *Wired.* Retrieved from http://archive.wired.com/wired/archive/5.05/ff_well_pr.html

Hajli, M. N. (2014). Developing online health communities through digital media. *International Journal of Information Management, 34*(2), 311–314. doi:10.1016/j.ijinfomgt.2014.01.006

Hall, J. (2014, May 21). Personal web page. links.net.

Hall, S. (1996). Who needs identity? In S. Hall & P. duGay (Eds.), *Questions of cultural identity* (pp. 1–17). London, UK: SAGE.

Hampton, K., Goulet, L. S., Marlow, C., & Rainie, L. (2012, February 3). Why most Facebook users get more than they give. *Pew Research Center.* Retrieved from http://www.pewinternet.org/2012/02/03/why-most-facebook-users-get-more-than-they-give/

Hampton, K., Goulet, L. S., Rainie, L., & Purcell, K. (2011, June 16). Social networking sites and our lives. *Pew Research Center.* Retrieved from http://www.pewinternet.org/2011/06/16/social-networking-sites-and-our-lives/

Hampton, K., Rainie, L., Lu, W., Dwyer, M., Shin, I., & Purcell, K. (2015, August 26). Social media and the "spiral of silence." *Pew Research Center.* Retrieved from http://www.pewinternet.org/2014/08/26/social-media-and-the-spiral-of-silence/

Hampton, K., Rainie, L., Lu, W., Shin, I., & Purcell, K. (2015). Social media and the cost of caring. *Pew Research Center.* Retrieved from http://www.pewinternet.org/2015/01/15/social-media-and-stress/

Hampton, K., & Wellman, B. (2003). Neighboring in Netville: How the internet supports community and social capital in a wired suburb. *City & Community, 2*(4), 277–311.

Hampton, K. N. (2007). Neighborhoods in the network society: The e-neighbors study. *Information, Communication and Society, 10*(5), 714–748. doi:10.1080/13691180701658061

Hampton, K. N. (2010). Internet use and the concentration of disadvantage: Glocalization and the urban underclass. *American Behavioral Scientist, 53*(8), 1111–1132.

Hampton, K. N. (2016). Persistent and pervasive community: New communication technologies and the future of community. *American Behavioral Scientist, 60*(1), 101–124.

Hampton, K. N., & Wellman, B. (1999). Netville online and offline: Observing and surveying a wired suburb. *American Behavioral Scientist, 43*(3), 475–492.

Hanna, B., Kee, K. F., & Robertson, B. W. (2017). Positive impacts of social media at work: Job satisfaction, job calling, and

Facebook use among co-workers. *SHS Web of Conferences*. EDP Sciences. 33. doi:10.1051/shsconf/20173300012

Haraway, D. (1998). The persistence of vision. In N. Mirzoeff (Ed.), *The visual culture reader* (pp. 191–198). London, UK: Routledge.

Hargittai, E., & Shaw, A. (2015). Mind the skills gap: The role of internet know-how and gender in differentiated contributions to Wikipedia. *Information, Communication & Society, 18*(4), 424–442.

Hargittai, E., & Walejko, G. (2008). The participation divide: Content creation and sharing in the digital age. *Information, Communication and Society, 11*(2), 239–256. doi:10.1080/13691180801946150

Harkin, J. (2003). *Mobilisation: The growing public interest in mobile technology*. London, UK: Demo.

Harrington, C. L., & Bielby, D. D. (1995). *Soap fans: Pursuing pleasure and making meaning in everyday life*. Philadelphia, PA: Temple University Press.

Harrington, S. (2014). Tweeting about the telly: Live TV, audiences, and social media. In K. Weller, A. Bruns, J. Burgess, M. Marht, & C. Puschmann (Eds.), *Twitter and society* (pp. 237–247). New York, NY: Peter Lang.

Harris, S., & Gerich, E. (1996, April). Retiring the NSFNET backbone service: Chronicling the end of an era. *Connexions, 10*(4). Retrieved from http://www.merit.edu/research/nsfnet_article.php

Hartzog, W., & Selinger, E. (2013, January 13). Obscurity: A better way to think about your data than "privacy." *The Atlantic*. Retrieved from http://www.theatlantic.com/technology/archive/2013/01/obscurity-a-better-way-to-think-about-your-data-than-privacy/267283/

Haythornthwaite, C. (2002). Building social networks via computer networks: Creating and sustaining distributed learning communities. In K. A. Renninger & W. Shumar (Eds.), *Building virtual communities: Learning and change in cyberspace* (pp. 159–190). Cambridge, UK: Cambridge University Press.

Haythornthwaite, C. (2005). Social networks and internet connectivity effects. *Information, Communication & Society, 8*(2), 125–147.

Haythornthwaite, C., & Hagar, C. (2005). The social worlds of the web. *Annual Review of Information Science and Technology, 39*(1), 311–346.

Haythornthwaite, C., & Kendall, L. (2010). Introduction: Third association of internet researchers. *Information, Communication & Society, 13*(3), 285–288.

Hess, A. (2014, January 6). Why women aren't welcome on the internet. *Pacific Standard*. Retrieved from http://www.psmag.com/health-and-behavior/women-arent-welcome-internet-72170

Hess, A. (2015). The selfie assemblage. *International Journal of Communication, 9*(19), 1629–1646. Retrieved from http://ijoc.org/index.php/ijoc/article/viewFile/3147/1389

Hesse, B. W., Nelson, D. E., Kreps, G. L., Croyle, R. T., Arora, N. K., Rimer, B. K., & Viswanath, K. (2005). Trust and sources of health information: The impact of the internet and its implications for health care providers: Findings from the first health information national trends survey. *Archives of Internal Medicine, 165*(22), 2618–2624.

Hewitt, J. (1989). *Dilemmas of the American self*. Philadelphia, PA: Temple University Press.

Hian, L. B., Chuan, S. L., Trevor, T. M. K., & Detenber, B. H. (2004). Getting to know you: Exploring the development of relational intimacy in computer-mediated communication. *Journal of Computer-Mediated Communication, 9*(3), 9–24.

Higgins, E. T. (1987). Self-discrepancy: A theory relating self and affect. *Psychological Review, 94*(3), 319–340.

Hilden, J. (2002, May 14). FindLaw forum: What legal questions are the new chip implants for humans likely to raise? *CNN.* Retrieved from http://edition.cnn.com/2002/LAW/05/columns/fl.hilden.chip/

Hillery, G. A. (1968). *Communal organizations: A study of local societies.* Chicago, IL: University of Chicago Press.

Himelboim, I., Sweetser, K. D., Tinkham, S. F., Cameron, K., Danelo, M., & West, K. (2016). Valence-based homophily on Twitter: Network analysis of emotions and political talk in the 2012 presidential election. *New Media & Society, 18*(7), 1382–1400. doi:10.1177/1461444814555096

Hmielowski, J. D., Hutchens, M. J., & Cicchirillo, V. J. (2014). Living in an age of online incivility: Examining the conditional indirect effects of online discussion on political flaming. *Information, Communication and Society, 17*(10), 1196–1211.

Hofer, B. K., & Moore, A. S. (2011). *The iConnected parent: Staying close to your kids in college (and beyond) while letting them grow up*. New York, NY: Simon & Schuster.

Holtzman, D. H. (2006). *Privacy lost: How technology is endangering your privacy.* San Francisco, CA: Jossey-Bass.

Hormuth, S. E. (1990). *The ecology of the self: Relocation and self-concept change.* Cambridge, UK: Cambridge University Press.

Horton, D., & Wohl, R. (1956). Mass communication and para-social interaction: Observations on intimacy at a distance. *Psychiatry, 19*(3), 215–229.

Hovenden, D., & Bartlett, C. (2013, February 26). The digital government. *Strategy + Business Magazine*, (70). Retrieved from http://www.strategy-business.com/article/00155? gko=f32f0&utm_source=taboola&utm_medium=referral

Hu, Y., Wood, J. F., Smith, V., & Westbrook, N. (2004). Friendships through IM: Examining the relationship between instant messaging and intimacy. *Journal of Computer-Mediated Communication, 10*(1), 38–48.

Huffaker, D. A., & Calvert, S. L. (2005). Gender, identity, and language use in teenage blogs. *Journal of Computer-Mediated Communication, 10*(2).

Huizinga, J. (1950). *Homo ludens: A study of the play element in culture.* Boston, MA: Beacon Press. (Original work published 1938)

Hunter, A. (1974). *Symbolic communities: The persistence and change of Chicago's local communities.* Chicago, IL: University of Chicago Press.

Hwang, T., & Levy, K. (2015, January 15). "The cloud" and other dangerous metaphors. *The Atlantic.* Retrieved from http://www.theatlantic.com/technology/archive/2015/01/the-cloud-and-other-dangerous-metaphors/384518/

International Telecommunication Union. (2014). The world in 2014: ICT facts and figures. *ICT Data and Statistics Bureau: Telecommunication Development Bureau.* Retrieved from http://www.itu.int/en/ITU-D/Statistics/Documents/facts/ICTFactsFigures2014-e.pdf

International Telecommunication Union. (2016). The world in 2016: ICT facts and figures. *ICT Data and Statistics Bureau: Telecommunication Development Bureau.* Retrieved from http://www.itu.int/en/ITU-D/Statistics/Documents/facts/ICTFactsFigures2016.pdf

Internet Society. (2017). History of the internet in Africa: Some African pioneers. *Internet Society.* Retrieved from https://www.internetsociety.org/history-internet-africa-some-african-pioneers

Ito, M., Baumer, S., Bittanti, M., boyd, d., Cody, R., Herr-Stephenson, B., . . . Tripp, L. (2010). *Hanging out, messing around, and geeking out: Kids living and learning with new media.* Cambridge, MA: MIT Press.

Ito, M., & Okabe, D. (2005). Technosocial situations: Emergent structurings of mobile email use. In M. Ito & D. Okabe (Eds.), *Personal, portable, pedestrian: Mobile phones in Japanese life* (pp. 257–273). Cambridge, MA: MIT Press.

Iyer, A., Jetten, J., & Tsivrikos, D. (2008). Torn between identities: Predictors of adjustment to identity change. In F. Sani (Ed.), *Self continuity: Individual and collective perspectives* (pp. 187–197). New York, NY: Psychology Press.

James, W. (1983). *The principles of psychology.* Cambridge, MA: Harvard University Press. (Original work published 1890)

Jary, D., & Jary, J. (1991). *The HarperCollins dictionary of sociology.* New York, NY: Harper Collins.

Jenkins, H. (1992). *Textual poachers: Television fans and participatory culture* (Studies in Culture and Communication). New York, NY: Routledge.

Jenkins, H. (2006). *Convergence culture: Where old and new media collide*. New York, NY: NYU Press.

Jenkins, H. (2009). *Confronting the challenges of participatory culture: Media education for the 21st century*. Cambridge, MA: MIT Press.

Jenkins, H., Ford, S., & Green, J. (2013). *Spreadable media: Creating value and meaning in a networked culture.* New York, NY: NYU Press.

John Dixon Technology. (2012a). History of the cellular (cell/mobile) phone. Retrieved from http://www.historyofthecellphone.com/

John Dixon Technology. (2012b). History of the cellular (cell/mobile) phone—people—Dr. Martin Cooper. *John Dixon Technology.* Retrieved from http://www.historyofthecellphone.com/people/martin-cooper.php

Johns, M. D. (2012). Voting "present": Religious organizational groups on Facebook. In P. H. Cheong, P. Fischer-Nielson, S. Gelfgren, & C. Ess (Eds.), *Digital religion, social media, and culture: Perspectives, practices, and futures* (pp. 151–168). New York, NY: Peter Lang.

Jones, S. G. (1995). Understanding community in the information age. In S. G. Jones (Ed.), *Cybersociety* (pp. 10–35). Thousand Oaks, CA: SAGE.

Junco, R., & Cotten, S. R. (2011). Perceived academic effects of instant messaging use. *Computers & Education, 56*(2), 370–378.

Junco, R., Heiberger, G., & Loken, E. (2011). The effect of Twitter on college student engagement and grades. *Journal of Computer Assisted Learning, 27*(2), 119–132.

Jurgenson, N. (2012a, January 13). The Facebook eye. *The Atlantic.* Retrieved from http://www.theatlantic.com/technology/archive/2012/01/the-facebook-eye/251377/

Jurgenson, N. (2012b, June 28). The IRL fetish. *The New Inquiry*. Retrieved from http://thenewinquiry.com/essays/the-irl-fetish/

Jurgenson, N. (2012c). When atoms meet bits: Social media, the mobile web and augmented revolution. *Future Internet, 4*(1), 83–91.

Juul, J. (2005). *Half-real: Video games between real rules and fictional worlds*. Cambridge, MA: MIT Press.

Kanter, R. M. (1972). *Commitment and community: Communes and utopias in sociological perspective*. Cambridge, MA: Harvard University Press.

Kaptein, M., Castaneda, D., Fernandez, N., & Nass, C. (2014). Extending the similarity-attraction effect: The effects of when-similarity in computer-mediated communication. *Journal of Computer-Mediated Communication, 19*(3), 342–357.

Katz, E., Haas, H., & Gurevitch, M. (1997). 20 years of television in Israel: Are there long-run effects on values, social connectedness, and cultural practices? *Journal of Communication, 47*(2), 3–20.

Katz, J. E. (2003). *Machines that become us: The social context of personal communication technology*. New Brunswick, NJ: Transaction.

Katz, J. E., & Aakhus, M. (2002). *Perpetual contact: Mobile communication, private talk, public performance*. Cambridge, UK: Cambridge University Press.

Katz, J. E., Barris, M., & Jain, A. (2013). *The social media president: Barack Obama and the politics of digital engagement*. New York, NY: Palgrave Macmillan.

Katz, J. E., & Sugiyama, S. (2006). Mobile phones as fashion statements: Evidence from student surveys in the US and Japan. *New Media and Society, 8*(2), 321–337. doi:10.1177/1461444806061950

Kauffman, R., & Wood, C. (2006). Doing their bidding: An empirical examination of factors that affect a buyer's utility in internet auctions. *Information Technology and Management*, 7(3), 171–190.

Kayany, J. M., Wotring, C. E., & Forrest, E. J. (1996). Relational control and interactive media choice in technology-mediated communication situations. *Human Communication Research, 22*(3), 399–421.

Kellerman, G. R. (2012, October 3). The extremely personal computer: The digital future of mental health. *The Atlantic*. Retrieved from http://www.theatlantic.com/health/archive/2012/10/the-extremely-personal-computer-the-digital-future-of-mental-health/263183/

Kelly, K. (2010). *What technology wants*. New York, NY: Penguin.

Kendall, L. (2002). *Hanging out in the virtual pub: Masculinities and relationships online*. Berkeley: University of California Press.

Kendall, L. (2010). Community and the internet. In R. Burnett, M. Consalvo, & C. Ess (Eds.), *The Blackwell handbook of internet studies* (pp. 310–325). Oxford, UK: Wiley-Blackwell.

Kendzior, S., & Pearce, K. (2012, May 11). How Azerbaijan demonizes the internet to keep its citizens offline. *Slate*. Retrieved from http://www.slate.com/blogs/future_tense/2012/05/11/azerbaijan_eurovision_song_contest_and_keeping_activists_and_citizens_off_the_internet_.html

Kennedy, H. (2006). Beyond anonymity: Future directions for internet identity research. *New Media and Society, 8*(6), 859–876.

Khazan, O. (2006, August 18). Lost in an online fantasy world. *Washington Post.* Retrieved from http://www.washingtonpost.com/wp-dyn/content/article/2006/08/17/AR2006081700625_pf.html

Kim, T., & Biocca, F. (1997). Telepresence via television: Two dimensions of telepresence may have different connections to memory and persuasion. *Journal of Computer-Mediated Communication, 3*(2).

Kim, Y., Kim, Y., Lee, J. S., Oh, J., & Lee, N. Y. (2015). Tweeting the public: Journalists' Twitter use, attitudes toward the public's tweets, and the relationship with the public. *Information, Communication and Society, 18*(4), 443–458. doi:10.1080/1369118X.2014.967267

Kirschner, P. A., & Karpinski, A. C. (2010). Facebook and academic performance. *Computers in Human Behavior, 26*(6), 1237–1245.

Kjuka, D. (2013, March 6). Digital jihad: Inside Al-Qaeda's social networks. *The Atlantic.* Retrieved from http://www.theatlantic.com/international/archive/2013/03/digital-jihad-inside-al-qaedas-social-networks/273761/

Klastrup, L., & Tosca, S. P. (2004). Transmedial worlds-rethinking cyberworld design. *Proceedings of the 2004 International Conference on Cyberworlds.* Retrieved from http://www.cs.uu.nl/docs/vakken/vw/literature/04.klastruptosca_transworlds.pdf

Koliska, M., & Roberts, J. (2015). Selfies: Witnessing and participatory journalism with a point of view. *International Journal of Communication, 9*(19), 1672–1685. Retrieved from http://ijoc.org/index.php/ijoc/article/viewFile/3149/1392

Korzenny, F. (1978). A theory of electronic propinquity: Mediated communications in organizations. *Communication Research, 5*(1), 3–24.

Kosenko, K., Luurs, G., & Binder, A. R. (2017). Sexting and sexual behavior, 2011–2015: A critical review and meta-analysis of a growing literature. *Journal of Computer-Mediated Communication, 22,* 141–160. doi:10.1111/jcc4.12187

Korthaus, A., & Dai, W. (2015). Opportunities and challenges for mobile crowdsourcing-conceptualisation of a platform architecture. *International Journal of High Performance Computing and Networking, 8*(1), 16–27.

Kreek, M. J., Nielsen, D. A., Butelman, E. R., & LaForge, K. S. (2005). Genetic influences on impulsivity, risk taking, stress responsivity and vulnerability to drug abuse and addiction. *Nature Neuroscience, 8*(11), 1450–1457.

Kumar, N. (2014). Facebook for self-empowerment? A study of Facebook adoption in urban India. *New Media and Society, 16*(7), 1122–1137. doi:10.1177/1461444814543999

Kurtzberg, T. R., & Gibbs, J. L. (2017). *Distracted: Staying connected without losing focus.* ABC-CLIO.

Lambert, J. (2013). *Digital storytelling: Capturing lives, creating community.* New York, NY: Routledge.

LaRose, R., Eastin, M. S., & Gregg, J. (2001). Reformulating the internet paradox: Social cognitive explanations of internet use and depression. *Journal of Online Behavior, 1*(2).

LaRose, R., Lin, C. A., & Eastin, M. S. (2003). Unregulated internet usage: Addiction, habit, or deficient self-regulation? *Media Psychology, 5*(3), 225–253.

Lee, H. (2005). Behavioral strategies for dealing with flaming in an online forum. *Sociological Quarterly, 46*(2), 385–403.

Lee, J., & Lee, H. (2010). The computer-mediated communication network:

Exploring the linkage between the online community and social capital. *New Media and Society, 12*(5), 711–727. doi:10.1177/1461444809343568

Leeper, T. J. (2014). The informational basis for mass polarization. *Public Information Quarterly, 78*(1), 27–46. doi:10.1093/poq/nft045

Leiner, B. M., Cerf, V. G., Clark, D. D., Kahn, R. E., Kleinrock, L., Lynch, D. C., & Wolff, S. (2009). A brief history of the internet. *ACM SIGCOMM Computer Communication Review, 39*(5), 22–31.

Lenhart, A. (2012, March 19). Teens, smartphones, and texting. *Pew Research Center.* Retrieved from http://www.pewinternet.org/2012/03/19/teens-smartphones-texting/

Lenhart, A., & Duggan, M. (2014, February 11). *Couples, the internet, and social media.* Pew Research Center. Retrieved from http://www.pewinternet.org/2014/02/11/couples-the-internet-and-social-media/

Lenhart, A., & Madden, M. (2006). Teen content creators and consumers. *Pew Internet and American Life Project.* Retrieved from http://www.pewinternet.org/files/old-media/Files/Reports/2005/PIP_Teens_Content_Creation.pdf.pdf

Lenhart, A., Purcell, K., Smith, A., & Zickuhr, K. (2010, February 3). Social media and mobile internet use among teens and young adults. *Pew Internet and American Life Project.* Retrieved from http://www.pewinternet.org/files/old-media//Files/Reports/2010/PIP_Social_Media_and_Young_Adults_Report_Final_with_toplines.pdf

Lessig, L. (2008). *Remix: Making art and commerce thrive in the hybrid economy.* London, UK: Penguin.

Lev-On, A. (2010). Engaging the disengaged: Collective action, media uses, and sense of (virtual) community by evacuees from Gush Katif. *American Behavioral Scientist, 53*(8), 1208–1227.

Lewan, T. (2007, March 17). Microchips in humans spark privacy debate. *USA Today.* Retrieved from http://usatoday30.usatoday.com/tech/news/surveillance/2007-07-21-chips_N.htm

Liang, H., & Fu, K.-W. (2017). Information overload, similarity, and redundancy: Unsubscribing information sources on Twitter. *Journal of Computer-Mediated Communication, 22,* 1–17. doi:10.1111/jcc4.12178

Licklider, J. C. R. (1960). Man-computer symbiosis. *IRE Transactions on Human Factors in Electronics, 1,* 4–11.

Licklider, J. C. R., & Taylor, R. W. (1968). The computer as a communication device. *Science and Technology, 76*(2), 20–41.

Lin, D. C. (2006). Sissies online: Taiwanese male queers performing sissinesses in cyberspaces. *Inter-Asia Cultural Studies, 7*(2), 270–288. doi:10.1080/14649370600673938

Lindsay, S., Smith, S., Bell, F., & Bellaby, P. (2007). Tackling the digital divide: Exploring the impact of ICT on managing heart conditions in a deprived area. *Information, Communication & Society, 10*(1), 95–114.

Ling, R. (2004). *The mobile connection: The cell phone's impact on society.* San Francisco, CA: Morgan Kaufmann.

Ling, R., & Stald, G. (2010). Mobile communities: Are we talking about a village, a clan, or a small group? *American Behavioral Scientist, 53*(8), 1133–1147. doi:10.1177/0002764209356245

Lingel, J. (2013). The digital remains: Social media and practices of online grief. *Information Society, 29*(3), 190–195. doi:10.1080/01972243.2013.777311

Livingstone, S. (2009). *Children and the internet.* Cambridge, UK: Polity.

Livingstone, S. (2017, August 16). No, the internet is not actually stealing kids' innocence. London School of Economics and Political Science *Parenting for a Digital Future* blog. Retrieved from http://blogs.lse.ac.uk/parenting4digitalfuture/2017/08/16/no-the-internet-is-not-actually-stealing-kids-innocence

Lobinger, K., & Brantner, K. (2015). In the eye of the beholder: Subjective views on the authenticity of selfies. *International Journal of Communication, 9*(19), 1848–1860. Retrieved from http://ijoc.org/index.php/ijoc/article/view/3151/1404

Lombard, M., & Ditton, T. (1997). At the heart of it all: The concept of presence. *Journal of Computer-Mediated Communication, 3*(2).

Luders, M., & Bae Brandtzaeg, P. (2017). "My children tell me it's so simple": A mixed-methods approach to understand older non-users' perceptions of social networking sites. *New Media & Society, 19*(2), 181–198. doi:10.1177/1461444814554064

Luders, M., & Gjevjon, E. R. (2017). Being old in an always-on culture: Older people's perceptions and experiences of online communication. *The Information Society, 33*(2), 64–75. doi:10.1080/01972243.2016.1271070

Lutz, A. (2012, June 14). These 6 corporations control 90% of the media in America. *Business Insider.* Retrieved from http://www.businessinsider.com/these-6-corporations-control-90-of-the-media-in-america-2012-6

Lyon, D. (2007). *Surveillance studies: An overview.* Cambridge, UK: Polity.

Machlup, F. (1962). *The production and distribution of knowledge in the United States.* Princeton, NJ: Princeton University Press.

MacKinnon, G., & Williams, P. (2006). Models for integrating technology in higher education: The physics of sound. *Journal of College Science Teaching, 35*(7), 22–25.

Madden, M., Cortesi, S., Gasser, U., Lenhart, A., & Duggan, M. (2012, November 20). Parents, teens, and online privacy. *Pew Research Center.* Retrieved from http://www.pewinternet.org/2012/11/20/main-report-10/

Madden, M., & Jones, S. (2008, September 24). Networked workers. *Pew Research Center.* Retrieved from http://www.pewinternet.org/2008/09/24/networked-workers/

Madden, M., & Lenhart, A. (2006, March 5). Online dating. *Pew Research Center.* Retrieved from http://www.pewinternet.org/2006/03/05/online-dating/

Madden, M., Lenhart, A., Cortesi, S., Gasser, U., Duggan, M., Smith, A., & Beaton, M. (2013, May 21). Teens, social media, and privacy. *Pew Research Center.* Retrieved from http://www.pewinternet.org/files/2013/05/PIP_TeensSocialMediaandPrivacy_PDF.pdf

Madianou, M., & Miller, D. (2011). *Migration and new media: Transnational families and polymedia.* Abingdon, NY: Routledge.

Mangen, A., Walgermo, B. R., & Brønnick, K. (2013). Reading linear texts on paper versus computer screen: Effects on reading comprehension. *International Journal of Educational Research, 58,* 61–68.

Mannheim, K. (1960). *Ideology and utopia: An introduction to the sociology of knowledge.* London, UK: Routledge. (Original work published 1929)

Markham, A. N., & Baym, N. K. (2009). *Internet inquiry: Conversations about method.* Thousand Oaks, CA: SAGE.

Markoff, J. (2005). *What the dormouse said.* New York, NY: Viking.

Markus, H., & Kunda, Z. (1986). Stability and malleability of the self-concept. *Journal of Personality and Social Psychology, 51*(4), 858–866.

Markus, H., & Nurius, P. (1986). Possible selves. *American Psychologist, 41*(9), 954–969.

Martey, R. M., Stromer-Galley, J., Banks, J., Wu, J., & Consalvo, M. (2014). The strategic female: Gender-switching and player behavior in online games. *Information, Communication & Society, 17*(3), 286–300.

Martin, F. (2014). The case for curatorial journalism . . . or, can you really be an ethical aggregator? In L. Zion & D. Craig (Eds.), *Ethics for digital journalists: Emerging best practices* (pp. 87–102). London, UK: Routledge.

Marvin, C. (1988). *When old technologies were new.* New York, NY: Oxford University Press.

Marwick, A. E. (2012). The public domain: Surveillance in everyday life. *Surveillance and Society, 9*(4), 378–393.

Marwick, A. E. (2014). Networked privacy: How teenagers negotiate context in social media. *New Media and Society, 16*(7), 1051–1067.

Marwick, A. E., & boyd, d. (2011). I tweet honestly, I tweet passionately: Twitter users, context collapse, and the imagined audience. *New Media & Society, 13*(1), 114–133.

Marwick, A., & Ellison, N. B. (2012). "There isn't Wi-Fi in heaven!" Negotiating visibility on Facebook memorial pages. *Journal of Broadcasting and Electronic Media, 56*(3), 378–400. doi:10.1080/08838151.2012.705197

Marx, K. (1887). *Capital.* London, UK: George Allen and Unwin Ltd.

Marx, K. (2012). *Economic and philosophic manuscripts of 1844.* Mineola, NY: Dover. (Original work published 1844)

Mascheroni, G., & Olafsson, K. (2013). Mobile internet access and use among European children. Initial findings of the Net Children Go Mobile project. Milano, Italy: Educatt.

Massanari, A. (2017). #Gamergate and The Fappening: How Reddit's algorithm, governance, and culture support toxic technocultures. *New Media & Society, 19*(3), 327–346. doi:10.1177/1461444815608807

Maximino, M. (2014, August 22). Does media fragmentation contribute to polarization? Evidence from lab experiments. *Journalist's Resource.* Retrieved from http://journalistsresource.org/studies/society/news-media/media-fragmentation-political-polarization-lab-experiments

Mazlish, B. M. (1989). *A new science.* New York, NY: Oxford University Press.

Mazur, E., Signorella, M. L., & Hough, M. (2018). The internet behavior of older adults. In *Encyclopedia of information science and technology, 4th Ed.* (pp. 7026–7035). Hershey, PA: IGI Global.

McCall, G. J., & Simmons, J. L. (1978). *Identities and interactions.* New York, NY: Free Press.

McCormick, A. (2009, August 5). Revolution's brief history of digital music. *Marketing.* Retrieved from http://www.marketingmagazine.co.uk/article/904234/revolutions-brief-history-digital-music

McCormick, T. (2013, December 9). The darknet: A short history. *Foreign Policy.* Retrieved from http://foreignpolicy.com/2013/12/09/the-darknet-a-short-history/

McCosker, A., & Darcy, R. (2013). Living with cancer: Affective labour, self-expression and the utility of blogs. *Information, Communication & Society, 16*(8), 1266–1285.

McDaniel, B. T., Drouin, M., & Cravens, J. D. (2017). Do you have anything to hide? Infidelity-related behaviors on social media sites and marital satisfaction. *Computers in Human Behavior, 66*, 88–95.

McEwan, R. (2014). Mediating sociality: The use of iPod touch devices in the classrooms of students with autism in Canada. *Information, Communication and Society, 17*(10), 1264–1279.

McHale, T. (2005). Portrait of a digital native: Are digital-age students fundamentally different from the rest of us? *Technology & Learning, 26*(2), 33–34.

McKenna, K. Y. A., Green, A. S., & Gleason, M. E. J. (2002). Relationship formation on the internet: What's the big attraction? *Journal of Social Issues, 58*(1), 9–31.

McKinsey & Company. (2014). Offline and falling behind: Barriers to internet adoption. *Technology, Media, and Telecom Practice.* Retrieved from http://www.mckinsey.com/insights/high_tech_telecoms_internet/offline_and_falling_behind_barriers_to_internet_adoption

McLuhan, M. (1964). *Understanding media: The extensions of man.* New York, NY: McGraw-Hill.

Mead, G. H. (2009). *Mind, self, and society: From the standpoint of a social behaviorist.* Chicago, IL: University of Chicago. (Original work published 1934)

Mehra, B., Merkel, C., & Bishop, A. P. (2004). The internet for empowerment of minority and marginalized users. *New Media and Society, 6*(6), 781–802. doi:10.1177/146144804047513

Mesch, G., & Talmud, I. (2010). Internet connectivity, community participation, and place attachment: A longitudinal study. *American Behavioral Scientist, 53*(8), 1095–1110. doi:10.1177/0002764209356243

Metz, C. (2012). Before Google and Go Daddy, there was Elizabeth Feiner. *Wired Magazine.* Retrieved from https://www.wired.com/2012/06/elizabeth-jake-feinler/

Meyrowitz, J. (1985). *No sense of place: The impact of electronic media on social behavior*. New York, NY: Oxford University Press.

Milgram, S. (1967). The small world problem. *Psychology Today, 2*(1), 60–67.

Miller, C. C. (2014, December 15). As robots grow smarter, American workers struggle to keep up. *The New York Times.* Retrieved from http://www.nytimes.com/2014/12/16/upshot/as-robots-grow-smarter-american-workers-struggle-to-keep-up.html? smid=tw-share&_r=0&abt=0002&abg=1

Miller, J. R. (2017, July 10). Alexa calls cops on man allegedly beating his girlfriend. *The New York Post.* Retrieved from http://nypost.com/2017/07/10/alexa-calls-cops-on-man-allegedly-beating-his-girlfriend/

Milner, R. M. (2013). Pop polyvocality: Internet memes, public participation, and the Occupy Wall Street movement. *International Journal of Communication,* 7, 2357–2390. Retrieved from http://ijoc.org/index.php/ijoc/article/view/1949/1015

Mitra, A. (2004). Voices of the marginalized on the internet: Examples from a website for women of South Asia. *Journal of Communication, 54*(3), 492–510.

Mitra, A. (2005). Creating immigrant identities in cybernetic space: Examples from a non-resident Indian website. *Media, Culture & Society, 27*(3), 371–390.

Miyata, K., Boase, J., Wellman, B., & Ikeda, K. (2005). The mobile-izing Yapanese: Connecting to the internet by PC and webphone in Yamanashi. In M. Ito, D. Okabe, & M. Matsuda (Eds.), *Personal, portable, pedestrian: Mobile phones in Japanese life, 1* (pp. 143–164). Cambridge, MA: MIT Press.

Morahan-Martin, J. (2005). Internet abuse: Addiction? Disorder? Symptoms? Alternative explanations? *Social Science Computer Review, 23*(1), 39–48.

Moreman, C. M., & Lewis, D. (2014). *Digital death: Mortality and beyond in the online age.* New York, NY: Praeger.

Morgan, C., & Cotten, S. R. (2003). The relationship between internet activities and depressive symptoms in a sample of college freshmen. *Cyberpsychology and Behavior, 6*(2), 133–142. doi:10.1089/109493103321640329

Morley, D., & Robins, K. (1995). *Spaces of identity: Global media, electronic landscapes and cultural boundaries.* London, UK: Routledge.

Mortensen, K. K. (2017). Flirting in online dating: Giving empirical grounds to flirtatious implicitness. *Discourse Studies.* doi:1461445617715179.

Napoli, P., & Obar, J. (2013). *Mobile leapfrogging and digital divide policy: Assessing the limitations of mobile internet access.* Fordham University School of Business Research Paper no. 2263800. Retrieved from https://static.newamerica.org/attachments/3911-mobile-leapfrogging-and-digital-divide-policy/MobileLeapfrogging_Final.8f720f33d8e349cfa5c22684815ddeb8.pdf

National Conference of State Legislatures. (2013, December 5). State cyberbullying and cyberharassment laws. *NCSL.* Retrieved from http://www.ncsl.org/research/telecommunications-and-information-technology/cyberstalking-and-cyberharassment-laws.aspx

Naughton, J. (2010, August 14). The internet: Is it changing the way that we think? *The Guardian.* Retrieved from http://www.theguardian.com/technology/2010/aug/15/internet-brain-neuroscience-debate

Naughton, J. (2012). *From Gutenberg to Zuckerberg: Disruptive innovation in the age of the internet.* New York, NY: Quercus.

Neff, G. (2012). *Venture labor: Work and the burden of risk in innovative industries.* Cambridge, MA: MIT Press.

Neimark, J. (1995). It's magical. It's malleable. It's . . . memory. *Psychology Today, 28*(1), 44–49.

Nelson, M. K. (2010). *Parenting out of control: Anxious parents in uncertain times.* New York, NY: NYU Press.

Nemer, D., & Freeman, G. (2015). Empowering the marginalized: Rethinking selfies in the slums of Brazil. *International Journal of Communication, 9*(19), 1832–1847. Retrieved from http://ijoc.org/index.php/ijoc/article/view/3155/1403

Newell, B. C., Moore, A. D., & Metoyer, C. (2015). Privacy in the family. In B. Roessler & D. Mokrosinska (Eds.), *The social dimensions of privacy* (pp. 104–121). Cambridge, UK: Cambridge University Press.

Newitz, A. (2011, June 23). William Gibson says cyberspace was inspired by 8-bit videogames. *io9*. Retrieved from http://io9.com/5815019/william-gibson-says-cyberspace-was-inspired-by-8-bit-videogames

Newman, J. (2014, October 17). To Siri, with love. *The New York Times*. Retrieved from http://www.nytimes.com/2014/10/19/fashion/how-apples-siri-became-one-autistic-boys-bff.html?_r=0

Newman, L., Biedrzycki, K., & Baum, F. (2012). Digital technology use among disadvantaged Australians: Implications for equitable consumer participation in digitally-mediated communication and information exchange with health services. *Australian Health Review, 36*(2), 125–129.

Ngulube, P. (2012). "Ghosts in our machines": Preserving public digital information for the sustenance of electronic government in sub-Saharan Africa. *Mousaion, 30*(2), 129–136.

Nippert-Eng, C. E. (1996). *Home and work: Negotiating boundaries through everyday life*. Chicago, IL: University of Chicago Press.

Nippert-Eng, C. E. (2010). *Islands of privacy*. Chicago, IL: University of Chicago Press.

Nissenbaum, A., & Shifman, L. (2017). Internet memes as contested cultural capital: The case of 4chan's/b/board. *New Media & Society, 19*(4), 483–501.

Nissenbaum, H. (2009). *Privacy in context*. Stanford, CA: Stanford University Press.

Nowak, K. L., Watt, J., & Walther, J. B. (2005). The influence of synchrony and sensory modality on the person perception process in computer-mediated groups. *Journal of Computer-Mediated Communication, 10*(3).

Ofcom. (2008). Social networking: A quantitative and qualitative research report into attitudes, behaviours and use. *Ofcom Office of Communications*. Retrieved from http://news.bbc.co.uk/2/shared/bsp/hi/pdfs/02_04_08_ofcom.pdf

O'Harrow, R. (2006). *No place to hide*. New York, NY: Simon & Schuster.

Oldenburg, R. (1989). *The great good place: Cafés, coffee shops, community centers, beauty parlors, general stores, bars, hangouts, and how they get you through the day*. New York, NY: Paragon House.

O'Leary, A. (2012, August 1). In virtual play, sex harassment is all too real. *The New York Times*. Retrieved from http://www.nytimes.com/2012/08/02/us/sexual-harassment-in-online-gaming-stirs-anger.html?_r=0.

O'Leary, M. B., Wilson, J. M., & Metiu, A. (2014). Beyond being there: The symbolic role of communication and identification in perceptions of proximity to geographically dispersed colleagues. *MIS Quarterly, 38*(4), 1219–1243. Retrieved from http://www18.georgetown.edu/data/people/mbo9/publication-77556.pdf

Ophir, E., Nass, C., & Wagner, A. D. (2009). Cognitive control in media multitaskers. *Proceedings of the National Academy of Sciences of the United States of America, 106*(37), 15583–15587. doi:10.1073/pnas.0903620106

Oreskovic, A. (2017, October 1). Mark Zuckerberg apologized for Facebook's role dividing people in a Yom Kippur message vowing to "do better." *Business Insider*. Retrieved from http://www.businessinsider.com/mark-zuckerberg-yom-kippur-apology-facebook-dividing-not-uniting-2017-10

Palfrey, J. G., & Gasser, U. (2008). *Born digital: Understanding the first generation of digital natives*. New York, NY: Basic Books.

Papacharissi, Z. (Ed.). (2010). *A networked self: Identity, community, and culture on social network sites*. New York, NY: Routledge.

Park, E. K., & Sundar, S. S. (2015). Can synchronicity and visual modality enhance social presence in mobile messaging? *Computers in Human Behavior, 45*, 121–128.

Parks, M. (2011). Social network sites as virtual communities. In Z. Paparachissi (Ed.), *A networked self: Identity, community, and culture on social network sites* (pp. 105–123). New York, NY: Routledge.

Pavlik, J. (1997). The future of online journalism. *Columbia Journalism Review, 36*, 30–38.

Pearson, R. (2010). Fandom in the digital era. *Popular Communication, 8*(1), 84–95.

Perreault, C., & Mathew, S. (2012). Dating the origin of language using phonemic diversity. *PLoS One*, 7(4), e35289.

Pew Research Center. (2014, November 6). Religion and electronic media. Retrieved from http://www.pewforum.org/files/2014/11/Religion-and-Electronic-media-11-06-full.pdf

Pew Research Center. (2015, March 19). Internet seen as positive influence on education but negative on morality in emerging and developing nations. Retrieved from http://www.pewglobal.org/files/2015/03/Pew-Research-Center-Technology-Report-FINAL-March-19-20151.pdf

Pew Research Center. (2016, February 22). Smartphone ownership and internet usage continues to climb in emerging economies. Retrieved from http://www.pewglobal.org/2016/02/22/internet-access-growing-worldwide-but-remains-higher-in-advanced-economies/

Pew Research Center. (2017, January 7). Social media fact sheet. Retrieved from http://www.pewinternet.org/fact-sheet/social-media/

Pew Research Center's Global Attitudes Project. (2012, December 12). Social networking popular across globe. *Pew Research Center.* Retrieved from http://www.pewglobal.org/2012/12/12/social-networking-popular-across-globe/

Plotkin, H. (2002, February 11). All hail Creative Commons: Stanford professor and author Lawrence Lessig plans a legal insurrection. *San Francisco Gate.* Retrieved from http://www.sfgate.com/news/article/All-Hail-Creative-Commons-Stanford-professor-2874018.php

Polgar, D. R. (2017, July 17). We've already developed Google brain—but what about Facebook heart? *Quartz.* Retrieved from https://qz.com/1024931/weve-already-developed-google-brain-but-what-about-facebook-heart/

Polk, E. (2014). Digital technology and the construction of "glocal" information flows: Social movements and social media in the age of sustainability. In J. Servaes (Ed.), *Technological determinism and social change: Communication in a tech-mad world* (pp. 125–141). New York, NY: Lexington Books.

Polson, E. (2013). A gateway to the global city: Mobile place-making practices by expats. *New Media & Society, 17*(4), 629–645. doi:10.1177/1461444813510135

Poor, N. (2013). Computer game modders' motivations and sense of community: A mixed-methods approach. *New Media & Society, 16*(8), 1249–1267.

Portwood-Stacer, L. (2012). Media refusal and conspicuous non-consumption: The performative and political dimensions of Facebook abstention. *New Media & Society.* Retrieved from http://lauraportwoodstacer.com/wp-content/uploads/2013/03/mediarefusalandconspicuousnonconsumption.pdf

Postman, N. (1993). *Technopoly*. New York, NY: Vintage Books.

Preece, J. (2000). *Online communities: Designing usability and supporting sociability.* New York, NY: John Wiley & Sons.

Preece, J., & Maloney-Krichmar, D. (2003). Online communities. In J. A. Jacko & A. Sears (Eds.), *Handbook of human-computer interaction* (pp. 596–620). Boca Raton, FL: CRC Press.

Prensky, M. (2001). Digital natives, digital immigrants. Part 1. *On the Horizon, 9*(5), 1–6.

Psychology Today. (2007, January/February). Texting Gr8 4U. *Psychology Today*, p. 14.

Quan-Haase, A., & Wellman, B. (2002, March 13–16). *Understanding the use of communication tools for ad-hoc problem-solving in mid-size organizations.* Paper presented at the Popular Culture Association and American Culture Association Conference: Electronic Culture and Communications Forum, Toronto, Ontario.

Raab, C. D., & Mason, D. (2004). Privacy, surveillance, trust and regulation. *Information, Communication & Society*, 7(1), 89–91.

Radway, J. (1984). *Reading the romance: Women, patriarchy, and popular culture.* Chapel Hill: University of North Carolina Press.

Rainie, L. (2006, September 28). New workers, new workplaces: Digital natives invade the workplace. *Pew Research Center.* Retrieved from http://www.pewinternet.org/2006/09/28/new-workers-newworkplaces-digital-natives-invade-theworkplace/

Rainie, L. (2011, December 2). The internet as a diversion and a destination. *Pew Research Center.* Retrieved from http://www.pewinternet.org/2011/12/02/the-internetas-a-diversion-and-destination/

Rainie, L., & Anderson, J. (2017, June 6). The internet of things connectivity binge: What are the implications? *Pew Research Center*. Retrieved from http://www.pewinternet.org/2017/06/06/the-internet-of-things-connectivity-binge-what-are-the-implications

Rainie, L., & Wellman, B. (2012). *Networked: The new social operating system.* Cambridge, MA: MIT Press.

Reeves, B., & Nass, C. (1996). *How people treat computers, television, and new media like real people and places.* Cambridge, UK: CSLI Publications and Cambridge University Press.

Rennie, J. (2012, January 9). The overdue death of cyberspace. *Smart Planet.* Retrieved from http://www.smartplanet.com/blog/the-savvy-scientist/the-overdue-death-of-cyberspace/

Renninger, K. A., & Shumar, W. (2002). Community building with and for teachers at the math forum. In K. A. Renninger & W. Shumar (Eds.), *Building virtual communities: Learning and change in cyberspace* (pp. 60–95). Cambridge, UK: Cambridge University Press.

Rettberg, J. W. (2014). *Seeing ourselves through technology: How we use selfies, blogs, and wearable devices to see and shape ourselves.* New York, NY: Palgrave Macmillan.

Rheingold, H. (1993). *The virtual community.* Reading, MA: Addison-Wesley.

Rheingold, H. (2002). *Smart mobs: The next social revolution.* New York, NY: Basic Books.

Rhoades, H., Wenzel, S., Rice, E., Winetrobe, H., & Henwood, B. (2017). No digital divide? Technology use among homeless adults. *Journal of Social Distress and the Homeless, 26*(1). doi:10.1080/10530789.2017.1305140

Ribitzky, R. (2017, April 10). Active monitoring of employees rises to 78 percent. *ABC News.* Retrieved from http://abcnews.go.com/Business/story?id=88319&page=1

Riley, T. (2013). Self-initiated (re) education of digital technology in retired content creators. *Northern Lights: Film & Media Studies Yearbook, 11*(1), 51–69. doi:10.1386/nl.11.1.51_1

Ritzer, G. (2009). *The McDonaldization of society.* Los Angeles, CA: Pine Forge Press.

Ritzer, G., Dean, P., & Jurgenson, N. (2012). The coming of age of the prosumer. *American Behavioral Scientist, 56*(4), 379–398.

Ritzer, G., & Jurgenson, N. (2010). Production, consumption, prosumption. *Journal of Consumer Culture, 10*(1), 13–36.

Roberts, L. D., & Parks, M. R. (1999). The social geography of gender-switching in virtual environments on the internet. *Information, Communication & Society, 2*(4), 521–540.

Robinson, L., & Schulz, J. (2013). Net time negotiations within the family. *Information, Communication and Society, 16*(4), 542–560.

Rogers, E. M. (2010). *Diffusion of innovations.* New York, NY: Simon & Schuster. (Original work published 1962)

Rose, E. (2010). Continuous partial attention: Reconsidering the role of online learning in the age of interruption. *Educational Technology Magazine, 50*(4), 41–46.

Rosenthal, J. (2017, July 24). Wisconsin company to implant microchips in employees. *KSTP.com.* Retrieved from http://kstp.com/news/wisconsin-company-to-implant-microchips-in-employees-three-square-market/4549459/

Rotman, D., & Preece, J. (2010). The "WeTube" in YouTube—creating an online community through video sharing. *International Journal of Web Based Communities, 6*(3), 317–333. doi:10.1504/IJWBC.2010.033755

Rowe, I. (2015). Civility 2.0: A comparative analysis of incivility in online political discussion. *Information, Communication and Society, 18*(2), 121–138. doi:10.1080/1369118X.2014.940365

Rudi, J., Dworkin, J., Walker, S., & Doty, J. (2015). Parents' use of information and communications technologies for family communication: Differences by age of children. *Information, Communication and Society, 18*(1), 78–93.

Rui, J. R., & Stefanone, M. A. (2013). Strategic image management online: Self-presentation, self-esteem and social network perspectives. *Information, Communication & Society, 16*(8), 1286–1305.

Rushkoff, D. (2013). *Present shock: When everything happens now.* New York, NY: Penguin.

Sadowski, J. (2013, November 14). The business of living forever. *Slate.* Retrieved from http://www.slate.com/articles/business/billion_to_one/2013/11/dmitry_itskov_2045_initiative_eternal_living_through_science.html

Sakkopoulos, E., Lytras, M., & Tsakalidis, A. (2006). Adaptive mobile web services facilitate communication and learning internet technologies. *IEEE Transactions on Education, 49*(2), 208–215.

Sanders, C., Field, T. M., Diego, M., & Kaplan, M. (2000). The relationship of internet use to depression and social isolation. *Adolescence, 35*(138), 237–242.

Sandvig, C. (2006). The internet at play: Child users of public internet connections. *Journal of Computer-Mediated Communication, 11*(4), 932–956.

Sandvig, C. (2015). Seeing the sort: The aesthetic and industrial defense of "the algorithm." *Media-N.* Retrieved from http://median.newmediacaucus.org/art-infrastructures-information/seeing-the-sort-the-aesthetic-and-industrial-defense-of-the-algorithm/

Sass, E. (2014, December 16). Social media helps fight aging. *Social Media and Marketing Daily*. Retrieved from http://www.mediapost.com/publications/article/240142/social-media-helps-fight-aging.html

Scherer, J. (1972). *Contemporary community: Sociological illusion or reality?* London, UK: Tavistock.

Schilling, D. R. (2013, April 19). Knowledge doubling every 12 months, soon to be every 12 hours. *Industry Tap*. Retrieved from http://www.industrytap.com/knowledge-doubling-every-12-months-soon-to-be-every-12-hours/3950

Scholz, T. (2012). Why does digital labor matter now? In T. Scholz (Ed.), *Digital labor: The internet as playground and factory* (pp. 1–10). New York, NY: Routledge.

Schradie, J. (2011). The digital production gap: The digital divide and web 2.0 collide. *Poetics, 39*(2), 145–168. doi:10.1016/j.poetic.2011.02.003

Schradie, J. (2012). The trend of class, race, and ethnicity in social media inequality: Who still cannot afford to blog? *Information, Communication & Society, 15*(4), 555–571.

Schrock, D., Holden, D., & Reid, L. (2004). Creating emotional resonance: Interpersonal emotion work and motivational framing in a transgender community. *Social Problems, 51*(1), 61–81.

Schuler, D. (1996). *New community networks: Wired for change*. Reading, MA: ACM Press/Addison-Wesley.

Schuler, D., & Day, P. (2004). *Shaping the network society: The new role of civil society in cyberspace*. Cambridge, MA: MIT Press.

Schutz, A. (1951). Making music together. A study in social relationship. *Social Research, 18*(1), 76–97.

Schutz, A. (1973). On multiple realities. In M. A. Natason (Ed.), *Collected papers of Alfred Schutz, Vol. 1*. The Hague, the Netherlands: Martinus Nijhoff.

Schwammlein, E., & Wodzicki, K. (2012). What to tell about me? Self-presentation in online communities. *Journal of Computer-Mediated Communication, 17*(4), 387–407.

Schwartz, J. (2002, December 29). The nation: Case-sensitive crusader; who owns the internet? You and I do. *The New York Times*. Retrieved from http://www.nytimes.com/2002/12/29/weekinreview/the-nation-case-sensitive-crusader-who-owns-the-internet-you-and-i-do.html

Schwartz, J. (2013, January 12). Internet activist, a creator of RSS, is dead at 26, apparently a suicide. *The New York Times*. Retrieved from http://www.nytimes.com/2013/01/13/technology/aaron-swartz-internet-activist-dies-at-26.html?_r=1

Schwartz, T. (1981). *Media, the second god*. New York, NY: Random House.

ScienceDaily.com. (2005). Internet dating much more successful than once thought. Retrieved from http://www.sciencedaily.com/releases/2005/02/050218125144.htm

Sedghi, A. (2014, February 4). Facebook: Ten years of social networking, in numbers. *The Guardian*. Retrieved from http://www.theguardian.com/news/datablog/2014/feb/04/facebook-in-numbers-statistics

Senft, T. M. (2008). *Camgirls: Celebrity and community in the age of social networks*. New York, NY: Peter Lang.

Senft, T. M., & Baym, N. K. (2015). What does the selfie say? Investigating a global phenomenon. *International Journal of Communication, 9*(19), 1588–1606. Retrieved from http://ijoc.org/index.php/ijoc/article/viewFile/4067/1387

Sengupta, S. (2012, October 2). Facebook delivers a confident sales pitch to advertisers. *The New York Times.* Retrieved from http://www.nytimes.com/2012/10/03/technology/facebook-delivers-confident-pitch-to-advertisers.html?_r=0

Šesek, L., & Pušnik, M. (2014). Reading popular literature and digital media: Reading experience, fandoms, and social networks. *Anthropological Notebooks, 20*(2), 103–126.

Shapin, S. (2007). What else is new? *The New Yorker.* Retrieved from http://www.newyorker.com/magazine/2007/05/14/what-else-is-new

Sharon, T. (2017). Self-tracking for health and the quantified self: Re-articulating autonomy, solidarity, and authenticity in an age of personalized healthcare. *Philosophy & Technology, 30*(1), 93–121.

Shaw, J. (2010). Philosophy of humor. *Philosophy Compass, 5*(2), 112–126. doi:10.1111/j.1747-9991.2009.00281.x

Shibutani, T. (1955). Reference groups as perspectives. *American Journal of Sociology, 60*(6), 562–569.

Shklovski, I., Burke, M., Kiesler, S., & Kraut, R. (2010). Technology adoption and use in the aftermath of Hurricane Katrina in New Orleans. *American Behavioral Scientist, 53*(8), 1228–1246. doi:10.1177/0002764209356252

Shklovski, I., Kraut, R., & Rainie, L. (2004). The internet and social participation: Contrasting cross-sectional and longitudinal analyses. *Journal of Computer-Mediated Communication, 10*(1).

Short, J., Williams, E., & Christie, B. (1976). *The social psychology of telecommunications.* New York, NY: John Wiley and Sons.

Silleson, L. B. (2014, November 5). Is this the web's first blog? *Columbia Journalism Review.* Retrieved from http://www.cjr.org/behind_the_news/justin_hall_blog_web.php? page=all

Silverblatt, A. (2004). Media as social institution. *American Behavioral Scientist, 48*(1), 35–41.

Simmel, G. (1898). The persistence of social groups. *American Journal of Sociology, 3*(5), 662–691.

Simmel, G. (1950). *The sociology of Georg Simmel.* (K. H. Wolff, Trans.). Glencoe, IL: Free Press. (Original work published 1908)

Simmel, G. (1962). *Conflict and the web of group affiliations.* New York, NY: Free Press. (Original work published 1908)

Sinnreich, A. (2010). *Mashed-up: Music, technology, and the rise of configurable culture.* Amherst: University of Massachusetts Press.

Sinnreich, A. (2013). *The piracy crusade: How the music industry's war on sharing destroys markets and erodes civil liberties.* Amherst: University of Massachusetts Press.

Smith, A. (2017, January 12). Record share of Americans now own smartphones, have home broadband. *Pew Research Center.* Retrieved from http://www.pewresearch.org/fact-tank/2017/01/12/evolution-of-technology/

Smith, A., & Duggan, M. (2013, October 21). Online dating and relationships. *Pew Research Center.* Retrieved from http://www.pewinternet.org/2013/10/21/online-dating-relationships/

Smith, A., Schlozman, K. L., Verba, S., & Brady, H. (2009). The internet and civic engagement. *Pew Research Center*. Retrieved from http://www.pewinternet.org/2009/09/01/the-internet-and-civic-engagement/

Solove, D. J. (2004). *The digital person: Technology and privacy in the information age*. New York, NY: NYU Press.

Somers, D. (2017, February 10). Do colleges look at your social media accounts? *US News and World Report*. Retrieved from https://www.usnews.com/education/best-colleges/articles/2017-02-10/colleges-really-are-looking-at-your-social-media-accounts

Song, L., Son, J., & Lin, N. (2011). Social support. In J. Scott & P. J. Carrington (Eds.), *The SAGE handbook of social network analysis* (pp. 116–128). Thousand Oaks, CA: SAGE.

Sproull, L., Conley, C. A., & Moon, J. Y. (2005). Prosocial behavior on the net. In Y. Amichai-Hamburger (Ed.), *The social net: Understanding human behavior in cyberspace* (pp. 139–161). Oxford, UK: Oxford University Press.

Srivastava, L. (2005). Mobile phones and the evolution of social behaviour. *Behaviour and Information Technology, 24*(2), 111–129.

Standage, T. (2013). *Writing on the wall.* New York, NY: Bloomsbury.

Statista. (2014). E-commerce: Statista dossier. *Statista, the Statistics Portal.* Retrieved from http://www.statista.com/study/10653/e-commerce-statista-dossier/

Statista. (2017a). Mobile phone user penetration as percentage of the population worldwide from 2013 to 2019*. Statista, the Statistics Portal. Retrieved from https://www.statista.com/statistics/470018/mobile-phone-user-penetration-worldwide/

Statista. (2017b). Number of social media users worldwide from 2010 to 2020 (in billions). Statista, the Statistics Portal. Retrieved from https://www.statista.com/statistics/278414/number-of-worldwide-social-network-users/

Stavrositu, C., & Sundar, S. S. (2012). Does blogging empower women? Exploring the role of agency and community. *Journal of Computer-Mediated Communication, 17*(4), 369–386.

Steinem, G. (2017, May 10). Lecture and discussion. *Media Mentoring Event.* New York, NY.

Stephenson, W. (1964a). The Ludenic theory of newsreading. *Journalism & Mass Communication Quarterly, 41*(3), 367–374.

Stephenson, W. (1964b). *The play theory of mass communication.* Chicago, IL: University of Chicago Press.

Stewart, B. (2012, July 3). What produsage is and why it matters. *The Theory Blog.* Retrieved from http://theory.cribchronicles.com/2012/07/03/what-produsage-is-and-why-it-matters/

Stewart, B. (2014). Living internet. *The Living Internet.* Retrieved from http://www.livinginternet.com/

Stokes, P. (2012). Ghosts in the machine: Do the dead live on in Facebook? *Philosophy and Technology, 25*(363), 379. doi:10.1007/s13347–011–0050–7

Stone, L. (2005). Linda Stone's thoughts on attention and specifically, continuous partial attention. Personal website. Retrieved from https://sites.google.com/a/lindastone.net/home/

Suellentrop, C. (2007, January/February). Playing with our heads. *Utne*, 58–63.

Retrieved from http://www.utne.com/community/playingwithourheads.aspx

Suler, J. (2004). The online disinhibition effect. *Cyberpsychology and Behavior,* 7(3), 321–326.

Tamkivi, S. (2014, January 24). Lessons from the world's most tech-savvy government. *The Atlantic.* Retrieved from http://www.theatlantic.com/international/archive/2014/01/lessons-from-the-worlds-most-tech-savvy-government/283341/

Tapscott, D. (2011). The eight net gen norms. In M. Bauerlein (Ed.), *The digital divide* (pp. 130–159). New York, NY: Tarcher Penguin.

Thomas, A. (2006). "MSN was the next big thing after Beanie Babies": Children's virtual experiences as an interface to their identities and their everyday lives. *E-Learning, 3*(2), 126–142.

Thomas, W. I., & Thomas, D. S. (1928). *The child in America.* New York, NY: Knopf.

Thompson, C. (2013). *Smarter than you think: How technology is changing our minds for the better*. New York, NY: Penguin.

Thurlow, C., Lengel, L., & Tomic, A. (2004). *Computer mediated communication.* London, UK: SAGE.

Tiidenberg, K. (2014). Bringing sexy back: Reclaiming the body aesthetic via self-shooting. *Cyberpsychology: Journal of Psychosocial Research on Cyberspace, 8*(1). Retrieved from http://cyberpsychology.eu/view.php?cisloclanku=2014021701&article

Toffler, A. (1980). *The third wave.* New York, NY: Morrow.

Tokunaga, R. S. (2011). Social networking site or social surveillance site? Understanding the use of interpersonal electronic surveillance in romantic relationships. *Computers in Human Behavior,* 27(2), 705–713.

Tufekci, Z. (2008). Grooming, gossip, Facebook and MySpace: What can we learn about these sites from those who won't assimilate? *Information Communication and Society, 11*(4), 544–564. doi:10.1080/13691180801999050

Tufekci, Z. (2010). Who acquires friends through social media and why? "Rich get richer" versus "seek and ye shall find." *Proceedings of the Fourth International AAAI Conference on Weblogs and Social Media.* Retrieved from http://citeseerx.ist.psu.edu/viewdoc/download?doi=10.1.1.465.314&rep=rep1&type=pdf

Tufekci, Z. (2012, April 25). Social media's small, positive role in human relationships. *The Atlantic.* Retrieved from http://www.theatlantic.com/technology/archive/2012/04/social-medias-small-positive-role-in-human-relationships/256346/

Tufekci, Z. (2014). Social movements and governments in the digital age: Evaluating a complex landscape. *Journal of International Affairs, 68*(1), 1–18.

Tufekci, Z., & Brashears, M. E. (2014). Are we all equally at home socializing online? Cyberasociality and evidence for an unequal distribution of disdain for digitally-mediated sociality. *Information, Communication and Society,* 17(4), 482–502.

Turkle, S. (1995). *Life on the screen: Identity in the age of the internet*. New York, NY: Simon & Schuster.

Turkle, S. (2012). *Alone together: Why we expect more from technology and less from each other.* New York, NY: Basic Books.

Turow, J. (2013). *The daily you: How the new advertising industry is defining your identity and your worth*. New Haven, CT: Yale University Press.

Turow, J., & Hennessy, M. (2007). Internet privacy and institutional trust insights from a national survey. *New Media & Society, 9*(2), 300–318.

van Dijk, J. A. (2005). *The deepening divide: Inequality in the information society*. Thousand Oaks, CA: SAGE.

van Oosten, J. M. F., Peter, J., & Boot, I. (2015). Exploring associations between exposure to sexy online self-presentations and adolescents' sexual attitudes and behavior. *Journal of Youth and Adolescence, 44*(5), 1078–1091.

Van Rooij, A. J., & Prause, N. (2014). A critical review of "internet addiction": Criteria with suggestions for the future. *Journal of Behavioral Addictions, 3*(4), 203–213.

van't Hooft, M., & Kelly, J. (2004). Macro or micro: Teaching fifth-grade economics using handheld computers. *Social Education, 68*(2), 165–168.

Vertesi, J. (2014, May 15). My experiment opting out of big data made me look like a criminal. *Time*. Retrieved from http://time.com/83200/privacy-internet-big-data-opt-out/

Vickery, J. R. (2015). "I don't have anything to hide, but . . . ": The challenges and negotiations of social and mobile media privacy for non-dominant youth. *Information, Communication & Society, 18*(3), 281–294.

Viken, R. J., Rose, R. J., Kaprio, J., & Koskenvuo, M. (1994). A developmental genetic analysis of adult personality: Extraversion and neuroticism from 18 to 59 years of age. *Journal of Personality and Social Psychology, 66*(4), 722–730.

Vinsel, L. (2014, September 23). How to give up the i-word, part 2. *Culture Digitally*. Retrieved from http://culturedigitally.org/2014/09/how-to-give-up-the-i-word-pt-2/

Vissers, S., & Stolle, D. (2014). The internet and new modes of political participation: Online versus offline participation. *Information, Communication and Society, 17*(8), 937–955.

Volti, R. (2014). *Society and technological change*. New York, NY: Worth.

Walther, J. B. (1996). Computer-mediated communication: Impersonal, interpersonal, and hyperpersonal interaction. *Communication Research, 23*(1), 3–43.

Walther, J. B. (1997). Group and interpersonal effects in international computer-mediated collaboration. *Human Communication Research, 23*(3), 342–369.

Walther, J. B., & Barazova, N. N. (2008). Validation and application of electronic propinquity theory to computer-mediated communication in groups. *Communication Research, 35*(5), 622–645. doi:10.1177/0093650208321783.

Wang, H., & Wellman, B. (2010). Social connectivity in America: Changes in adult friendship network size from 2002 to 2007. *American Behavioral Scientist, 53*(8), 1148–1169.

Wasko, M., & Faraj, S. (2000). "It is what one does": Why people participate and help others in electronic communities of practice. *The Journal of Strategic Information Systems, 9*(2), 155–173.

Watts, D. J., & Strogatz, S. H. (1998). Collective dynamics of "small-world" networks. *Nature, 393*(6684), 440–442.

Weber, M. S. (2012). Newspapers and the long-term implications of hyperlinking. *Journal of Computer-Mediated Communication, 17*(2), 187–201.

Wei, R., Lo, V., Xu, X., Chen, Y. K., & Zhang, G. (2014). Predicting mobile news use among college students: The role of press freedom in four Asian cities. *New Media and Society, 16*(4), 637–654.

Weinschank, S. (2012, September 11). Why we're all addicted to texts, Twitter, and Google. *Psychology Today.* Retrieved from http://www.psychologytoday.com/blog/brain-wise/201209/why-were-all-addicted-texts-twitter-and-google

Wellman, B., & Hampton, K. (1999). Living networked on and offline. *Contemporary Sociology, 28*(6), 648–654. doi:10.2307/2655535

Wellman, B., Smith, A., Wells, A., & Kennedy, T. (2008, October 19). Networked families. *Pew Research Center.* Retrieved from http://www.pewinternet.org/2008/10/19/networked-families/

Wellman, B., & Tindall, D. (1993). Reach out and touch some bodies: How social networks connect telephone networks. *Progress in Communication Sciences, 12,* 63–93.

Whitty, M. T. (2005). The realness of cybercheating: Men's and women's representations of unfaithful internet relationships. *Social Science Computer Review, 23*(1), 57–67.

Willson, M. (2010). Technology, networks, communities: An exploration of network and community theory and technosocial forms. *Information, Communication and Society, 13*(5), 747–764.

Wilson, B., & Atkinson, M. (2005). Rave and straightedge, the virtual and the REAL: Exploring online and offline experiences in Canadian youth subcultures. *Youth and Society, 36*(3), 276–311. doi:10.1177/0044118X03260498

WIN-Gallup International. (2012). Global index of religiosity and atheism. *WIN-Gallup International.* Retrieved from http://www.wingia.com/web/files/news/14/file/14.pdf

Wolfe, A. (1989). *Whose keeper? Social science and moral obligation.* Berkeley: University of California Press.

Wolfson, T., & Funke, P. N. (2013). Communication, class and concentric media practices: Developing a contemporary rubric. *New Media and Society, 16*(3), 363–380. doi:1461444813481199

Wood, R. T., & Williams, R. J. (2007). Problem gambling on the internet: Implications for internet gambling policy in North America. *New Media & Society, 9*(3), 520–542.

World Energy Outlook. (2016). World energy outlook electricity access database. *World Energy Outlook.* Retrieved from http://www.worldenergyoutlook.org/resources/energydevelopment/energyaccessdatabase/

Yang, C., Brown, B. B., & Braun, M. T. (2013). From Facebook to cell calls: Layers of electronic intimacy in college students' interpersonal relationships. *New Media and Society, 16*(1), 5–23. doi:1461444812472486

Young, A. L., & Quan-Haase, A. (2013). Privacy protection strategies on Facebook: The internet privacy paradox revisited. *Information, Communication and Society, 16*(4), 479–500.

Young, S. (2006). Student views of effective online teaching in higher education. *The American Journal of Distance Education, 20*(2), 65–77.

Yu, X., Anaya, G. J., Miao, L., Lehto, X., & Wong, I. A. (2017). The impact of smartphones on the family vacation experience. *Journal of Travel Research.* doi:0047287517706263

Yuan, E. J. (2013). A culturalist critique of "online community" in new media studies. *New Media & Society, 15*(5), 665–679.

Zawacki, K. (2015, January 22). Why can't computers understand sarcasm? *The Atlantic.* Retrieved from http://www.theatlantic.com/technology/archive/2015/01/why-cant-robots-understand-sarcasm/384714/

Zerubavel, E. (1981). *Hidden rhythms: Schedules and calendars in everyday life.* Chicago, IL: University of Chicago Press.

Zevallos, Z. (2011, October 11). The sociology of unfollowing on Twitter. *Other Sociologist.* Retrieved from http://othersociologist.com/2011/10/18/twitter-unfollow/

Zezulka, L. A., & Seigfried-Spellar, K. C. (2016). Differentiating cyberbullies and internet trolls by personality characteristics and self-esteem. *Journal of Digital Forensics, Security and Law*, *11*(3), 7–26.

Zhao, S. (2005). The digital self: Through the looking glass of telecopresent others. *Symbolic Interaction*, *28*(3), 387–405. doi:10.1525/si.2005.28.3.387

Zhao, S. (2006). Do internet users have more social ties? A call for differentiated analyses of internet use. *Journal of Computer-Mediated Communication*, *11*(3), 844–862. doi:10.1111/j.1083-6101.2006.00038.x

Zickuhr, K., Purcell, K., & Rainie, L. (2014, March 13). From distant admirers to library lovers—and beyond. *Pew Research Center.* Retrieved from http://www.pewinternet.org/2014/03/13/library-engagement-typology/

Zickuhr, K., & Smith, A. (2013, August 26). Home broadband 2013. *Pew Research Center.* Retrieved from http://www.pewinternet.org/2013/08/26/home-broadband-2013/

Zittrain, J. L. (2014). Reflections on internet culture. *Journal of Visual Culture*, *13*(3), 388–394.

INDEX